STARK

TRAINING Grundwissen ENGLISCH

Rainer Jacob

Übertritt in die Oberstufe

STARK

Bildnachweis
S. 10, 30, 44, 90, 98, 170, 181: © Cinetext
S. 24, 51, 63, 84, 135, 151: © ullstein – ullstein bild
S. 79: © Dirk De Kegel 2004 (Sabam Belgium), www.sxc.hu
S. 103: Quelle: http://moray.ml.duke.edu/faculty/read/nessie.html
S. 110: © Frank Laumen, www.kornkreisphaenomen.de
S. 119: © Stefan Diel, www.dlrptour.de

ISBN 978-3-89449-249-6

D-85318 Freising · Postfach 1852 · Tel. (0 81 61) 1790
Auflage 2008

Inhalt

Fortsetzung siehe nächste Seite

Fortsetzung siehe nächste Seite

Autor: Rainer Jacob

Vorwort

Liebe Schülerin, lieber Schüler,

beim Übertritt in die Oberstufe kommt eine Reihe neuer Anforderungen auf Sie zu. Mit dem vorliegenden Buch können Sie sich optimal auf diese Anforderungen vorbereiten, denn es behandelt in kompakter und übersichtlicher Form das, was die Oberstufenarbeit im Fach Englisch ausmacht: **Wortschatz**, **Grammatik**, **Textverständnis** und **Textproduktion**.

Damit Sie sich gut zurechtfinden, sind alle Kapitel dieses Buches wie folgt aufgebaut:

- In der **Textbox** können Sie anhand eines informativen und zugleich spannenden Textes Ihr **Textverständnis** verbessern und grundlegende Verfahren der **Texterschließung** üben.
- Die Unterkapitel **Word Power** und **Language Corner** sollen Ihren **aktiven und passiven Wortschatz** erweitern und festigen und Ihnen ein Gespür dafür vermitteln, wie Sie Wörter in der englischen Sprache richtig einsetzen – „spenden" heißt eben nicht „to spend"!
- Der **Grammar Spot** aktiviert und trainiert Ihre Kenntnisse in den grammatischen Bereichen, die für die Klausuren in der Oberstufe unabdingbar sind: *ing*-Formen, Zeiten, Aktiv–Passiv, *if*-Sätze etc.
- Ganz sicher werden Sie auch vom **Writing Desk** profitieren: In jedem Kapitel wird eine Aufgabenform aus dem Bereich der **Textproduktion** vorgestellt, an Beispielen erklärt und ausführlich geübt. Wie beantwortet man Fragen zum Text? Wie schreibt man einen „Comment" oder einen „Letter to the Editor"? Wenn Sie die entsprechenden Abschnitte durchgearbeitet haben, wird es Ihnen nicht mehr schwer fallen, sich in englischer Sprache schriftlich zu äußern.
- Die Rätsel im Unterkapitel **Fun and Games** dienen der Wiederholung des Wortschatzes und sorgen dafür, dass der Spaß bei der Arbeit nicht zu kurz kommt.
- Dass es zu allen Aufgaben auch **Lösungen** gibt, versteht sich von selbst.

Viel Spaß und viel Erfolg!

Rainer Jacob

Born in the wrong age

1 Text box

Prison life in the 19th century

The year is 1831. Andrew Simms and Tom Roberts of Challacombe near Bodmin in Cornwall (S. W. England) are both 14. The boys come from extremely poor families. Andrew's father died six years ago and his mother was left to bring up the five children herself. Tom has four brothers and two sisters. His father lost his farm more than three years ago because of his heavy drinking. He was not able to work the farm properly, that's why he ran into debt. In the end he and his family were driven off the farm. He now works as a farmhand in Dartmeed.

One day the boys meet Henry Cuthbert, who is 21. Henry has been in trouble with the police more than once. He is a pickpocket and persuades the boys "to work" with him on a busy market day in Bodmin. The youngsters cannot resist the temptation of a quick penny. However, they are caught by the police when they try to steal a woman's purse at a baker's stall in the market square. Shortly after, a judge sentences them to three months imprisonment for stealing.

Andrew and Tom are taken to Bodmin gaol, which is the county prison, to serve their sentence. They know Bodmin gaol quite well – until today only from the outside. Two months ago they had stood in a large crowd to watch the public hanging of the Lightfoot Brothers, who had murdered a store owner. Originally, the idea behind public hangings had been to teach everyone a lesson: Crime does not pay.

Hangings were meant as a deterrent. But most people enjoyed the thrill of a public hanging. Crowds from all over Devon and Cornwall gathered hours before the execution was to take place. The spectators were entertained by jesters and jugglers. Public hangings were regarded as a source of entertainment.

Bodmin prison was built seventy years before in 1776. In the meantime the stone building has become much too small for its 165 inmates: 112 men, 41 women and 12 juveniles and children. Andrew and Tom are taken to a part of the prison called Bridewell where prisoners found guilty of minor offences are housed. Their dark cell is 8 feet by 6 feet; there is a bed, straw for bedding and two blankets. It's very damp and cold, as the prison cannot be heated. There is no water to wash hands. Hygienic conditions are terrible, so diseases often break out: typhoid, measles, fever, diarrhoea.

The prisoners are fed three meals a day: breakfast, dinner and supper. The meals consist of water, bread and gruel, a kind of porridge. If prisoners don't keep to the prison regulations or if they don't work well, they get less to eat, are beaten or are taken to a permanently dark cell. Prisoners are not allowed to talk to each other. They have to keep their cells clean – which is impossible – and work.

Those serving the longest sentences must do hard labour: they work at the Treadwheel or in the nearby quarry for eight hours a day. Other inmates work in the gardens, saw wood or make shoes. Women spin and weave cloth or work in the laundry of the prison; children have to work, too.

Andrew and Tom meet other juvenile inmates under sixteen. Every morning a prison clerk tries to teach the children the three "R's": reading, writing and arithmetic. For some of them this is the first teaching they have ever received. After the lessons the children have to go back to their work. Andrew and Tom are released after serving two months – and they promise to keep up their schooling and never to return to that dreadful prison again!

In 1854 Parliament passed a new law: The Youthful Offenders Act. From then on juvenile offenders were no longer thrown into prisons like Bodmin. They were taken to special houses called "correction centres" or reformatories, the forerunners of the Borstals.

657 words

Exercise 1 Understanding the text

Match questions and answers.

A Why didn't Mrs Simms have anybody to help her raise her children?

B Why did Tom's family lose their farm?

C Why did the boys work together with Henry Cuthbert?

D Why did the boys know Bodmin gaol quite well?

E In which way had the original idea of allowing people to watch a hanging changed?

F What sort of prisoners were housed in the Bridewell section of Bodmin gaol?

G Why did so often diseases break out in the gaol?

1 In that part of the prison were people who had committed less serious crimes.

2 Her husband had died, so she had to bring up the children herself.

3 There was not enough water with which the inmates could keep themselves and their cells clean. In addition, the prisoners were underfed because they didn't get enough good food.

4 They thought they could earn money quickly and easily.

5 They had been to a public hanging outside the prison.

6 Tom's father drank more than he could take. Consequently he couldn't work his farm and lost it.

7 When people were first allowed to watch a hanging it was thought that they would be shocked; they should be taught a lesson. Now they saw it as an entertainment.

A	B	C	D	E	F	G

2 Word power

2.1 Some words to remember

(to) abolish	abschaffen
accusation	Beschuldigung, Anklage
(to) appeal	appellieren, (dringend) um Hilfe bitten; Berufung gegen ein Urteil einlegen
(to) arrest	festnehmen
aware	bewusst
bail	Kaution
(to) betray	verraten
bribery	Bestechung
burglary	Einbruch
capital punishment	Todesstrafe
charge	Beschuldigung, Anklage
(to) condemn	verdammen, verurteilen
confession	Geständnis
(to) confiscate	beschlagnahmen
conspiracy	Verschwörung
convict	Sträfling
conviction	Verurteilung; Überzeugung
court	Gerichtshof
credibility	Glaubwürdigkeit
criminal record	Strafregister
cross-examination	Kreuzverhör
custody	Haft
death penalty	Todesstrafe
debt	Schuld
defendant	Angeklagter
denial	Leugnen, Ablehnung
(to) deny	leugnen
district attorney	Staatsanwalt

dreadful	fürchterlich, schlimm
emotion	Gefühl
evidence	Beweis, Beweismaterial
experience	Erfahrung
gaol	Gefängnis
(to) increase	zunehmen
injustice	Ungerechtigkeit
inmate	Häftling
innocent	unschuldig
(to) introduce	vorstellen, einführen
investigation	Ermittlung
judicial system	Rechtssystem, Rechtswesen
juror	der Geschworene
jury	die Geschworenen
lawyer	Rechtsanwalt
merchant	Kaufmann
misery	Elend
murderer	Mörder
offence	Vergehen, Delikt, Gesetzesübertretung
offender	Täter(in), Straffällige(r)
penalty	Strafe
perjury	Meineid
(to) plead	plädieren
prison	Gefängnis
prosperity	Wohlstand
responsible	verantwortlich
riot	Krawall
search	Suche
sentence	Urteil; Satz
trial	Prozess
(to) be on trial for	vor Gericht stehen wegen
underprivileged	Benachteiligte

2.2 Useful phrases

to take s.o. to court	If you don't stop that terrible noise every night I'll take you to court for disturbing the peace.	jdn. verklagen
to sue for damages	After the tanker accident in Alaska the fishermen sued the Exxon company for damages.	auf Schadenersatz verklagen
to commit a crime	Alf Windmill committed the burglary.	ein Verbrechen begehen
to take an oath	Before the witness testified he had to take an oath to tell the truth and nothing but the truth.	einen Eid leisten
to be charged with	the defendant was charged with the murder of his ex-wife.	eines Vergehens beschuldigt werden, eines Verbrechens angeklagt werden
to be convicted of a crime	According to a new law, anyone convicted of two violent crimes must be jailed for 25 years.	wegen eines Verbrechens verurteilt (worden) sein
to plead guilty/ not guilty	The defendant pleaded not guilty.	sich schuldig/nicht schuldig bekennen
to find s.o. guilty	After four hours' discussion the jury returned a verdict "not guilty".	jdn. schuldig sprechen/ für schuldig erklären
to be sentenced to	He was sentenced to two years' imprisonment.	verurteilt werden zu
to be sent to prison	He was sent to prison for two years.	zu einer Gefängnisstrafe verurteilt werden

Exercise 2 Vocabulary grid: Law

Fill the squares with words from the list "Some Words to Remember". The down column with the darker squares will give you a word we use for people who have less rights and opportunities than the rest of us.

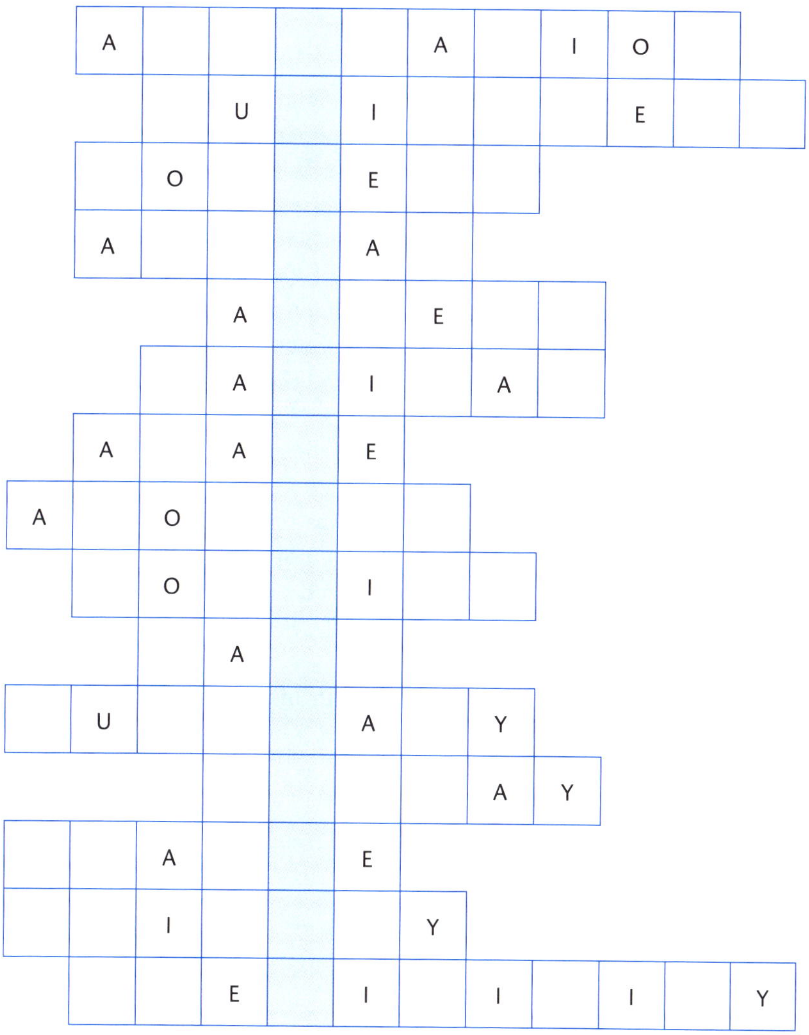

Exercise 3 Cloze-Test: Working for social reforms

Complete the text with words from this list.

aware	experienced	merchants	search
century	increased	misery	underprivileged
debts	injustices	prison	wages
dreadful	introduce	responsible	

The 19th ______________[1] – the Victorian Age – was a time of great prosperity in England. The population ______________[2] tremendously: in 1811 England had 12 million inhabitants, by 1851 that number had risen to 21 million. The Industrial Revolution and the growth of the Empire made factory-owners and ______________[3] rich. Under the golden surface there was a lower class whose life was characterized by poverty, ______________[4] and crime. Thousands of workers left the countryside in ______________[5] of jobs in the towns. What they found were low ______________[6] and badly built houses. The little money they earned was not enough to support themselves and their families. If they could not pay their ______________[7], they had to go to______________[8]. Gradually, more and more ______________[9] people became aware of the great ______________[10] and the social problems of the age and tried to ______________[11] reforms. An important member of that reform movement was one of the greatest writers of English literature: Charles Dickens. In his very popular novels Dickens described the ______________[12] conditions in which poor people had to live. He wanted to make his readers ______________[13] that social reforms were necessary to improve the lives of the ______________[14] masses. Dickens knew very well what he was writing about because in his early childhood he had ______________[15] what it meant to be poor.

Exercise 4 Translation: Charles Dickens

Translate into English or German respectively.

Charles Dickens was born in Portsmouth in 1812. His father John Dickens, who worked as a ______________[1] (Büroangestellter) for the government, was rather careless with money. He ran into *debt* (______________)[2] and brought about the financial ruin of the family. In 1824 John Dickens was *arrested* (______________)[3] and imprisoned. Young Charles could no longer go to school because he had to earn his *living* (______________)[4] by himself. He worked in a ______________[5] (Lager) where he filled pots of black boot polish. While the rest of his family lived together with his father in the debtors' ______________[6]

(Gefängnis), young Charles lived alone like an *orphan* (__________)[7] in a lodging house in North London. That shameful __________[8] (Erfahrung) of being poor and being left alone was so terrible for Dickens that he kept it as a secret all his life. He never talked about those *dreadful* (__________)[9] years. However, later in his life, he described what he had seen and how he had felt in his novel *David Copperfield* (1849).
Eventually (__________)[10], Dickens could go back to school. In 1827 he took a job in a law firm, taught himself shorthand and became a journalist and reporter in the __________[11] (Gerichten). In December 1833 Dickens started publishing a number of essays for which he used his observations of the city of London and its inhabitants: *Sketches by Boz.* He became so popular that his readers asked for more and more stories.
All *novels* (__________)[12] of Charles Dickens appeared in monthly instalments, which means every month a small part of the novel was published. Since these small segments were __________[13] (billig) to produce and to buy, they guaranteed a large readership – and a rich and wealthy publisher and author. Dickens used his popularity to tell his readers about the darker sides of life. He made them *familiar* (__________)[14] with the lives of people in trouble and thus paved the path for social __________[15] (Verbesserungen). Two of his most famous novels were *Oliver Twist* (1837–39) and *Great Expectations* (1860/61).

Exercise 5 C-Test: Oliver Twist – The boy from the workhouse

In the following text some words are incomplete. Only one or a couple of letters are given. Try to complete with words that fit the context.

"Workhouses" in England were first set up to help poor people. The idea was to give them a place to go to where they could find work to keep them off the streets. But by the end of the 18th century workhouses had become the most terrible places you could think of. Families could not stay together, husbands and wives were separated and children were without care. Because of the dreadful hygienic conditions illnesses were widespread and there was not enough food.

This is the story of Oliver Twist as told by Charles Dickens: Oliver Twist is bo________[1] in a workhouse. His mother dies, nobody knows her name. Oliver, now an orp________[2], is raised in the workhouse. Mr Bumble, the supervisor of the workhouse, and Mrs Mann rece________[3] money to buy food for the children. However, they never give the children eno________[4] to eat because they spend less money on food than they are given. They make a pro________[5] by not feeding the children properly. When Oliver says that he is still hun________[6] he is beaten and thrown into a dark ce________[7].

Even________[8] Mr Bumble is so fed up with the boy's complaints about food that Oliver is sent away as an appren________[9] to the undert________[10] Mr Sowerberry and his wife. When they come to coll________[11] him they give him some bits to eat that their dog hadn't wanted. Oliver is so hungry that he quickly eats up the dog's meal.

"I wish that people who have enough to eat and who talk about reform but don't do anything about it could have seen Oliver devouring the dog's bits. I also wish that these people would be made to eat dogs' food, too!" says Dickens.

At the undertaker's Oliver has to sleep among the coffins and is trea________[12] so badly that he escapes. In London he meets a gang of pickp________[13]. The boys take Oliver to where they live and to the man who takes ca________[14] of them, Fagin, who thinks of all these boys as his sons.

When Oliver is caught pickpocketing the wal________[15] of wealthy Mr Brownlow, he almost goes to ja________[16]. But Brownlow decides to take the child instead, which compl________[17] changes Oliver's life. The pickpockets want Oliver to become a crim________[18] and stay a member of their gang. But Oliver wants to lead an honest life. In a happy ending Oliver his rewarded for this behav________[19]: Mr Brownlow adopts him as his son.

3 Language corner: False friends

Es gibt einige Wörter, die im Englischen und im Deutschen fast die gleiche Form aufweisen und nahezu gleich geschrieben werden. In der Bedeutung jedoch sind sie grundverschieden. Also Vorsicht vor diesen „falschen Freunden".

undertaker ≠ Unternehmer

- *undertaker* = Leichenbestatter, Bestattungsunternehmer

When Oliver worked at the undertaker's he had to sleep among coffins.
Als Oliver beim Leichenbestatter arbeitete, musste er zwischen Särgen schlafen.

- Unternehmer = *entrepreneur; industrialist; employer* (Arbeitgeber)

Henry Ford was a successful industrialist.
Henry Ford war ein erfolgreicher Unternehmer.

warehouse ≠ Warenhaus

- *warehouse* = das Lager

Young Charles Dickens worked in a warehouse where he filled pots of black boot polish.
Der junge Charles Dickens arbeitete in einem Lager, wo er Töpfe mit schwarzer Stiefelwichse füllte.

- Warenhaus = *department store*

One of the best-known British department stores is Marks & Spencer.
Eines der bekanntesten britischen Warenhäuser ist Marks & Spencer.

novel ≠ Novelle

- *novel* = Roman

In his novels Dickens described how poor people had to live in the early 19th century.
In seinen Romanen beschrieb Dickens, wie die armen Leute zu Anfang des 19. Jahrhunderts leben mussten.

- Novelle = *novella, short story*

We've just read Heinrich von Kleist's famous novella "Das Bettelweib von Locarno".
Wir haben gerade Heinrich von Kleists berühmte Novelle „Das Bettelweib von Locarno" gelesen.

4 Grammar spot

4.1 Questions

Questions without question word

Entscheidungsfragen sind Fragen, die man mit *yes* oder *no* beantworten kann. Sie werden durch ein **Hilfsverb** (*do/have/be*) oder **Modalverb** (*can/may/ must /shall/will*) eingeleitet.

Hilfs-/Modalverb	Subjekt	Vollverb	Objekt/Ergänzungen
Do	you	work	in Dartmeed?
Can	your brother	help	you with your work?

Questions with question word

Die **Fragewörter** sind:

who = wer	*when* = wann	*how* = wie
what = was	*where* = wo	*how often* = wie oft
which = welche(r, s, n)	*why* = warum	*how much* = wie viel

how many friends = (zahlbares Substantiv) wie viele Freunde
how much salt = (nicht zählbares Substantiv) wie viel Salz

Fragewort	Hilfs-/Modalverb	Subjekt	Vollverb
Where	do	you	live?

Questions without auxiliary verb

Wenn das **Fragewort Subjekt** des Satzes ist, wird **kein Hilfsverb** verwendet. Außerdem bleibt die normale Satzgliedstellung erhalten.

Subjekt	Prädikat	Objekt/Ergänzungen
Who	caught	the thieves?
What	happened	in the market square?

Questions with auxiliary verb

In **Fragesätzen**, die **mit einem Fragewort** eingeleitet werden, muss ein **Hilfsverb** (*do/have*) verwendet werden.

Fragewort	Hilfsverb	Subjekt	Vollverb	Objekt/Ergänzungen
Why	do	you	work	in Dartmeed?
When	did	you	meet	Tom?
What	have	you	done	with the money?

Wenn die Hilfsverben *to do, to have* in Redewendungen als Vollverben verwendet werden, wird auch die Frage mit *to do* umschrieben. Die wichtigsten Redewendungen mit *to do* sind auf Seite 179 zusammengestellt. Die entsprechenden Formen mit *to have* finden Sie auf Seite 111.

Fragewort	Hilfsverb	Subjekt	Hilfsverb als Vollverb	Objekt/Ergänzungen
Where	did	the women	do	the washing?
When	did	you	have	a rest?

4.2 Question tags

Frageanhängsel (deutsch: …, nicht?; …, nicht wahr?; …, oder?) werden verwendet, um den Zuhörer zu veranlassen, eine Aussage zu bestätigen. Frageanhängsel werden mit dem Hilfs- bzw. Modalverb des Hauptsatzes gebildet. Ist im Hauptsatz kein Hilfsverb vorhanden, werden Frageanhängsel mit *to do* gebildet.

Ist der **Aussagesatz bejaht**, wird das **Frageanhängsel verneint**.

They can be very strict with young offenders, can't they?
You know you are wrong, don't you?

Ist der **Aussagesatz verneint**, wird das **Frageanhängsel bejaht**.

The police cannot blame me, can they?
I didn't do anything wrong, did I?

Exercise 6 Asking questions

Ask questions for the underlined parts of speech.

a) Andrew Simms and Tom Roberts of Challacombe were both 14 years old.

____

b) Tom's father lost his farm more than three years ago.

____

c) Tom's father lost his farm more than three years ago.

____

d) He lost his farm because of his heavy drinking.

____

e) One day the boys met <u>Henry Cuthbert</u>.

____

f) <u>A judge</u> sentenced the boys to three months' imprisonment for stealing.

____

g) Crowds gathered <u>hours before the execution</u>.

____

h) Bodmin prison was built <u>in 1776</u>.

____

i) The prisoners were fed <u>three</u> meals a day.

____

j) <u>After the lessons</u> the children went back to their work.

____

k) <u>In 1854</u> Parliament passed the Youthful Offenders Act.

____

Exercise 7 Question tags

Add question tags.

a) You didn't help your mother much, ______________________?

b) You feel awful for what you did, ______________________?

c) You didn't really want to rob that old lady, ______________________?

d) You could tell the old lady that you are sorry, ______________________?

e) You can't expect to get away with stealing, ______________________?

f) You should have kept away from Henry, ______________________?

g) This prison sentence is meant as a serious warning for others, __________?

h) You won't ever get into trouble with the law again, ______________________?

5 Writing desk

5.1 How to find synonyms, opposites and definitions

Synonyms

Was wird verlangt?
Im Aufgabenbereich Language/Vocabulary einer Textaufgabe begegnen Ihnen diese Arbeitsanweisungen: *Give synonyms* oder *Replace the underlined word by a synonymous expression.* Sie werden aufgefordert, für bestimmte Wörter im Text Synonyme zu finden.

Synonyme sind Wörter, die in einem bestimmten Zusammenhang **dieselbe Bedeutung** haben, z. B. die Verben *to shut* und *to close*. Es ist unerheblich, ob ich sage: *Please, shut the door* oder *Please, close the door.*

Meist bezeichnet man Synonyme heute auch als „sinnverwandte" Wörter, um zu verdeutlichen, dass es absolute Bedeutungsgleichheit und Austauschbarkeit nicht gibt.
Für den Fremdsprachenbereich gilt: Diese Aufgabenstellung testet Ihren Wortschatz! Meist steht im Originaltext ein schwierigeres Wort (d. h. ein Wort, das auf einer gehobeneren Stilebene angesiedelt ist), das Sie durch ein einfacheres ersetzen sollen.

Beispiel The Queen delivered a speech. → The Queen made/gave a speech.

Wie gehen Sie vor?
Lesen Sie die Textstelle sehr genau! Sie sollen ein Synonym finden, das an dieser Stelle in den Text eingesetzt werden kann. Nicht jedes Synonym passt! Erst der Kontext macht klar, welche Bedeutung vorliegt.

Beispiel Poor emigrants assembled their families to sail across the ocean. → gathered, called together, collected
In this factory they assemble TV sets. → put together

Beachten Sie besonders:
- Ihre Lösung soll genau in den Text passen, d. h. Sie müssen die richtige Form wählen, sonst gibt es Punktabzüge: Verben müssen in der entsprechenden Zeitform angegeben werden (siehe obiges Beispiel), Substantive in der Singular- oder Pluralform.

Noch ein Tipp!
- Wenn Ihnen die Bedeutung des Wortes, für das Sie ein Synonym angeben sollen, nicht geläufig ist, nutzen Sie die Information, die der Kontext bietet. Kombinieren Sie, raten Sie! Überlegen Sie sich, was das Wort ungefähr bedeuten könnte/müsste.

Opposites

Opposites oder *antonyms* sind Wörter, die das **Gegenteil des Ausgangsworts** bedeuten: *bright – dark, new – old.*

Für die Aufgabe „*Find opposites*" oder „*Give antonyms*" gilt dasselbe Vorgehen wie bei den *synonyms*.

Definitions

Was wird verlangt?
Auch die Aufgabenstellung „*Give a definition of …*", „*Define …*", „*Explain …*" testet Ihren Wortschatz. Sie sollen zeigen, dass Sie das Ausgangswort verstehen und mit Ihren eigenen Worten eine Erklärung geben können.

Wie gehen Sie vor?
Verwenden Sie das Ausgangswort in Ihrer Einleitung, z. B. „*a robber is …*" oder „*by the word sentence we understand …*". Gehen Sie dann vom Allgemeinen zum Besonderen. Versuchen Sie, einen allgemeinen Nenner, einen Oberbegriff zu finden, d. h. eine Klasse, in die das Wort gehört. Danach geben Sie eine eingrenzende, genauere Beschreibung und eventuell ein Beispiel.

Beispiel

Wort	**allgemeiner Nenner**	**nähere Beschreibung**
a robber is	a person/someone	who steals things from people
a sentence is	a punishment	which a judge gives to a criminal, for example a thief or murderer
a fine is	a sum of money	which you have to pay as a penalty when you have broken the law, for example when you have parked your car in the wrong place.

5.2 Example: Finding synonyms and writing definitions

Crime today

In 1993 two 10-year-old schoolboys killed a little boy of two in the North of England. Not only the British nation was deeply shocked. All the world asked: Why did they commit such a horrible crime? What makes young people commit brutal crimes? Surely, this special murder case can be regarded as a dramatic exception. But more and more people fear that ours is a violent society.

The crime rate at schools has risen dramatically: at some schools in the US, pupils are searched for weapons before they are allowed on to the school grounds to make sure that hooligans won't hurt their school-mates.

Why do these kids try to bring knives and guns to school? Is violent behaviour becoming acceptable? Are criminals getting younger?

a) Find synonyms for these words:
killed (line 1) / All the world (line 2) / horrible (line 3) / Surely (line 4)

b) Explain these words:
weapons (line 8) / criminals (line 11)

Key

a) Synonyms:

killed	=	murdered
all the world	=	everybody
horrible	=	dreadful, terrible
surely	=	certainly

b) Explanations/definitions:

weapon	=	A weapon is an instrument with which one can hurt someone else, for example a gun.
criminal	=	A criminal is a person who breaks the law.

Exercise 8 Give synonyms and definitions: Child crime

Criminologists say that – in the majority of cases – violent crimes are committed by youngsters who come from a poor background. Even more important than the depressing economic situation, is the sad fact that most young delinquents come from broken homes. They grow up without love. Nobody tells them what is right and what is wrong. They have the feeling that nobody is really interested in them, no-one cares. When they play truant and don't turn up at school – nobody seems to mind and exercise some sort of control.

Another explanation for child crime is that young people learn violent behaviour. By watching violence in films or videos which are meant "for adults only" kids get used to brutality and find it entertaining. Very often parents do not care what sort of films or videos their children watch.

Some teachers argue that computer games have a negative influence on young children. Those computer games which offer brutality are popular and can be bought quite easily. Children can become aggressive by constantly playing such computer games.

a) Find synonyms for the following words:
youngsters (line 2) / depressing (line 3) / delinquents (line 4) / homes (line 4) / entertaining (line 10)

b) Explain what these words mean:
criminologist (line 1) / to play truant (line 6)

Exercise 9 Guided writing: David Copperfield's childhood

Shortly before David Copperfield is born his father dies. He leaves his young widow Clara with an annual income of £ 105. David's early years are happy ones.

Now you go on and complete the story of David Copperfield. Use all the words in their correct forms. You may have to add articles, prepositions etc. Make sure to use the right tense, too. Sometimes a passive form may be necessary.

Example:

One day / Pegotty, the servant / take / him / an excursion / the port of Yarmouth / her brother Daniel / live.	One day Pegotty, the servant, takes him on an excursion to the port of Yarmouth, where her brother Daniel lives.

a) When / he / come back / Yarmouth / David / discover / his mother / marry / Edward Murdstone.

____

____

b) Mr Murdstone / bring / his sister Jane / live with them.

____

____

c) Together the Murdstones / make life / David and his mother / unbearable.

d) David / bite / Mr Murdstone / the hand / immediately / send / Salem House school.

e) He / put / under the care of Mr Creakle / a sadistic headmaster.

f) David / make / a few friends / the terrible school.

g) Suddenly/ his mother / die / childbirth.

h) Pegotty / leave / get married.

i) David / leave alone / neglect / his stepfather.

j) When / ten years old / David / send / to London / earn his living / the counting house of Murdstone and Grinby / he / almost starved to death.

k) His job / wash and label / wine bottles / a warehouse.

l) The warehouse / dirty, dark / full of rats.

m) David / lodge / the optimistic Mr Micawber / be / always / great financial trouble.

____

____

n) Mr Micawber / finally / throw / debtor's prison / David / again alone and without a home.

____

____

o) David / leave / London for Dover / his great-aunt Betsey Trotwood / live.

____

____

From then on things are getting better and David makes it to the top. In the end he marries Agnes, the woman he has always loved and becomes a highly successful author.

6 Fun and games

Exercise 10

Wordsearch

Try to find the hidden words.

```
            U R I R Z H A
          Y N S Y N O B C P
        R N D P C N J R C R P
      E H Y E E A O L U U T A E
    S C L R R N R I U I S J J E A
  I B U T A P A I S L R A T L E S L
M D R S N L R L P S D Q T B I O T T L
N O I T A G I T S E V N I O C C N R A
Y I B O D R V Y N F Q S O O I Y E I I
E A E D N U I P O N N R N V E R C A N
E W R Y E B L H C O M F N O E U O L E
B G Y T F J E O P C I O E D G J N C D
R I R W E O G S A S C T R H O R N F B
  E A A D B E Q C G A U C F T E I F
    Y R H R D A Z M M J F R T O G
      W R C T T N N M E D N O C
        A E V I D E N C E Z M
          L S N Y C V S B C
            X T E R X A T
```

Exercise 11 Crossword puzzle

Try to solve the crossword puzzle.

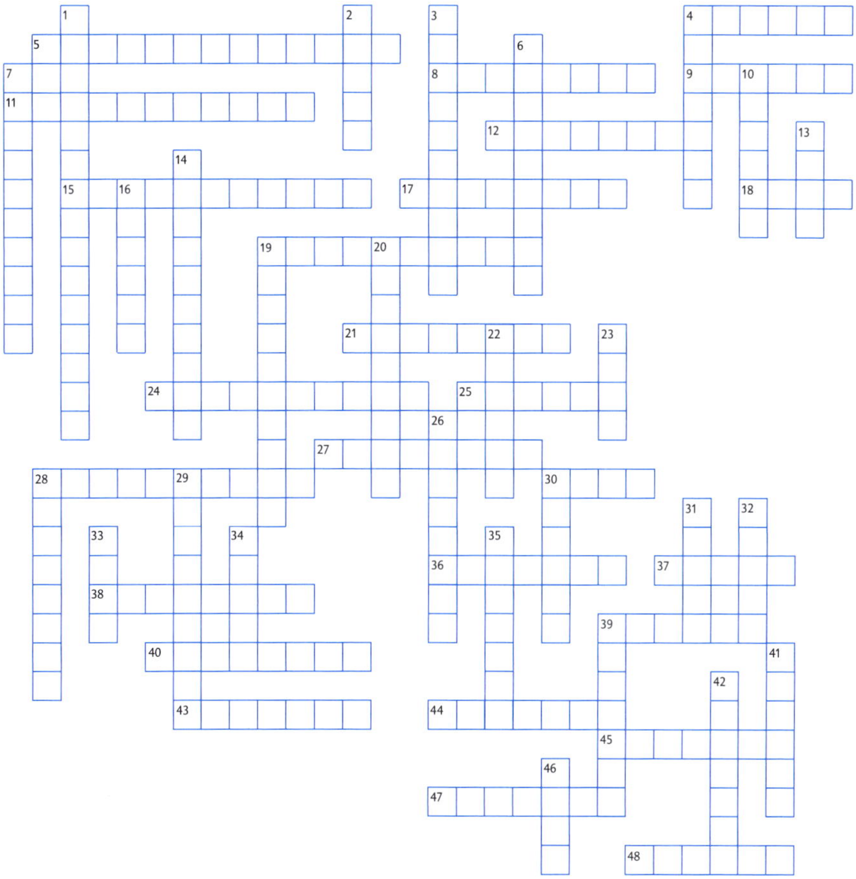

Across

4. verraten
5. Ermittlung
8. Täter(in), Straffällige(r)
9. Häftling
11. Glaubwürdigkeit
12. Urteil; Satz
15. verantwortlich
17. fürchterlich, schlimm
18. Krawall
19. Verurteilung; Überzeugung
21. Einbruch
24. beschlagnahmen
25. Gefängnis
27. zunehmen
28. Erfahrung
30. Schuld
36. abschaffen
37. Prozess
38. unschuldig
39. Beschuldigung, Anklage
40. Mörder
43. Gefühl
44. Sträfling
45. Vergehen, Delikt, Gesetzesübertretung
47. Meineid
48. Rechtsanwalt

Down

1. benachteiligt
2. Gerichtshof
3. Wohlstand
4. Bestechung
6. Angeklagter
7. Beschuldigung, Anklage
10. Elend
13. Gefängnis
14. Geständnis
16. Suche
19. Verschwörung
20. Ungerechtigkeit
22. festnehmen
23. leugnen
26. Kaufmann
28. Beweis, Beweismaterial
29. vorstellen, einführen
30. Leugnen, Ablehnung
31. der Geschworene
32. bewusst
33. Kaution
34. plädieren
35. verdammen, verurteilen
39. Haft
41. appellieren
42. Strafe
46. die Geschworenen

Detectives of the past

1 Text box

In search of a lost city: Heinrich Schliemann

By 1863 businessman Heinrich Schliemann had become rich. He was 41 and gave up work as a merchant in the import and export trade. For the remaining 23 years of his life he tried to make a dream come true he had had as a boy: to find the ancient city of Troy. When he was seven he had heard the tale of the battle between Greeks and Trojans for the first time. The classic story by the Greek poet Homer had fascinated him. As a wealthy man he now had enough time to prove that Homer's report was not pure fantasy but that it was based on fact.

Heinrich Schliemann was born on January 6, 1822, in Neubukow (Mecklenburg). His father was a poor vicar, rather moody and strict – but an excellent story teller. Young Heinrich had a lively fantasy and took great interest in the legends and ghost stories of his home county told to him by his father. When Heinrich was seven his father presented him with a book that was to change his life: *Illustrierte Weltgeschichte* by Ludwig Jerrer. It contained a picture of the destroyed city of Troy in flames. At the end of the famous war only a few Trojans escaped. One of them was Aeneas, who led the other survivors to Italy. The old Schliemann told his son that the story of the Trojan War was only a Greek legend, but young Heinrich was convinced that the enormous city walls could not have been destroyed completely. Remains must be buried under ground somewhere. His dream had started: "One day I will find those Trojan walls!"

Schliemann's childhood was soon over: At the age of 14 he had to leave school to earn his living and started an apprenticeship with a grocer's. He was very ambitious and full of energy, saved all his money, lived in cheap and dirty rooms. He studied his beloved Homer – and learned foreign languages. Schliemann was very clever at teaching himself a new language. In 1845 his company wanted to send him to St. Petersburg. So he had to learn Russian. He went into a shop, bought himself a Russian text-book and a dictionary. He then read the story, looking up all the words he did not know – and remembered them for ever. He had such a fantastic memory that he never had to look up a word twice. He learnt whole pages by heart, and said them out aloud. His neighbours often complained about the noise, so he had to move to different flats more than once. It usually took Schliemann six months to learn a new language. Using the same method he taught himself English, French, Dutch, Spanish, Italian, Portuguese.

In 1870 Schliemann started digging on the hill of Hissarlik, in Turkey, where he thought he would find the remains of the ancient city of Troy. He discovered several layers which he believed to be the Troy of Homer. Later, however, archaeologists proved that the ruins were those of an even earlier settlement. In one of the graves which Schliemann excavated in Greece from 1876 to 1878, he found a gold mask. Schliemann believed it belonged to King Agamemnon.

Many people have criticized Schliemann as a mere treasure hunter, who destroyed much valuable evidence with his rather rough methods of digging and excavating. However, even critics admit: Schliemann made many people become interested in lost civilisations and paved the way for others who introduced more scientific methods. Because of his enthusiasm and his energy he holds an important place as a pioneer in field archaeology. Heinrich Schliemann died in Italy in 1890. That same year the German chancellor Otto von Bismarck was dismissed by Emperor William II. *620 words*

Exercise 1

Understanding the text

Decide if these statements are true. Correct the false ones.

		true	false
a)	Schliemann had earned a fortune as a businessman.	☐	☐
b)	Schliemann wanted to try his luck searching for gold in Greece.	☐	☐
c)	Schliemann thought that Homer's epic was the true historical report of a war between Greeks and Romans.	☐	☐
d)	Young Heinrich bought a book called *Illustrierte Weltgeschichte* for his father.	☐	☐
e)	Schliemann was certain that remains of the old Trojan city walls could still be found in the ground somewhere.	☐	☐
f)	Schliemann was very talented for learning foreign languages.	☐	☐
g)	In Greece Schliemann found remains of old walls which he thought had been part of Troy.	☐	☐
h)	Archaeologists later proved that the walls Schliemann had discovered were older still.	☐	☐
i)	Schliemann also excavated the gold coffin of King Agamemnon.	☐	☐
j)	Although Schliemann did not use proper scientific methods he is important for the development of archaeology.	☐	☐

2 Word power: Some words to remember

(to) afford	sich leisten
ambitious	ehrgeizig
ancient	sehr alt, antik
apprentice	Lehrling
burial	Begräbnis
(to) bury	beerdigen, begraben
chamber	Kammer
coffin	Sarg
(to) contain	enthalten
curse	Fluch
(to) decay	zer-, verfallen
decease	Ableben
department	Ministerium
descent	Abstammung
desert	Wüste
(to) destroy	zerstören
determination	Entschlossenheit, Resolutheit
(to) dig	graben
discovery	Entdeckung
(to) display	zeigen, ausstellen
(to) disturb	stören
draftsman, draughtsman	Zeichner
dreadful	furchtbar, schrecklich
effort	Anstrengung
(to) embalm	einbalsamieren
evidence	Beweis
(to) evolve	(sich, etwas) entwickeln, entstehen
(to) excavate	ausgraben
exploration	Erforschung

funeral	Begräbnis
grave	Grab
layer	(Erd-, Luft-) Schicht
link	Bindeglied
merchant	Kaufmann
mummy	Mumie
patience	Geduld
pottery	Töpferwaren
(to) preserve	erhalten, bewahren
(to) prove	beweisen
recovery	Bergung
remains	Reste, Überbleibsel, Spuren
resin	Harz
(to) rule	herrschen
scientific	wissenschaftlich
settlement	Siedlung
(to) supervise	überwachen
survivor	Überlebende(r)
tomb	Grab
treasure	Schatz
valley	Tal
(to) wrap	einwickeln

Exercise 2 Definitions: Archaeology

Match the definitions with the corresponding words. Please note that there are more words than definitions.

battle	dig	grave	pave
burial	dismiss	hill	pharaoh
civilisation	evidence	method	scientific
dictionary	excavate	mummy	treasure

a) a body of a human being or animal embalmed for burial, esp. in ancient Egypt ____________
b) to break up and remove or turn over soil with a tool or one's hands ____________
c) ruler of ancient Egypt, also the title of this ruler ____________
d) a long fight between armed forces ____________
e) a book that lists and explains the words of a language or gives equivalent words in another language ____________
f) the way you choose to do something ____________
g) to send someone away ____________
h) a naturally raised area of land, not as high as a mountain ____________
i) gold, silver, jewels and other valuable things ____________
j) to remove earth carefully and look for the remains of pots, bones or buildings ____________
k) an advanced stage or system of social development ____________
l) to cover a street ____________

Exercise 3

Vocabulary grid: Archaeology

Find the words for these definitions and write them into the squares across. The down column in the centre will tell what Howard Carter's job was when he joined Sir William Flinders Petrie. Here's some help: All words can be found in the list "Some Words to Remember".

a) to have enough money to buy something
b) a beginner; a learner; someone who is learning a trade or occupation
c) to show a great desire for success, to be eager
d) the act or process of putting a dead person into a grave
e) a hole in the earth where a dead body is put
f) a room in a house, especially a bedroom
g) very old
h) a source or cause of evil; wishing someone bad things to happen
i) government branch or division of a large organization
j) to hold within itself
k) box in which a dead body is put

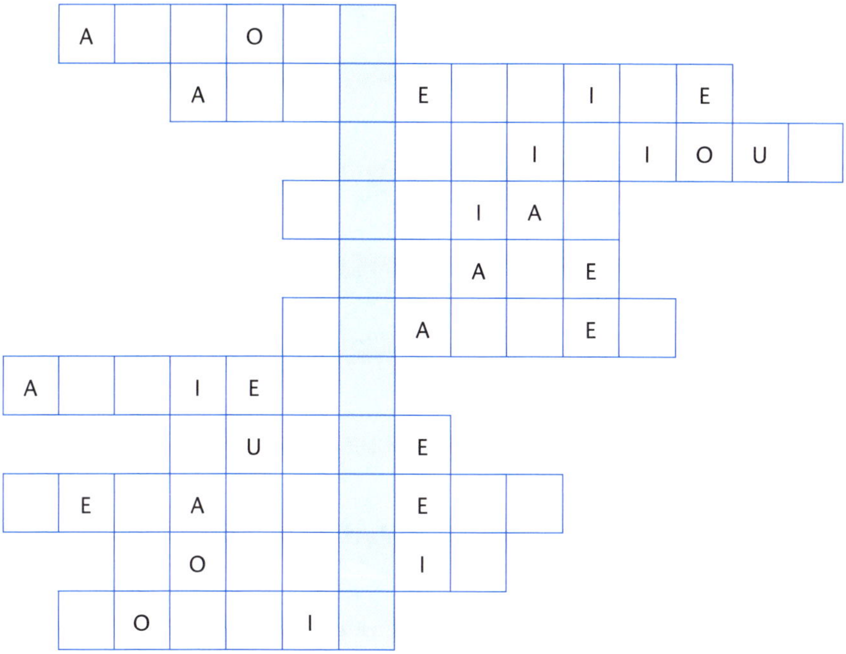

Exercise 4 Cloze-Test: The tomb of Tutankhamen

Complete the text with words from this list.

across	curse	graves	pharaoh
age	desert	hand	received
assistant	destroy	hole	rewarded
beginning	discoveries	joined	ruled
blood	display	Kings	scientist
buried	eventually	masterpiece	took
candle	give	objects	untouched

Sir William Flinders Petrie became the father of a new kind of archaeology, very different from the treasure-hunters. He was the first archaeologist who used scientific methods to study ancient Egyptian remains, such as pottery.
In 1891 an 18-year-old young man ______________ [1] Flinders' Egypt Exploration Fund as a draughtsman. His name was Howard Carter. He ______________ [2] training in excavation and surveying from Sir William and worked as his ______________ [3] during several excavations in Egypt. Carter was an extremely talented and careful ______________ [4]. In 1899 he became inspector general of

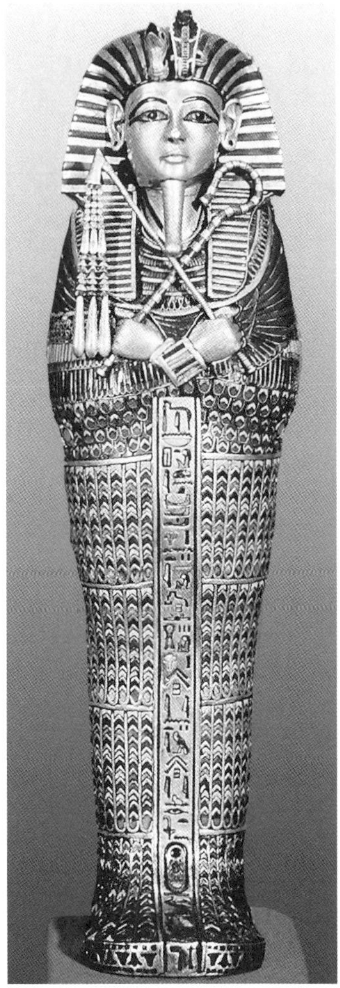

the antiquities department of the Egyptian government. He supervised a number of tomb excavations in the Valley of the ____________[5].
Carter knew that valley like the back of his ____________[6] and was convinced that there must still be some undiscovered ____________[7]. As he himself didn't have the financial means, Carter ____________[8] found George Herbert, 5th Earl of Carnarvon, an English Egyptologist and collector of antiquities, who put up the money for the excavations. After many frustrating years of careful searching in the Egyptian ____________[9] in Luxor, Carter and Lord Carnarvon were about to ____________[10] up. In November 1922, however, they were ____________[11] for their patience and determination. Carter made one of the greatest archaeological ____________[12] of the 20th century. His workmen had started digging under some huts ____________[13] in the ground and suddenly came ____________[14] steps leading down.
Right from the ____________[15] Carter was sure that he had found something really important. So he ____________[16] every effort not to dig too quickly and ____________[17] valuable evidence. Three weeks after the first step was discovered, Carter made a ____________[18] into the wall of a burial chamber and held a ____________[19] through it. What he saw was breath-taking: the room was filled with hundreds of valuable ____________[20] and fabulous burial treasure. Carter and Lord Carnarvon had found a tomb that had been lying ____________[21] for more than 3,000 years: the tomb of the Egyptian ____________[22] Tutankhamen. For months Carter and his men worked on the scientific recovery and exploration of the tomb. Suddenly Lord Carnarvon died of ____________[23] poisoning and pneumonia, before the royal sarcophagus was opened. With this death a new legend was

born: the legend of Tutankhamen's ____________[24] on those who disturbed his tomb.
Tutankhamen had become pharaoh at the ____________[25] of nine in the 14th century BC. He ____________[26] for only nine years. The excavation of his tomb is still regarded as one of the scientific triumphs of archaeology, as a ____________[27] of careful investigation. The treasures of Tutankhamen are now on ____________[28] in the Egyptian Museum in Cairo.

Exercise 5 C-Test: Mummies and tomb robbers

In the following text some words are incomplete. Only one or a couple of letters are given. Try to complete with words that fit the context.

The Ancient Egyptians believed that after death they would enter the next world in which they would live in the same way as they did on this earth. They believed that the spi________[1] of the deceased returned to the body when visiting the tomb. So they took every eff________[2] to avoid that their bodies would dec________[3]. The technique developed by the Egyptian embalmers is known as mummification – and it sounds rather cru________[4] and dreadful.
The cor________[5] was cut open on its left side. All the organs were taken out and prese________[6] separately in the so-called Canopic jars. Only the heart was left in place. The brain was dra________[7] out of the head through the nose. The body was then cleaned and fil________[8] with spices and herbs to make it smell swe________[9]. Bags of white powder, natron, was used to dry the body for about 35 days. Fina________[10] it was wrapped in many lay________[11] of linen bandages and coated with salts, oils and res________[12]. A mask was put over the face. The body was then put into a coffin which, in turn, was put into another coffin-like box to keep it sa________[13]. Several coffins were used to protect the pharaoh's mummy. The outer coffin was finely deco________[14] and painted. The most beautiful and valu________[15] death mask is that of Tutankhamen.

From now on some words are scrambled. Try to restore the original word. To help you the first letter is given.

In a burial (p-icsnreoos) ____________[16] the dead pharaoh was taken to his resting place, a specially built tomb in the (d-teers) ____________[17]. The most famous complex can still be (v-eiidts) ____________[18] today at Giza, near modern Cairo, where the 4th-dynasty (p-yiasdrm) ____________[19] of

Kings Cheops, Chephren, and Mycerinus lie close to each other. The tomb was filled with (f-nrutuire) ____________[20], food and everything that might be needed in the next world.
As all that was an (e-rlxmeyet) ____________[21] costly affair only pharaohs and rich Egyptians could (a-odfrf) ____________[22] to have their bodies mummified and buried in special places. Clever and brilliant tricks were (a-eplipd) ____________[23] by the architects of the pharaoh's tomb to protect the grave from robbers. They hid (e-nrenscat) ____________[24], built underground passages, blocked the burial (c-shemrba) ____________[25] with huge stones – but all in vain. Very often the burial place was robbed not long after the (f-eaunrl) ____________[26]. Most treasure buried with the pharaohs has long been dug up by tomb robbers. Only one grave was left untouched until 1922, when the British (a-rhelsgicoaot) ____________[27] Howard Carter (d-vcidresoe) ____________[28] the tomb of Tutankhamen.

3 Language corner: False friends

become ≠ bekommen

• *to become* = werden	By 1863 businessman Heinrich Schliemann had <u>become</u> rich. *Als das Jahr 1863 kam, war der Geschäftsmann Heinrich Schliemann reich <u>geworden</u>.*
• bekommen = *to get, to obtain*	In 1845 he <u>obtained</u> an important post in St. Petersburg. *1845 <u>bekam</u> er einen wichtigen Posten in St. Petersburg.*

actually ≠ aktuell

• *actually* = in Wirklichkeit, eigentlich, tatsächlich	The ruins were <u>actually</u> those of an even earlier settlement. *Die Ruinen gehörten <u>tatsächlich</u> zu einer früheren Siedlung.*
• aktuell = *topical, current, of current interest; up-to-date*	The poverty in Third World countries is a <u>topical</u> problem. *Die Armut in den Entwicklungsländern ist ein <u>aktuelles</u> Problem.*

eventually ≠ eventuell

• *eventually* = schließlich	After years of frustrating digging Carter and Lord Carnarvon were eventually rewarded for their patience. *Nach Jahren vergeblichen Grabens wurden Carter und Carnarvon schließlich für ihre Geduld belohnt.*
• eventuell = *perhaps, probably, possibly, if necessary*	Perhaps it would be better to give all ancient monuments back to the original owner countries. *Vielleicht wäre es besser, alle Denkmäler an die ursprünglichen Besitzerstaaten zurückzugeben.*

Exercise 6 Usage: Early elephant hunters

Use one of these words in the empty spaces: become – obtain / actually – current / eventually – perhaps, probably.

From fossils found in Spain scientists can __________[1] prove that by 300,000 BC early people had become elephant hunters. The men __________[2] lay in wait for the animals which passed through their valley. They waited for the animals to come near and __________[3] set fire to the grass on the hills. The elephants __________[4] frightened and stampeded down the valley. Marshy land __________[5] made it impossible for the animals to escape. The hunters waited until the animals __________[6] died in the marshes. Then they __________[7] used hand-axes made of stone and __________[8] some other tools to cut them open.

Exercise 7 Usage: The curse of the dead pharaoh

Use one of these words in the empty spaces: become – obtain / actually – current / eventually – perhaps.

The early death of Lord Carvarvon, sponsor of Howard Carter, __________[1] the starting point of a legend: that of “the curse of the pharaoh”. Shortly after its discovery in 1922 the tomb of the pharaoh had __________[2] the status of a world sensation. Millions of readers wanted to know everything about the __________[3] state of the excavations. Thousands of visitors __________[4] travelled to Egypt to have a look at the site themselves. __________[5] a journalist got so bored with ordinary reports on the diggings. So when yet another member of Carter's crew – Archibald Reid – died, he invented a sensational headline: "Has Reid ____________[6] another victim of the curse of Tutankhamen?" Thus the journalist ____________[7] the father of a new "mystery": Everyone who had taken part in the opening of the tomb would not ________[8] old. The ghost of the dead pharaoh would ____________[9] cause his early death. That was the punishment for those who had ____________[10] access to the burial chamber. In the 1930s the general public had ____________[11] so interested in the mysterious deaths that Hollywood producers ____________[12] made films on the subject. The film "The Mummy" (1932) was to _________[13] a horror classic. Because of his convincing acting as the monster in "Frankenstein" (1931) Boris Karloff ____________[14] the title role of the film. Today we know that all 20 people of Carter's crew who died after the discovery ____________[15] died natural deaths: due to infections, illnesses or even suicide.

4 Grammar spot

4.1 Adjective and adverb

• Das **Adjektiv** steht bei einem **Substantiv** oder einem **Pronomen** und bestimmt es näher.	More than 100 million years ago different kinds of dinosaurs lived on our earth. They were too slow to react to changing conditions.
• Das **Adverb** bestimmt ein **Verb** oder ein **Adjektiv** genauer.	The process in which animals change slowly is called evolution. Darwin showed that no two animals were exactly alike.

4.2 Comparison of adjectives

Adjektive werden mit *-er/-est* gesteigert (germanische Steigerung) oder mit *more/most* (romanische Steigerung).

Comparison with *-er/-est*

Einsilbige Adjektive und zweisilbige Adjektive, die auf *-y*, *-le*, *-ow* oder *-er* enden, werden mit *-er/-est* gesteigert.

Grundform (Positiv)	**Komparativ**	**Superlativ**
fast	faster	fastest
easy	easier	easiest
simple	simpler	simplest
narrow	narrower	narrowest
clever	cleverer	cleverest

Comparison with *more/most*

Die meisten zweisilbigen und alle mehrsilbigen Adjektive werden mit *more/ most* gesteigert.

Grundform (Positiv)	**Komparativ**	**Superlativ**
famous	more famous	most famous
interesting	more interesting	most interesting

Irregular comparison

Grundform (Positiv)	**Komparativ**	**Superlativ**
bad	worse	worst
far	farther/further	farthest/furthest
good	better	best
late	later	latest (letzte, neueste)
		last (das Letzte in der Reihenfolge)
little (wenig)	less	least
little (klein)	smaller	smallest
many (viele)	more	most
much (viel)	more	most
near	nearer	nearest (das Nächste in der Entfernung)
		next (das Nächste in der Reihenfolge)

4.3 Adjective or adverb?

Nach diesen Verben steht das Adjektiv (nicht das Adverb):

• *to become, to get, to grow, to keep, to look* (= aussehen), *to remain, to seem*	All the boys remained quiet.
• *to smell, to sound, to taste*	Your cakes always taste delicious. The new CD sounds great.

Adjektiv und Adverb mit unterschiedlicher Bedeutung:

Adjektiv		**Adverb**	
fair	gerecht	*fairly*	ziemlich
hard	schwer	*hardly*	kaum
high	hoch	*highly*	sehr
just	gerade	*justly*	zu Recht
late	spät	*lately*	kürzlich, in letzter Zeit
near	nahe	*nearly*	beinahe

Exercise 8 Comparison of adjectives: The origins of man

Use comparative or superlative forms of the adjectives in brackets.

The ____________[1] (recent) discovery of human bone fragments in Africa are a scientific sensation. The bones which were discovered in Ethiopia are 500,000 years ____________[2] (old) than any human remains found before. These fossils represent our ____________[3] (old) direct human ancestors. With these bones scientists will be able to carry out the ____________[4] (detailed) investigation into the origins of man. The ____________[5] (fascinating) aspect of the discovery are the 20 teeth which were excavated. The findings suggest that those humans were ____________[6] (likely) vegetarians. It is ____________[7] (likely) that they ate plants and fruit than that they hunted animals. They ____________[8] (certainly) made no stone tools.

Exercise 9 Adjective or adverb?: Conserving the past

Decide whether to use adjectives or adverbs in these sentences.

Shirley Binghall works as a conservator in the British Museum. Her job is to keep the ____________[1] (valuable) objects in ____________[2] (good) condition so that they look ____________[3] (beautiful) when they are displayed

__________[4] (public). Because of her __________[5] (extreme) __________[6] (long) experience Shirley knows __________[7] (exact) how to look after the artefacts __________[8] (proper). Last week she was given an __________[9] (exceptional) __________[10] (difficult) job. German archaeologists in Troy had __________[11] (careful) unearthed __________[12] (numerous) pieces of a __________[13] (probable) Greek pot. Although the dirty-brown pieces looked __________[14] (fair) __________[15] (worthless) at first sight, Shirley knew __________[16] (immediate) that the Germans had found a __________[17] (real) beauty. Shirley __________[18] (careful) placed all the pieces on her working table. There they look __________[19] (just) like a jigsaw puzzle. Then Shirley __________[20] (cautious) cleaned the pieces and tried to fit them together. For several days she worked __________[21] (regular) on the mending of the object. Using sellotape, plaster and wax, Shirley __________[22] (final) succeeded in sticking the pieces into place. Although several pieces were missing, she didn't find it __________[23] (hard) to date the pot __________[24] (correct). She __________[25] (hard) ever tries to paint over the missing pieces in order to give the visitors a __________[26] (clear) picture of which parts are old and which have __________[27] (recent) been added.

Exercise 10 Countries – Inhabitants – Languages

Fill in the missing forms.

Country	Inhabitant	Language
Austria		
Belgium		
Brazil		
Britain		
Canada		
Denmark		
England		
Finland		
France		
Germany		
Greece		

Holland / Netherlands	______________	______________
Hungary	______________	______________
India	______________	______________
Ireland	______________	______________
Italy	______________	______________
Japan	______________	______________
Norway	______________	______________
Poland	______________	______________
Portugal	______________	______________
Russia	______________	______________
Scotland	______________	______________
Spain	______________	______________
Sweden	______________	______________
Switzerland	______________	______________
Turkey	______________	______________
USA	______________	______________
Wales	______________	______________

5 Writing desk: Wordformation with suffixes

In nahezu jeder **erweiterten Textaufgabe** werden Sie einer oder mehreren Aufgaben des folgenden Typs begegnen: „*Give nouns, Give adjectives …*". Es gilt, von einem bestimmten Ausgangswort (Grundwort) eine andere Wortart zu bilden. Die Sprache geht hier ökonomisch vor: Grundwörter werden durch bestimmte unselbstständige Bildungselemente abgewandelt, d. h. durch Partikel, die in dieser Form nicht alleine auftauchen (*-ment*, *-able* etc.). Durch Ableitungen mit Vorsilben (Präfixen) oder Endsilben (Suffixen) entstehen neue Wörter. In diesem Abschnitt werden Sie damit vertraut gemacht, wie mithilfe von Suffixen Substantive (Nomina) und Adjektive gebildet werden können. Ein zweiter Teil im Kapitel „Adventures at Sea" (S. 58) zeigt Ihnen dann, wie durch die Verwendung von Vorsilben das Gegenteil ausgedrückt werden kann.

Wordformation with suffixes: Nouns

-ance/-ence	-ation	-dom	-hood
distance	operation	wisdom	childhood
difference	representation	freedom	neighbourhood

-ment	-ness	-ty
treatment	blindness	honesty
fulfilment	darkness	cruelty

Wordformation with suffixes: Adjectives

-ly	-ic(al)	-ous	-ful	-able/-ible	-al/-ial
lovely	historic(al)	dangerous	careful	drinkable	educational
yearly	economic(al)	glorious	beautiful	responsible	essential

Exercise 11

Give nouns

Add a suffix to these words to form nouns.

manage	______________
certain	______________
employ	______________
enter	______________
foolish	______________
free	______________
pay	______________
real	______________
sick	______________
tender	______________

Exercise 12 Give adjectives

Add a suffix to these nouns or verbs to form adjectives.

centre	________	read	________
classic	________	act	________
comfort	________	agree	________
comic	________	eat	________
courage	________	forget	________
duty	________	harm	________
fashion	________	pay	________
mountain	________	poison	________
music	________	think	________
noise	________	use	________

Exercise 13 Word families

Word families: Supply the missing forms.

noun (abstract)	**noun** (concrete)	**verb**	**adjective**
________	________	to explore	________
________	believer	________	________
collection	________	________	________
________	-----	________	convincing, convincible
________	destroyer	________	
________	________	to discover	-----
________	-----	to enter	-----
________	-----	-----	poor
________	preparer	________	________
remains, remainder	-----	to remain	-----
________	-----	________	safe
science	________	-----	________
________	________	to supervise	-----
________	________	to tell	-----

6 Fun and games

Exercise 14 Wordsearch

Try to find the hidden words.

D	E	T	E	R	M	I	N	A	T	I	O	N	E	V	O	L	V	E	H
H	Y	X	E	I	D	E	P	A	R	T	M	E	N	T	C	F	V	Y	P
P	G	S	P	Z	C	S	M	P	M	A	S	U	O	I	T	I	B	M	A
T	I	B	T	L	I	I	O	P	R	S	E	F	F	Z	D	F	D	E	T
N	D	I	S	C	O	V	E	R	Y	H	T	I	E	E	Y	L	U	R	I
E	R	U	S	A	E	R	T	E	G	M	T	H	N	B	U	Y	E	C	E
C	Y	E	O	H	J	E	A	N	Q	N	L	C	G	F	R	B	F	H	N
S	P	M	V	B	R	P	V	T	E	Y	E	A	D	U	M	N	M	A	C
E	P	O	M	R	P	U	A	I	I	R	M	A	B	A	A	R	J	N	E
D	V	O	T	U	E	S	C	C	P	O	E	N	H	M	C	R	J	T	K
O	T	K	Y	T	M	S	X	E	T	R	N	C	G	M	E	O	D	X	C
Q	T	R	E	S	E	D	E	R	D	E	T	I	O	R	S	V	W	U	X
C	O	F	F	I	N	R	C	R	E	E	R	E	Q	V	A	I	W	R	W
J	F	F	F	D	U	O	Y	M	P	Y	S	N	C	F	E	V	O	R	P
M	K	L	O	Y	I	F	B	D	N	I	A	T	N	O	C	R	E	E	O
I	B	R	R	D	R	F	U	N	E	R	A	L	R	O	E	U	Y	U	I
A	T	Y	T	Q	I	A	R	P	W	C	M	Y	P	O	D	S	R	D	N
M	H	F	F	Y	R	U	I	R	E	M	A	I	N	S	Y	K	C	S	Q
M	H	G	Y	E	L	L	A	V	C	O	J	Y	K	N	I	L	R	M	E
U	Q	L	N	E	M	P	L	M	F	A	X	R	P	L	P	D	G	Y	R

Exercise 15 Crossword puzzle

Try to solve the crossword puzzle.

Across
2. Zeichner
6. Erforschung
7. Grab
8. Fluch
9. Lehrling
13. Mumie
14. Ministerium
16. herrschen
17. wissenschaftlich
20. Siedlung
23. Töpferwaren
25. enthalten
28. Entdeckung
29. erhalten, bewahren
32. Kaufmann
34. Geduld
35. graben
37. Überlebende(r)
38. Grab
39. Schatz
40. Begräbnis

Down
1. Entschlossenheit
3. einbalsamieren
4. sehr alt, antik
5. beerdigen, begraben
10. ehrgeizig
11. Wüste
12. (sich, etwas) entwickeln, entstehen
15. Abstammung
18. überwachen
19. Ableben, Tod; sterben

21. Beweis
22. ausgraben
24. Harz
26. furchtbar, schrecklich
27. Reste, Überbleibsel, Spuren
30. einwickeln
31. Bergung
33. Anstrengung
36. Begräbnis

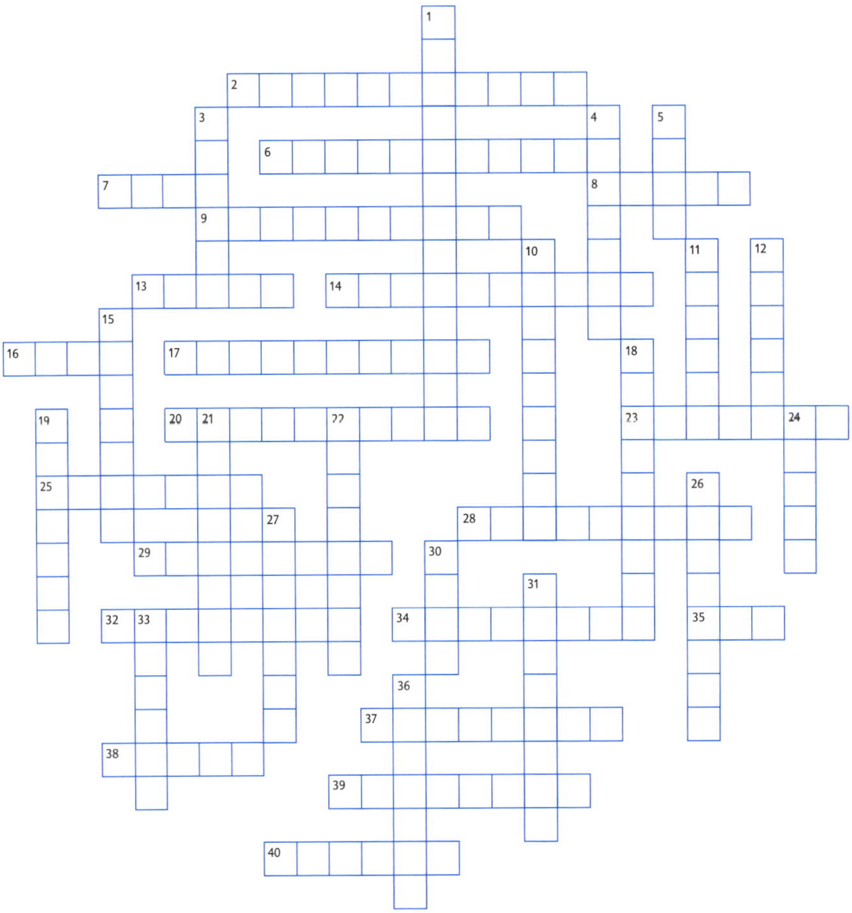

Adventures at sea

1 Text box

The mutiny on the Bounty

The famous mutiny on the H. M. S. Bounty happened in April 1789. The mutineers under Fletcher Christian complained about the severe treatment by their captain, William Bligh. Bligh and 18 men were put out in a small boat in the middle of the Pacific Ocean with few provisions. The story was used by American writers Charles Nordhoff (1887–1947) and James Hall (1887–1951) in their novel *Mutiny on the Bounty* (1932). Three films were also based on the story. One of them brought fame to actors Charles Laughton and Clark Gable. In most pictures William Bligh is portrayed as the hardhearted, unfair and incompetent tyrant. The reality, though, was quite different.

Bligh was born on September 9, 1754, in Plymouth where his father held a post in His Majesty's Customs Service. William grew up in one of the greatest ports of the time and very soon developed a love for the sea and the navy. Consequently he chose a career in the Royal Navy. As he was a bright young man, he quickly made his way to the top. Bligh was only twenty-three when the great Captain James Cook chose him as his navigator on his second voyage of discovery to the Pacific. In 1787 Bligh was appointed to command the H.M.S. Bounty. He was to sail to Tahiti to collect plants of the bread fruit tree and take them to the West Indies. The owners of the sugar plantations there wanted to use them as a cheap source of food for the slaves.

The whole crew of the Bounty consisted of volunteers. Friends and seamen who had sailed with Captain Bligh before asked him to join. One of them was Fletcher Christian. He was born in 1764 and when he was sixteen he had run away to sea. In 1782 he sailed together with Bligh for the first time. Fletcher respected the older man for his abilities as a seaman. Bligh taught Fletcher how to use instruments and how to draw charts.

On choosing his crew Bligh made a serious mistake. To please friends he accepted the applications of more sailors than he really needed. Some of them were young (several were only fourteen, fifteen years old) and lazy and not fit enough for a long demanding journey. Others turned out to be troublemakers. With a crew of forty-six the ship was overcrowded.

It all started as a happy voyage. It is true, there were some complaints about the food, but grumbling about food was quite normal in those days. Bligh's reactions were always insulting and aggressive. He was not a diplomatic and tactful man. As a captain he was more concerned about the general health of his crew. He had learnt the proper methods from Captain Cook, who had never lost a man. Bligh, too, never had a case of scurvy in his ship.

The Bounty arrived at Tahiti on October 26, 1788. After months of hardship and suffering the crew settled down to an idyllic and easy life in paradise. They had to wait for the right time to take the bread fruit plants. During the stay on the island the discipline of the men got worse. Some of them forgot that they were still in the navy. Several sailors were whipped because they did not obey orders. On April 4, 1789, the Bounty eventually left Tahiti for the West Indies. Many of the crew would have liked to stay. As the ship carried over a thousand bread fruit plants, conditions on board became rather cramped. The crew were dissatisfied. Bligh, on the other hand, was furious about them, saying they were all criminals, that he would kill half of them and make the officers jump overboard. An argument between Bligh and Christian in front of the men finally led to the catastrophe. Bligh and 18 crew members who remained loyal to him were set out in an open boat. The last words Bligh said were, "This is mutiny, Mr Christian, mutiny. You shall hang, you hear me, you shall hang."

The mutineers knew that from now on they were hunted men. After a long search for a safe place to hide, nine mutineers and nineteen Polynesians finally escaped to the uninhabited Pitcairn Island. They burned the Bounty so that they would not be discovered. In 1793 Christian and five other mutineers were murdered by natives. The survivors of the mutiny were not found until 1808. Their descendants still live on Pitcairn.

Bligh's voyage in an open boat is a masterpiece in courage and navigation. After a dangerous and terribly exhausting journey Bligh reached Timor in the East Indies. In 45 days he had sailed across 3,600 miles of open sea. He had lost seven of his 18 men. At the following investigations and inquiries it was confirmed that Bligh had acted correctly according to the rules and regulations of the Royal Navy. The mutiny was completely unjustified. In 1805 William Bligh was appointed governor of New South Wales, Australia. He died in 1817 and is buried in London.

844 words

HMS or H.M.S. (abbreviation) = Her, or His, Majesty's Ship
scurvy = a disease caused by a lack of vitamin C (= "Skorbut")

Exercise 1 Understanding text passages

Which phrases in the text tell you that ...

a) Bligh and his men did not have much to eat and drink in their open boat?
b) even as a young child William Bligh wanted to be a sailor?
c) Bligh was a very successful young marine officer?
d) only later it was discovered that some crew members were criminals?
e) there was not much space for the sailors on the ship?
f) Bligh did not answer to complaints in a friendly way?
g) not all crew members were against Bligh?
h) Fletcher and his supporters were wrong in what they did?

Exercise 2 **Questions on the text**

Answer the following question in your own words. Do not copy from the text.

a) Why did Fletcher Christian and his supporters start the mutiny?

b) How is William Bligh usually described in novels and films about the mutiny?

c) What facts prove that Bligh was an exceptionally good sailor and navigator?

d) What was the aim of Bligh's voyage to Tahiti?

e) Describe the relationship between Bligh and Christian when they first got to know each other.

f) Why was the Bounty so overcrowded?

g) Why did the discipline get worse during the stay on Tahiti?

h) What did the admirals and judges at the inquiry in England think about Bligh's behaviour as a captain?

2 Word power

2.1 Some words to remember

advanced	modern, fortschrittlich
apparently	offensichtlich
application	Bewerbung
attempt	Versuch
career	Laufbahn
chart	Karte
(to) complain	sich beschweren, beklagen
(to) conclude	schließen, schlussfolgern
consequently	folglich
(to) convince	überzeugen
cramped	(räumlich) eng
(to) delay	verzögern, verspäten
demanding	anspruchsvoll, anstrengend
descendant	Nachkomme

(to) desert	im Stich lassen
exhausting	erschöpfend
experienced	erfahren
(to) grumble	murren
hardship	Not, Entbehrung
incompetent	unfähig
insult	Beleidigung, beleidigen
invincible	unbesiegbar
lead [e]	Blei
loyal	treu, ergeben
mutineer	Meuterer
mutiny	Meuterei
native	Eingeborene(r)
navigator	Seefahrer
poisoning	Vergiftung
precaution	Vorsichtsmaßnahme
provision	Proviant, Lebensmittel
regulation	Vorschrift
settlement	Siedlung
sledge	Schlitten
source	Quelle
sufficient	ausreichend
survivor	Überlebender
trace	Spur
treatment	Behandlung
troublemaker	Unruhestifter, Störenfried
uninhabited	unbewohnt
vessel	Schiff
whip	Peitsche, peitschen
wreckage	Wrackteile

2.2 Useful phrases

to make one's way to the top	As he was a bright young man, he quickly made his way to the top.	Erfolg haben, Karriere machen
it is true … but	It is true, there were some complaints about the food, but grumbling about food was quite normal among sailors.	zwar … aber; freilich
to be concerned about	As a captain he was more concerned about the health of his crew.	sich Sorgen machen, sich kümmern um
to be appointed (governor, chairman, etc.)	In 1805 William Bligh was appointed governor of New South Wales, Australia	zum (Gouverneur, Vorsitzenden usw.) ernannt werden
to contract a disease	Drake contracted dysentery ("Ruhr") and died on Jan. 28, 1596.	sich eine Krankheit zuziehen, erkranken an

Exercise 3 **Words in a new context**

Here are words from the text box "The Mutiny on the Bounty". They are used in different contexts. Use the words in the right places. Please note there are more words listed than you actually need.

accept	appointment	ask	demand
act	argument	cruel	developed
application	arrived	dangerous	discipline

a) The two boys began an ________________ over who was to play first.
b) I must hurry; I have an ________________ with my dentist.
c) She knew he would not come back, but it was very hard for her to ________________ it.
d) I have an important question to ________________ you.
e) Now that he had starred in two successful films, he felt that he had ________________.
f) The ________________ for computers is steadily increasing.
g) Without this rule, there would be no ________________ at all.
h) People should not be ________________ to animals.
i) Meryl has just handed in her ________________ for a job with the HSCB Bank.
j) The trade relations between the two countries have ________________ favourably.

Exercise 4 Vocabulary grid: Sea

Fill the squares with words from the list "Some words to remember". The word down in the bold squares is used for people (or generations) who come after you.

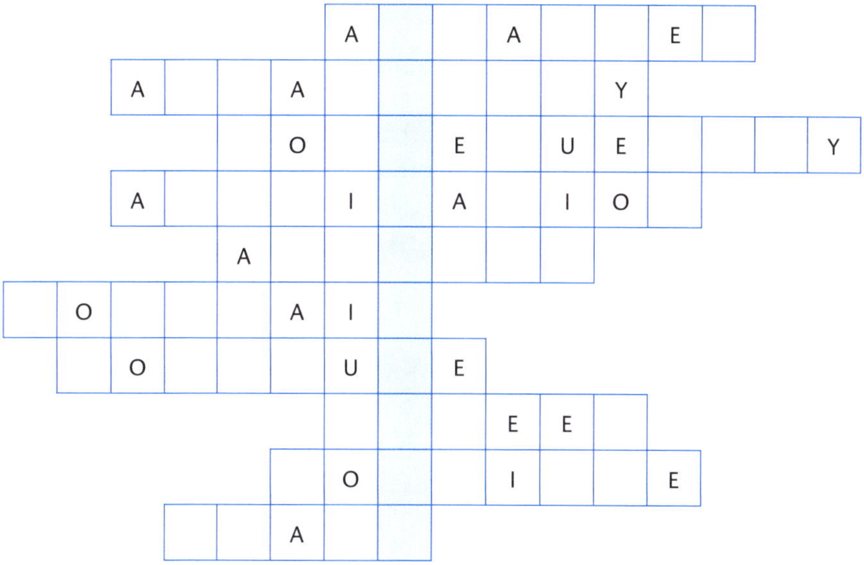

Exercise 5 Words with several meanings

Which word fits into all sentences of a group?

a) Robert went to the information desk to ________________ about an Intercity train to Glasgow.
Why did you ________________ him? He won't know anything about it.
Miss Marple ________________ the inspector to come in and have a nice cup of tea.
The Taylors ________________ their friends to dinner.

b) Jimmy Greaves has a valuable ________________ of foreign stamps.
The church uses the money it gets from ________________ to help elderly people.
The Tate Gallery has a large ________________ of portraits of famous people.
Have you posted your letter yet? Hurry, the next ________________ is at 3 pm.

c) The employees agreed to the ________________ stipulated in the contract.
Weather ________________ were excellent; so we went on a mountain tour.

I'll lend you these CDs on the ________________ that you give them back to me by next Friday.
He has flu; he is in no ________________ to go on the excursion with us.

d) There have been a number of economic ________________ caused by the introduction of the computer.
Is it of much ________________ to the government that their party lost the latest by-election?
As a ________________ of the rather poor productivity of our factory in Nottingham we are forced to reduce the number of jobs there.
You must apologize for your bad behaviour or face the ________________.

Exercise 6 Cloze-Test: The real Robinson Crusoe

Complete the text with words from this list.

alone	control	hunt	quarrelling
ashore	discipline	lonely	shoemaker
attract	enjoyed	navigator	uninhabited
became	everyone	near	vegetation
civilization	expeience	own	vessels

Alexander Selkirk was the son of a ________________[1] born in Largo in the Fife region, Scotland. As a young boy he was hard to ________________[2] and got into trouble with almost ________________[3]. After ________________[4] with many of his neighbours he left home and ran away to sea. Selkirk was 19 then. In 1703 he ________________[5] sailing master on the pirate ship Cinque Ports, one of the two ____________[6] of an expedition under the English ____________[7] William Dampier. Selkirk could not stand the ____________[8] on board. After an argument with the captain of the ship he asked to be put ____________[9] on the nearest island. He wanted to live on his ____________[10]. The ship at that point was ________________[11] the Juan Fernández Islands, off the coast of Chile. In October 1704 Selkirk was left behind on the ________________[12] island. Juan Fernández was a beautiful place with rich ________________[13]. There were plenty of goats which Selkirk could ________________[14] with his rifle he had taken with him. There were no people on the island and Selkirk ____________[15] the solitude. After more than four years of being ____________[16], though, he decided that he had had enough. In February 1709 he saw two ships off the coast and lit a signal fire to ________________[17] their attention.

One of the ships sent a boat ashore to pick up Alexander Selkirk and take him back to ________________[18] again. He died in 1721.
The English writer Daniel Defoe heard the story of Selkirk's stay on the ________________[19] island and wrote a novel based on the ________________[20] of Alexander Selkirk. He called it *The Life and Strange Surprising Adventures of Robinson Crusoe* (1719).

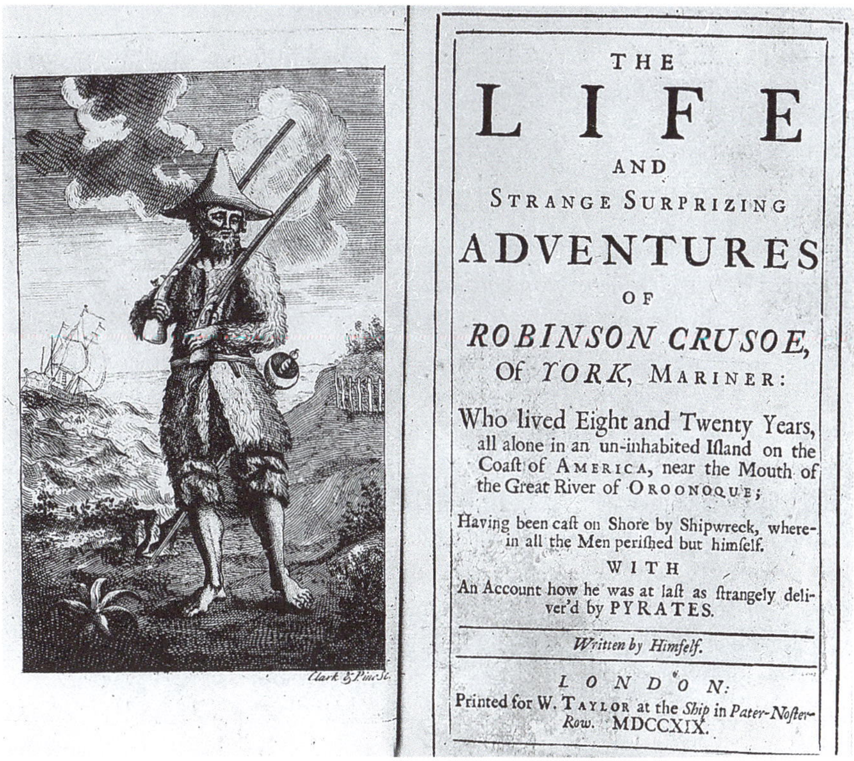
THE
LIFE
AND
STRANGE SURPRIZING
ADVENTURES
OF
ROBINSON CRUSOE,
Of *YORK*, MARINER:
Who lived Eight and Twenty Years, all alone in an un-inhabited Iſland on the Coaſt of AMERICA, near the Mouth of the Great River of OROONOQUE;
Having been caſt on Shore by Shipwreck, wherein all the Men periſhed but himſelf.
WITH
An Account how he was at laſt as ſtrangely deliver'd by PYRATES.
Written by Himſelf.
LONDON:
Printed for W. TAYLOR at the *Ship* in *Pater-Noſter-Row*. MDCCXIX.

Exercise 7 C-Test: Francis Drake fighting the Spaniards

In the following text some words are scrambled. Try to restore the original word. To help you the first letter is given.

Francis Drake became the first Englishman to (s-ali) ________________[1] around the globe. That historic (v-eoayg) ________________[2] took place between 1577 and 1580. In England Drake was regarded as a (h-oer) ________________[3] not so much for his achievements as a (n-ioaagtvr) ________________[4] but for the many attacks he carried out on Spanish (p-tors) ______________[5] and ships. In 1587, Queen Elizabeth and her advisors were (c-onevcnid) ______________[6] that war with Spain would break out soon. She sent Drake to (d-oetysr) ______________[7] the stores and the ships of the Spaniards in the harbour of Cadiz. Drake completed most of the (m-sionsi) ______________[8]. He described the attack on the Spanish (f-elte) ______________[9] in its own port as "the singeing of the King of Spain's beard". The Spaniards had to rebuild their ships, which (d-aeeldy) ______________[10] their attack on England for a year. On May 11, 1588, the "Invincible" Armada sailed from Lisbon to (c-qeonru) ______________[11] England.

Exercise 8 C-Test: The defeat of the Armada (1588)

In the following text some words are incomplete. Only one or a couple of letters are given. Try to complete with words that fit the context.

In 1588 Francis Drake ser__________[1] as vice admiral of the English fleet. While awaiting news of the coming of the Spanish Armada he was pla__________[2] bowls on Plymouth Hoe. When he was told that the Spanish ships had ent__________[3] the English Channel, Drake said, "There is plenty of time to fin__________[4] the game, and beat the Spaniards."
Lord Howard in his fla__________[5] Ark Royal and Drake in the Revenge led the att__________[6] against the Spaniards. The Armada was defe__________[7] in the Battle of Gravelines. Three great Spanish ships sa__________[8], a dozen more were badly dam__________[9]. The Spaniards lost more than 600 men, at least 800 were wou__________[10]. The English won a great victory and took the place of the Span__________[11] as the world's most important sea p__________[12].
In 1595 the queen sent Drake on an expe__________[13] against the Spanish forces in the West Indies. This mission was a fai__________[14]. Drake fell seriously ill (he contr__________[15] dysentery) in the Caribbean and died on Jan. 28, 1596. His body was bur__________[16] at sea.

to singe = versengen, ansengen
dysentery = a disease causing severe diarrhoea with blood and mucus (= "Ruhr")

3 Language corner

3.1 Usage of words

Für ein deutsches Wort gibt es im Englischen zuweilen mehrere Entsprechungen. Welche Variante die richtige ist, ergibt sich aus dem jeweiligen Sinnzusammenhang. Der deutsche und der englische Sprachgebrauch (*usage*) sollen in diesem Abschnitt an einigen Wörtern aus dem Haupttext erläutert werden.

bringen = to bring, to take

Das deutsche Wort **bringen** kann im Englischen entweder durch ***to bring*** oder durch ***to take*** wiedergegeben werden.

- Man verwendet *to bring*, wenn etwas **zum Sprecher** gebracht werden soll.

  Marian, could you bring me that book, please?
  Marian, kannst du mir bitte dieses Buch herbringen?

- Man verwendet *to take*, wenn etwas **vom Sprecher weg**gebracht werden soll.

  Please take this parcel to the post-office.
  Bitte bringe dieses Päckchen zur Post.

3.2 Combinations and collocations

Prägen Sie sich diese Wortkombinationen gut ein!

Phrases with *to take*

to take place	stattfinden
to take advantage of	ausnutzen
to take up	etwas anfangen
to take for granted	als selbstverständlich hinnehmen
to take into account	etwas berücksichtigen
to take interest in	sich interessieren für
to take care of	für jemanden sorgen
to take time	Zeit für etwas verwenden, dauern

Exercise 9 Usage: to take – to bring

Use a form of "to take" or "to bring" in these sentences.

a) The film *Mutiny on the Bounty* ______________ fame to the actors Charles Laughton and Clark Gable.
b) We are having a party on Saturday. Please come and ______________ your girlfriend Eve, too.
c) Let's finish our meal and then I'll ______________ you home.
d) Could you ______________ this parcel to the post-office, please.
e) James, please ______________ me your trousers. I must have a look to see if they have to be ______________ to the cleaners'.
f) Laura doesn't feel very well, Dave. Could you please ______________ her home now?
g) Could you ______________ me that book over there, please.
h) As it was getting rather late my Father ______________ Anne and Robert to the station in his car.
i) John visited me in hospital and ______________ me some lovely flowers.
j) It's Jennifer's birthday. I think I'll ______________ her some nice chocolates this time.
k) Our history teacher is ______________ us on a trip to Rome next month.

Exercise 10 Phrases with "to take"

Match the phrases with the corresponding synonymous expressions.

phrase	**synonymus expression**
A to take place	1 to make good use of (a favourable circumstance); to exploit or outwit (a person), esp. unfairly
B to take advantage of	2 to believe that something is true or valid
C to take up	3 to consider
D to take for granted	4 to look after; to keep safe
E to take into account	5 to occur, to happen
F to take care of	6 to require or to use up, to last
G to take time	7 to start, to begin

A	B	C	D	E	F	G

Exercise 11 **Some more phrases with "to take"**

Use a phrase with "take" in these sentences.

a) The next performance of "Macbeth" will ________________ on Friday 12, at 8 o'clock.

b) You can wait for your shoe to be repaired; it will only ________________ a short ________________.

c) Don't rush; ________________ for the job.

d) People in the industrialised countries ________________ all their luxuries ________________.

e) When we try to introduce birth control in Third World countries we must ________________ the religious beliefs of the population.

f) How can we ________________ the positive sides of nuclear energy?

g) We're going to the cinema tonight. Could you ________________ our two boys till we come back, please.

h) Henry has been extremely helpful to us; let's not ________________ his kindness too much.

i) Young Heinrich Schliemann ________________ great ________________ the legends and ghost stories told to him by his father.

4 Grammar spot: The passive (1)

Passive ordinary

Das Passiv wird gebildet mit einer Form von ***to be* + Partizip Perfekt**.

A new film is made about the mutiny on the Bounty.
Ein neuer Film über die Meuterei auf der Bounty wird gedreht.

Tense	Passive Active	Passive
Present	The film star signs the contract.	The contract is signed by the film star.
Past	The film star signed the contract yesterday.	The contract was signed by the film star yesterday.
Present perfect	The film star has signed the contract already.	The contract has already been signed by the film star.
Past perfect	The film star had signed the contract before.	The contract had been signed by the film star before.

Future I	The film star will sign the contract next month.	The contract will be signed by the film star next month.
Future II	The film star will have signed the contract before long.	The contract will have been signed by the film star before long.
Conditional I	The film star would sign the contract …	The contract would be signed by the film star …
Conditional II	The film star would have signed the contract …	The contract would have been signed by the film star …

Passiv progressive

Die Verlaufsform des Passivs wird gebildet mit ***to be + being* + Partizip Perfekt**. Diese Form gibt es nur im Präsens und im Präteritum.

At present the Oscars are being presented to the winners.
Die Oscars werden im Moment den Siegern überreicht.

Tense	Active	Passive
Present	The BBC is televising the Oscar ceremony.	The Oscar ceremony is being televised by the BBC. *Die Oscarfeier wird (gerade) von der BBC übertragen.*
Past	The BBC was televising the Oscar ceremony.	The Oscar ceremony was being televised by the BBC. *Die Oscarfeier wurde (über eine längere Zeit) von der BBC übertragen.*

Exercise 12 Active and passive

Put these sentences into Passive Voice.

Example:

James Cook chose him as his navigator.	He was chosen as navigator by James Cook.

a) The plantations owners use the bread fruit trees as a cheap source of food.

____

b) All his friends will ask him to join.

____

c) Fletcher respected the older man for his abilities as a seaman.

d) The old sailor is teaching his son how to draw a chart.

e) The lazy sailors did not obey orders.

f) The mutineers had burnt the ship.

g) We regard Bligh's voyage as a masterpiece in navigation.

h) He lost seven of his 18 men.

i) In 1817 they buried him in London.

j) Two American writers have used the story for a novel.

k) The MGM film company is still making a profit with the film on the mutiny.

Exercise 13

Passive and active

Remember the old Egyptians? They had developed the strange art of embalming their deceased. The following text tells you about the method they used. It may sound a bit crude in places. But this is how it really worked.

Put these sentences into Active Voice. Use "The Egyptian embalmers" (or "they") as subject of the Active sentences.

a) All the organs were taken out and preserved separately.

b) Only the heart was left in place.

c) The brain was drawn out of the head through the nose.

d) The body was cleaned and filled with spices and herbs.

____

e) Bags of white powder, natron, was used to dry the body.

____

f) Finally it was wrapped in many layers of linen bandages.

____

g) A mask was put over the face.

____

h) The body was then put into a coffin.

____

i) Several coffins were used to protect the mummy.

____

j) The outer coffin was finely decorated.

____

5 Writing desk: Wordformation with prefixes

Die Aufgabe „*Give opposites*" bzw. „*Give antonyms*" können Sie leicht lösen, wenn Sie die wichtigsten Präfixe (Vorsilben) kennen, mit denen sich bei Substantiven, Verben und Adjektiven das Gegenteil des Ausgangswortes bilden lässt. Eine Besonderheit stellt die Vorsilbe *in-* dar: Vor *p* wird *in-* zu *im-* (*i**m**possible*), vor *r* zu *ir-* (*i**r**relevant*) und vor *l* zu *il-* (*i**l**literate*). Es lassen sich keine allgemein gültigen Regeln angeben, ob nun **un-** oder **in-** als Präfix verwendet wird. Lösen Sie die Übungsaufgaben mithilfe Ihres Wörterbuchs und prägen Sie sich die Formen ein.

Wordformation with prefixes expressing the opposite

	nouns	verbs	adjectives
un-	**un**employment	**un**tie	**un**fair
in-/im-	**in**dependence/ **im**possibility	**in**activate	**im**polite
ir-	**ir**regularity	---	**ir**responsible
mis-	**mis**fortune	**mis**behave	**mis**taken
dis-	**dis**like	**dis**obey	**dis**honest

Exercise 14 Give opposites: Nouns

Add a prefix to these nouns to give them the opposite meaning.

a) advantage ______________________
b) ability ______________________
c) appearance ______________________
d) armament ______________________
e) balance ______________________
f) decision ______________________
g) honour ______________________
h) importance ______________________
i) literacy ______________________
j) patience ______________________

Exercise 15 Give opposites: Verbs

Add a prefix to these verbs to give them the opposite meaning.

a) guide ______________________
b) agree ______________________
c) appear ______________________
d) believe ______________________
e) chain ______________________
f) connect ______________________
g) do ______________________
h) fasten ______________________
i) like ______________________
j) plug ______________________
k) print ______________________
l) understand ______________________

Exercise 16 Give opposites: Adjectives

Add a prefix to these adjectives to give them the opposite meaning.

a) convenient ____________________
b) able ____________________
c) agreeable ____________________
d) breakable ____________________
e) dependent ____________________
f) direct ____________________
g) educated ____________________
h) effective ____________________
i) happy ____________________
j) kind ____________________
k) legal ____________________
l) lucky ____________________
m) pleasant ____________________
n) safe ____________________

Exercise 17 Text production: Francis Drake, the pirate

Try to put the sentences into the right order to form a paragraph on Francis Drake's early years as a pirate.

a) His first ship, the Judith, was one of a fleet led by Sir John Hawkins, on a slave-trading voyage in the Gulf of Mexico.
b) He was sent next to Ireland to help crush the rebellion there from 1573 to 1576.
c) The English navigator and explorer Francis Drake was born near Tavistock in 1541.
d) The year following his voyage to the West Indies Drake commanded two vessels in a piracy expedition against Spanish ports in the Caribbean Sea.
e) On its way to the Gulf the Judith and the other English ships were attacked by the Spaniards and all but two ships of the expedition were lost.
f) After capturing two ports in the Caribbean and destroying the town of Portobello, Drake returned to England with a valuable load.

g) Because of the great wealth he had brought to England Drake enjoyed a reputation as a brilliant pirate.
h) During this voyage to the Caribbean, Drake saw the Pacific Ocean for the first time.
i) In his early years he served an apprenticeship as a seafarer.
j) His two ships were full of Spanish silver.
k) In 1570 and 1571 Drake made two profitable trading voyages to the West Indies.
l) When he was 25 years old he was given his first command.

1	2	3	4	5	6	7	8	9	10	11	12

6 Fun and games

Exercise 18 Wordsearch

Try to find the hidden words.

Y	L	T	N	E	U	Q	E	S	N	O	C	D	J	E	D	J	I	T	S
L	E	R	B	N	O	I	T	U	A	C	E	R	P	A	L	O	Y	A	L
T	S	O	E	D	U	L	C	N	O	C	W	D	R	S	O	U	R	C	E
N	S	U	L	J	T	N	A	D	N	E	C	S	E	D	T	Q	F	S	D
E	E	B	K	G	C	W	R	E	C	K	A	G	E	L	B	M	U	R	G
R	V	L	M	C	G	N	I	T	S	U	A	H	X	E	A	F	O	Y	E
A	R	E	S	O	P	R	U	I	A	G	B	D	D	E	F	Y	E	D	E
P	M	M	Z	M	E	I	D	B	R	N	O	I	S	I	V	O	R	P	M
P	U	A	P	P	L	I	C	A	T	I	O	N	C	R	A	M	P	E	D
A	K	K	X	L	B	A	W	H	I	P	O	I	S	O	N	I	N	G	G
F	F	E	C	A	I	N	T	N	E	M	E	L	T	T	E	S	L	W	W
Q	E	R	C	I	C	N	K	I	G	N	I	D	N	A	M	E	D	T	B
Z	S	J	Y	N	N	S	S	N	T	D	A	O	E	G	L	A	F	R	J
Y	T	U	G	F	I	D	A	U	S	E	X	V	M	I	D	U	V	E	C
U	I	P	R	K	V	V	B	Y	L	O	I	T	T	V	W	G	G	S	H
R	Z	A	M	V	N	G	N	H	V	T	A	R	A	A	C	C	V	E	A
C	R	G	F	E	I	I	F	O	A	T	A	N	E	N	K	T	L	D	R
T	F	Y	M	G	T	V	C	N	C	C	C	A	R	E	E	R	G	C	T
L	F	P	J	U	Q	T	O	R	E	E	N	I	T	U	M	G	I	I	F
V	U	F	M	E	I	H	A	R	D	S	H	I	P	B	P	J	P	E	H

Exercise 19 Crossword puzzle

Try to solve the crossword puzzle.

Across
1. folglich
4. offensichtlich
7. Zeitgenosse; zeitgenössisch
8. sich beschweren, beklagen
9. schließen, schlussfolgern
11. Unruhestifter, Störenfried
13. Knochen
14. Bewerbung
16. Skelett
17. erschöpfend
19. verzögern, verspäten
22. unbewohnt
23. verurteilen, verdammen
24. drängen
26. Ausrottung
29. Siedlung
32. Vorsichtsmaßnahme
35. Kaiser
37. ausstatten
38. Vorschrift
41. Wrackteile (eines Schiffes); Trümmer
45. Seefahrer
47. streng, hart
48. überzeugen
49. Förderer; fördern
50. Meuterer

Down
2. begeistert
3. Bleivergiftung
5. erfahren (adj.)
6. Hunger, Hungersnot
10. Nachkomme
12. treu, ergeben
15. einheimisch
18. Vorfahren, Ahnen
20. ansteckend
21. Behandlung
23. Laufbahn
25. murren
27. unbesiegbar
28. anspruchsvoll, anstrengend
30. ausreichend
31. Proviant, Lebensittel
32. Vorschlag
33. sich beziehen auf
34. erwerben
36. modern, fortschrittlich
39. Völkermord
40. im Stich lassen
42. Geleit, Geleitzug
43. Blei
44. Überbleibsel
46. Schiff

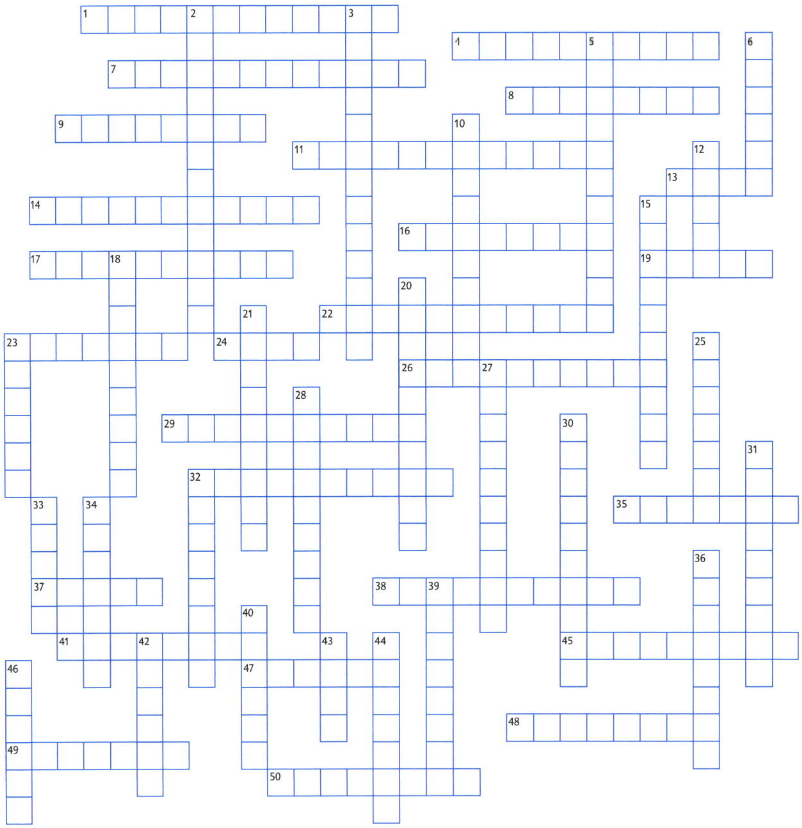

Discoveries

1 Text box

The discovery of the New World

When he died at the age of 54, he was ill and almost forgotten by his contemporaries. Today every child knows his name and what he achieved. Some recognize him as the bravest discoverer of a new world, others condemn him as the man whose arrival in the New World marked the beginning of a tragedy. Yet it would be just as unfair to hold Christopher Columbus responsible for the extinction of thousands of natives as to credit him alone with the expansion of the Old World. He should be seen as what he was: "The first European visitor to middle America."

Christopher Columbus was born in Genoa, Italy. In those days Genoa was an independent city-state and a busy port. His father was a weaver. Christopher, who had two brothers, received little education. Only much later as an adult did he learn to read and write. He went to sea and started a career as a commercial agent. When, in 1476, he sailed with a convoy to England, the fleet was attacked by pirates off the coast of Portugal. Columbus's ship was destroyed and sank, but he managed to swim to shore and sought refuge in Lisbon.

On his journeys Christopher Columbus had often listened to reports of legendary westward voyages beyond Madeira and the Azores. So now he tried to get hold of books and charts to acquire more information. Having studied the new charts Columbus was convinced that Asia could be reached quickly by sailing west. According to his calculations Japan was about 4,800 km (3,000 miles) to the west of Portugal – a distance that could be sailed in existing ships. In 1484 he submitted his theories to John II, king of Portugal, asking him to finance a westward crossing of the Atlantic Ocean. His proposal to search a route to Asia was rejected.

Soon after, Columbus moved with his son Diego to Spain. For almost seven years he tried to find sponsors for his expedition. Yet his plan to reach the Indies by a westward route was again rejected by a royal commission. Columbus, however, did not give up. He continued to seek support, and in April 1492 he reached his aim: The Spanish monarchs, Ferdinand V, king of Castile, and Queen Isabella, agreed to finance the proposed voyage. In an agreement with the crown Columbus was granted everything he wanted – three ships, a title and one-tenth of all riches he acquired for Spain. He departed from Palos, Spain, on August 3, 1492. What he did not know at his departure was that the discoveries he was to make would be more important and valuable than the route he failed to find.

For his first voyage Columbus had received three rather small and simple ships: the Santa María, a decked ship about 30 m long and two small caravels, the Pinta and the Niña, each about 15 m long. The Santa María sailed under his command, the caravels were commanded by two brothers, Martín Pinzón and Vicente Pinzón. On September 6, after a brief stop at the Canary Islands, the three vessels sailed west. After more than four weeks at sea and still sailing west, the crews got increasingly nervous, thinking their foreign commander had lost his way. Then, at last, on October 12 land was sighted! The expedition landed on Guanahaní, an island in the Bahamas, and was met by Arawak, a friendly local population that Columbus called Indians because he believed he had reached the East Indies. Columbus renamed the island San Salvador ("Holy Saviour"). Some days later the expedition sailed on to Cuba to seek the court of the Mongol emperor of China and gold. Columbus began his homeward journey in December 1492, arriving back in Spain in March 1493. The people and the court regarded him as a hero and received him enthusiastically.

Columbus made three more voyages on which he discovered Puerto Rico and explored Venezuela. Then his luck changed. He lost the support of the monarchs as he failed to find the gold they had hoped for. He was replaced as governor general of all new lands in 1500. He was even put in chains and returned to Spain.

Christopher Columbus died on May 20, 1506, still fighting for his rights, still believing that he had reached Asia. *718 words*

Exercise 1 Understanding the text

Match questions and answers.

A What do people today think about the arrival of Columbus in the "New World"?

B How did Columbus come to Lisbon?

C Who or what gave Columbus the idea that there could be land beyond the travelled routes in the West?

D What did Columbus ask from the king of Portugal?

E Why did Columbus not get very good ships for this first voyage?

F Which facts prove that Columbus really thought he had found the sea route to Asia?

G Why did Columbus lose the support of the monarchs?

1 As he himself didn't have any money to finance an expedition Columbus turned to the king to find a sponsor for the enterprise.

2 Columbus had received information from sailors and navigators. Many seafarers talked about the new land, but nobody was really sure.

3 First of all he gave the natives he met on the Bahamas the name "Indians"; secondly, he sailed on in order to find the court of the Emperor of China.

4 They were dissatisfied, because they had hoped Columbus would bring back lots of gold from the new lands.

5 Some are of the opinion that Columbus was a hero, others think that by discovering the New World he brought misery and death to millions of natives.

6 The monarch thought the risk was too high for a better-equipped expedition. He did not want to lose so much money and too many ships; that's why he gave Columbus simple vessels.

7 He was shipwrecked off the coast of Portugal and went to Lisbon.

A	B	C	D	E	F	G

2 Word power

2.1 Some words to remember

(to) abuse	misshandeln, missbrauchen
(to) acquire	erwerben
ancestors	Vorfahren, Ahnen
(to) award	jdm. (einen Preis) verleihen
bone	Knochen
brief	kurz, knapp
(to) condemn	verurteilen, verdammen
consequently	folglich
contemporary	Zeitgenosse; zeitgenössisch
convoy	Geleit, Geleitzug
(to) desert	verlassen, aufgeben, im Stich lassen
emperor	Kaiser
enthusiastic	begeistert
(to) equip	ausstatten
extinction	Ausrottung
famine	Hunger, Hungersnot
genocide	Völkermord
indigenous	einheimisch
infectious	ansteckend
lead poisoning	Bleivergiftung
native	eingeboren
precaution	Vorsichtsmaßnahme
proposal	Vorschlag
(to) refer	sich beziehen auf
refuge	Zuflucht
(to) reject	zurückweisen, ablehnen
remains	Überbleibsel
severe	streng, hart
(to) sight	sichten; Sicht

skeleton	Skelett
sledge	Schlitten
(to) sponsor	fördern; Förderer
supply	Vorrat; Versorgung
trace	Spur
(to) urge	drängen
vessel	Schiff
wreckage	Wrackteile (eines Schiffes); Trümmer

2.2 Useful phrases

to make a landfall	A landfall was made on the morning of Oct. 12, 1492, at an island in the Bahamas, which Columbus named San Salvador.	Land sichten
to hold s.o. responsible for sth.	We cannot hold Christopher Columbus responsible for the extinction of thousands of natives.	jdn. für etwas verantwortlich machen
to credit s.o. with sth.	It would be unfair to credit Columbus alone with the expansion of the Old World.	jdm. das Verdienst zuschreiben an
to set off	In 1502 Columbus set off on his last voyage with four caravels.	aufbrechen

Exercise 2

Cloze-Test: The search for the Northwest Passage

Complete the text with words from this list.

appointed	discover	preparations	trace
awarded	experienced	renewed	traders
chosen	frozen	route	unthinkable
convinced	led	supplies	urged
decided	part	survive	voyages

Sailors were always ________________[1] that there was a route for ships from Europe to China through the waterways of Northern Canada. They called it the Northwest Passage. Efforts to ____________________[2] the legendary passage

began in the 1490s with the ______________[3] of John Cabot. However, Cabot did not find the ______________[4]. Many later attempts were unsuccessful, too. For some time the idea of a Northwest passage was given up, but it was ______________[5] in the 19th century.
Merchants and ______________[6] were interested in the commercial possibilities of a quick sea route to China. They ______________[7] the King and the Royal Navy to take up the search again. It was ______________[8] to start the biggest and best-equipped expedition to find the Northwest Passage. The admirals chose one of the most ______________[9] navigators to take the command: Sir John Franklin.
Franklin was born in Spilsby, Lincolnshire, England in 1786. During the Napoleonic Wars he took ______________[10] in the battles of Copenhagen (1801) and Trafalgar (1805). In 1818 he made his first voyage to the Arctic as captain of the ship Trent. From 1819 to 1827 he ______________[11] several expeditions to explore the northern coast of Canada and North America. In 1829 Franklin was knighted and ______________[12] the gold medal of the Geographical Society of Paris for his services.
Because of his frequent journeys along the Canadian Arctic coast Franklin knew that area like nobody else. In 1845 he was ______________[13] commander of an expedition to discover the Northwest Passage. He controlled all the ______________[14] for the expedition. His ships Erebus and Terror were equipped with the most advanced technology of the time. Sufficient food and ______________[15] were taken on board to make sure the voyage would be a success. The crew of 129 officers and men was carefully ______________[16]. Franklin and the admirals did not allow any mistake to be made. Finally, the most modern and best-equipped expedition sailed from England to Canada. Despite all the precautions that were taken the ______________[17] happened: the expedition was last seen by a whaling vessel on July 26, 1845, in Baffin Bay – and then it was lost.
Searches for Franklin and his men were started almost immediately. It was thought that their ships were ______________[18] in the ice. The world hoped that he would ______________[19] somewhere in the ice – he had taken enough food to get through severe winters. Numerous searching expeditions returned from the Arctic. None found a ______________[20] of Franklin and his men.

Exercise 3 C-Test: The tragic end of the Franklin expedition

In the following text some words are incomplete. Only one or a couple of letters are given. Try to complete with words that fit the context.

Lady Jane Franklin (1792–1875), Franklin's second wife, tried ever_______[1] to keep up the search for her mis_______[2] husband and his men. She collected money to pay for the equi_______[3] of a ship called Fox. In July 1857 the ship sailed from England. The search party finally succeeded in disc_______[4] the history of Franklin's unlucky expedition. From Eskimos in Boothia Peninsula they recei_______[5] many remains of the Franklin expedition. Notes that were found told of the activities of the expl_______[6] up to April 25, 1848. According to this record, the two ships Erebus and Terror had been stop_______[7] by ice between Victoria Island and King William Island in 1846. From September 1846, the two ships were fro_______[8] among the ice. 9 officers and 15 men died. Among them was Franklin, who died on June 11, 1847. The surv_______[9] men left the ships on April 22, 1848 and tried to reach an Eskimo sett_______[10] on foot. But apparently no one was strong enough to make it through the cold and ice. All men died some days after they had des_______[11] the ships. In 1880 a US expedition discovered the wreckage of one of Franklin's ships and skel_______[12] of members of his party.

One hundred years later, in the 1980s, a Canadian anthropologist exa_______[13] the bones of the crew. He found tra_______[14] of lead and concluded that they had most likely died of lead pois_______[15]. The theory was that the tins which had cont_______[16] the food (vegetable, fruit) had given off the poisonous lead. But today it is still not clear whether this theory really expl_______[17] the end of Franklin and his men.

In the following lines some words are scrambled. Try to restore the original word. To help you the first letter is given.

Without (k-wnnoig) ___________[18] it Sir John Franklin had almost (f-noud) ___________[19] the Northwest Passage. In 1854 Robert McClure and his (c-wre) ___________[20] completed a passage from west to (e-tas) ___________[21], but partly by foot and (s-dleeg) ___________[22] because of the thick ice. Finally, in 1903–06, the Norwegian (e-lxrroep) ___________[23] Roald Amundsen led an expedition which made the first (t-irnats) ___________[24] of the passage. In 1969 a US icebreaking oil (e-akrtn) ___________[25], the Manhattan, became the first large (c-lriommcae) ___________[26] vessel to cross the passage. Today the Northwest Passage is not commercially (u-sfleu) ___________[27].

Exercise 4 Vocabulary grid: Explorers

Fill the squares with words from the list "Some words to remember". The word down in the bold squares is used for people who live at the same time.

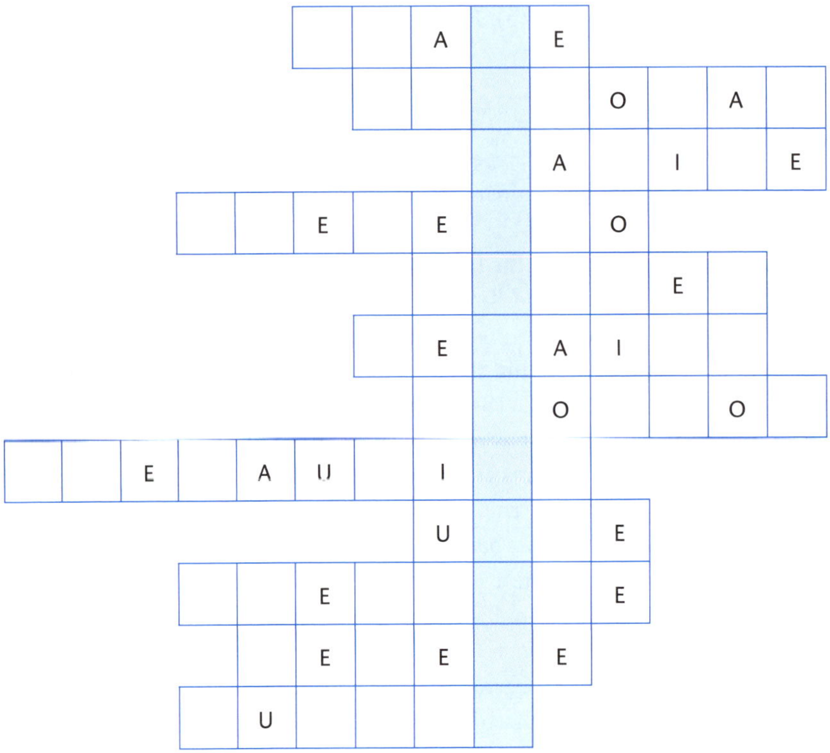

Exercise 5 Anagram: Discovery

The letters of these words have been jumbled. Write down the original words using the definitions as your help.

Anagram	Word	Definition
a) ACHERS	______________	to look through or go over thoroughly to find something
b) AGAVNTROI	______________	an explorer by sea
c) CYOVNO	______________	a group of ships travelling together or under protection
d) GEUERF	______________	a safe place from danger or trouble

e)	INMAFE	______________	the extreme lack of food; hunger, starvation
f)	PAOLRPSO	______________	an offer, a suggestion
g)	YLPUPS	______________	a store of things needed
h)	TCARE	______________	a track or a mark left by something or someone that has passed by

3 Language corner: Usage of words

historic – historical / economic – economical

Von zahlreichen Substantiven werden Adjektive abgeleitet, die auf *-ic* oder *-ical* enden: *musical, mechanical, logical, systematic, tragic, public*. Einige Wörter haben beide Formen, ohne dass wesentliche Bedeutungsunterschiede bestehen: *geometric(al), fantastic(al)*. Man kann aber sagen, dass neuere Wortschöpfungen überwiegend auf *-ic* enden: *electronic, cosmic, cosmetic*.

Von einigen Substantiven gibt es zwei verschiedene Adjektivformen, die unterschiedliche Bedeutungen haben:

history		
historic	October 12, 1492 is the **historic** date when Columbus landed in the New World.	historisch (= von historischer Bedeutung)
historical	Was the Trojan war a **historical** fact?	geschichtlich
economy		
economic	The **economic** situation of the Native Americans is not improving.	wirtschaftlich
economical	My new car is very **economical**.	sparsam
classic		
classic	The pyramids are a **classic** example of Egyptian engineering.	ein klassisches Beispiel (= typisch für)
classical	Schliemann was interested in **classical** languages.	klassische Sprachen (= Griechisch und Latein)

a lot of/lots of/plenty of – much – many

Besonders in der Umgangssprache verwendet man *much* und *many* vor allem bei Fragen und in verneinten Aussagesätzen. In bejahten Sätzen wird *a lot of/lots of/plenty of* bevorzugt. *Much* und *many* werden jedoch immer nach *too, as, very* und *how* gebraucht.

a lot of/lots of/plenty of	The King had hoped Columbus would bring back **lots of** gold from the new lands.	viel, viele
much	The King did not want to lose so **much** money that's why he gave Columbus simple vessels.	viel (wird verwendet mit nicht zählbaren Substantiven z. B. wine, salt, butter, gold)
many	The monarch did not want to lose too **many** ships; that's why he gave Columbus only three old vessels.	viele (wird verwendet mit Substantiven im Plural z. B. eggs, bottles, ships, islands)

Exercise 6 Usage: economic – economical/historic – historical

Use the right word in the empty spaces.

a) I'm sorry, but I can't give you any more pocket money. Try to be more __________ (economic – economical)!

b) The government is worried about the __________ (economic – economical) situation of people in the poorer areas of London.

c) It is more __________ (economic – economical) for an advertising agency to buy printing paper in larger quantities.

d) There is __________ (historic – historical) evidence that William arrived in England in 1066.

e) There seems to be much __________ (historic – historical) truth in Homer's epic poem.

f) An enormous amount of __________ (historic – historical) research has been carried out in the Valley of the Kings.

g) The world __________ (economic – economical) system has changed profoundly over the last ten years.

h) The industrialised countries experience an __________ (economic – economical) growth.

i) Fred's new car is rather __________ (economic – economical). It does more than 100 miles to the gallon.

j) People in the Third World countries have given up waiting for an _______________ (economic – economical) miracle.

k) Annie is a very _______________ (economic – economical) housewife: she uses up all the left-overs from the day before.

Exercise 7

Usage: a lot of/lots of/plenty of – much – many

Use the proper word in these sentences.

John Red Cloud Walcott is a 35-year-old native American activist. He works for an improvement of the situation of Native Americans in the reservations. In 1992 he said in his speech to commemorate the 500th anniversary of the landing of Columbus on American:

"Even the US President admits that there is too _______________[1] poverty among the Native Americans. But why doesn't anyone do anything? We all know what happened in the past. There have been _______________[2] TV reports about the cruel treatment of American Indians by the pioneers. _______________[3] people know that the arrival of the Europeans did not do the Indians _______________[4] good! For so _______________[5] years have they been neglected. How _______________[6] longer do they have to wait for better opportunities? Why don't they receive as _______________[7] support as other ethnic minorities? Is it because there aren't too _______________[8] left of us to have political influence? Most politicians do _______________[9] talking and don't offer _______________[10] help. There aren't _______________[11] US Indian families who live a comfortable and wealthy life. Native Americans have _______________[12] trouble when they try to find a job. How _______________[13] employers prefer a coloured applicant to a white jobseeker?"

4 Grammar spot: The passive (2)

Verbs with two objects

Die Grundregel bei der Umformung eines Aktivsatzes in einen Passivsatz lautet: Das **Objekt** des **Aktivsatzes** wird zum **Subjekt** des **Passivsatzes**.

	Subject	Predicate	Object
Active	Pirates	attacked	the ship.
Passive	The ship	was attacked	by pirates.

Es gibt Verben, die zwei Objekte nach sich führen können, z. B. *to give, to hand, to offer, to send, to show.*

Bei **Verben mit zwei Objekten** kann prinzipiell jedes der beiden Objekte zum Subjekt des Passivsatzes werden. Bevorzugt wird eine Passivbildung mit dem indirekten Personalobjekt des Aktivsatzes (= Variante 1).

	Subject	Predicate	Indirect object	Direct Object
Active	The King	gave	Columbus	a new ship.

Passive	Subject	Predicate	Object	Agent
Variant 1	Columbus	was given	a new ship	by the King.
Variant 2	A new ship	was given	to Columbus	by the King.

Verbs with prepositional object

Eine Reihe von Verben bildet mit Präpositionen eine Bedeutungseinheit. Man nennt diese Verbgruppe *prepositional verbs*. Bei der Umformung eines Aktivsatzes in einen Passivsatz muss diese Einheit erhalten bleiben.

Die feste Bindung zwischen Verb und Präposition bleibt auch im Passiv erhalten.

	Subject	Predicate	Object
Active	The King and Columbus	agreed on	a new contract.
Passive	A new contract	was agreed on	by the King and Columbus.

List of prepositional verbs

agree on	sich einigen auf	*look at*	anschauen
ask for	bitten um	*pay for*	zahlen für
complain of	sich beklagen über	*rely on*	sich verlassen auf
deal with	behandeln	*send for*	schicken nach
dream of	träumen von	*speak about/of*	sprechen von
hear about/of	hören von	*speak to*	sprechen mit
laugh at	lachen über	*talk about/of*	sprechen von
listen to	zuhören	*think about/of*	denken über
look after	sorgen für	*take care of*	sorgen für

Expercise 8 Put into passive: Mixed tenses

Put these sentences into Passive Voice.

a) Columbus opened the way to the "New World".

____

b) The European invaders abused the Indians.

____

c) Most US citizens recognize the destructive effects of colonisation.

____

d) An Indian civil rights activist will receive a medal of honour.

____

e) The Government expects more Indians to vote in the next election.

____

f) The United Nations has started a fund to help the indigenous peoples in America.

____

g) Kevin Costner produced the film "Dances With Wolves".

____

h) The film "Dances With Wolves" portrays the Indians as Noble Savages.

____

i) The Indian tribes speak completely different languages.

____

j) In 1930 archaeologists started a search for two old caravels of Columbus.

____

k) In 1991 deep-sea divers discovered the two ships of Columbus off the Jamaican coast.

____

l) The Jamaican government is stressing the importance of the discovery for the tourist industry.

____

Exercise 9 Put into passive: Two objects

Use the underlined object as subject of your passive sentence.

a) The natives offered <u>the European colonists</u> food.

____

b) The friendly Indians showed <u>the pioneers</u> the way through the desert.

____

c) The Indian chief Red Cloud sent <u>the settlers</u> a warning.

____

d) The settlers handed <u>the Indian chief</u> a new rifle.

____

e) Some Indian tribes denied <u>women</u> equal rights.

____

f) The Nobel Committee awarded <u>Wangari Maathai</u> the Nobel Peace Prize.

____

Exercise 10 Put into passive: Prepositional verbs

a) Latin American governments agreed on the creation of a development fund for Indians.

____

b) The administration will take care of newcomers to the reservation.

____

c) We must look after the young people in the Indian reservations.

____

d) The committe will deal with all complaints as quickly as possible.

____

5 Writing desk: Linkage words

Ein Text besteht nicht einfach aus einer gewissen Anzahl von beliebig aneinander gereihten Sätzen. Vielmehr stellt er ein enges Geflecht von aufeinander bezogenen Einzelteilen dar. Logische Verweise halten die Elemente – die Sätze – zusammen. Mithilfe der Satzverknüpfungen kann der Leser ein sinnvolles Ganzes erschließen. Wenn Sie aufgefordert werden, einen zusammenhängenden Text zu schreiben (*Comment, Summary, Letter, Story*), müssen Sie sich diese Grundeinsicht besonders bewusst machen.

> Bei der Textproduktion muss deutlich werden, dass die Einzelsätze in einer logischen Beziehung zueinander stehen, dass sie miteinander verbunden sind. Erst durch eine angemessene und richtige Verwendung der so genannten **linkage words** (to link = verbinden) wird aus Einzelsätzen ein zusammenhängender Text.

Ein kurzer Beispieltext soll Ihnen zeigen, wie die einzelnen Sätze eines Abschnitts miteinander verbunden sein können:

Beispiel Columbus believed that he had reached the East Indies. <u>Consequently</u>, <u>he</u> called the inhabitants of the islands 'Indians'. For a long time <u>this</u> term was in general use when people referred to the indigenous peoples of North, Central, and South America. We now call <u>them</u> 'Native Americans'.

Eine Analyse der Satzfunktionen macht das Beziehungsgeflecht und die Verweise klar:

Satz 1:	Columbus believed that he had reached the East Indies.	
Satz 2:	**Consequently, he** called the inhabitants of the islands 'Indians'.	eine doppelte Verbindung zum vorherigen Satz: **Consequently** = Folge aus erstem Satz; **he** = Bezug auf die im ersten Satz genannte Person ‚Columbus'
Satz 3:	For a long time **this** term was in general use when people referred to the indigenous peoples of North, Central, and South America.	bezieht sich auf ‚Indians' in Satz 2
Satz 4:	We now call **them** 'Native Americans'.	verweist auf ‚indigenous peoples' in Satz 3

Im Folgenden werden Ihnen einige wichtige Möglichkeiten aufgezeigt, wie Sie Sätze – je nach Aussageabsicht – verbinden können.

Aussageabsicht	linkage words
• einen **Gedanken** hinzufügen:	in addition, further, furthermore, also, besides, in the same way
• einen **Gedanken** neu formulieren:	in other words, that means, that is, that is to say
• einen **Gedankengang** abschließen:	in conclusion, in brief, in short, on the whole
• die **Reihenfolge** verdeutlichen:	first, second, next, finally, in the end
• das **Gegenteil** ausdrücken:	yet, however, on the other hand, on the contrary, in contrast, in spite of
• einen **Vergleich** anstellen:	similarly, in the same way, likewise
• eine **Folgerung** ausdrücken:	consequently, therefore, as a result, hence
• eine **Einräumung** ausdrücken:	although, though, even if, after all, in any case
• eine **Bedingung** ausdrücken:	if, unless, provided that, in case that
• eine zeitliche **Verbindung** knüpfen:	after, before, while, eventually, recently, lately, at last, in the end, in the past, when, as soon as
• eine **Begründung** anführen:	therefore, that is why, for this reason, because, since
• ein **Beispiel** anführen:	for example, for instance, in other words

Exercise 11 Linking sentences: American Indians today

Choose the linkage word that you think fits best.

What the Spaniards and the other conquerors did to the native population and their culture has not been forgotten. The 500th anniversary of the explorer's first landing on American shores (1992) had been planned as a great celebration. (However – Therefore – Besides) ____________[1] Columbus Day, October 12, became a day of protest. Native Americans and other groups staged big demonstrations (although – because – unless) ____________[2] they wanted to remind the world of the genocide of their people. (That means – On the whole – Secondly) ____________[3] they see the arrival of Columbus and his successors as the tragic beginning of the extinction of many indigenous peoples of America.

(Lately – In the past – In the end) ______________[4] to the soldiers and settlers of the westward movement the Indians were wild, stupid creatures. (But – Since – Hence) ______________[5] words like those of Indian Chief Seattle prove that the Indians really knew better: "We know that the white man does not understand our ways. One portion of land is the same to him as the next, (for – however – while) ______________[6] he is a stranger who comes in the night and takes from the land whatever he needs. The earth is not his brother,

(though – besides – but) ______________[7] his enemy, and (when – provided that – although) ______________[8] he has conquered it, he moves on."

Today the two million American Indians form one of the smallest ethnic groups in the United States. (As a result – In contrast – In addition) ______________[9] they have hardly any influence on modern American society. (Though – Unless – For instance) ______________[10] all of us support the just cause of the Native Americans their life in the reservations will still be characterized by extreme poverty, mass unemployment, alcoholism and teenage suicide.

Exercise 12 Text reconstruction: Killing off the native population

Put the sentences together in a logical order.

a) The colonists robbed them of their land, driving native people away into the less fertile areas, decimating their population.

b) Only a hundred years after the discovery of the island the greater part of the Arawak Indians had been killed.

c) Whole tribes had disappeared completely.

d) Many died of infectious diseases, such as measles, brought by the Europeans.

e) He and those who came after him abused the natives.

f) Others did not survive the cruel treatment they suffered as slaves.

g) Their ancestors had settled in the Americas thousands of years earlier, among them the Mayas, Aztecs and the Incas.

h) About 100,000 Arawak Indians lived on the islands when Columbus set foot on the Bahamas.

i) However, just two hundred years after Columbus' arrival there were only 4 million natives left.

j) At the end of the 15th century there were about 100 million Native Americans.

1	2	3	4	5	6	7	8	9	10

Exercise 13

Extracting information from a text

Use the information of the two texts on John Franklin and his search for the Northwest Passage and prepare a chronological list of events. Use the Present Tense. Start like this:

1786 John Franklin is born in Spilsby, Lincolnshire, England.

______ ______________________________

______ ______________________________

______ ______________________________

______ ______________________________

______ ______________________________

______ ______________________________

______ ______________________________

______ ______________________________

______ ______________________________

______ ______________________________

6 Fun and games

Exercise 14 Crossword puzzle

Try to solve the crossword puzzle.

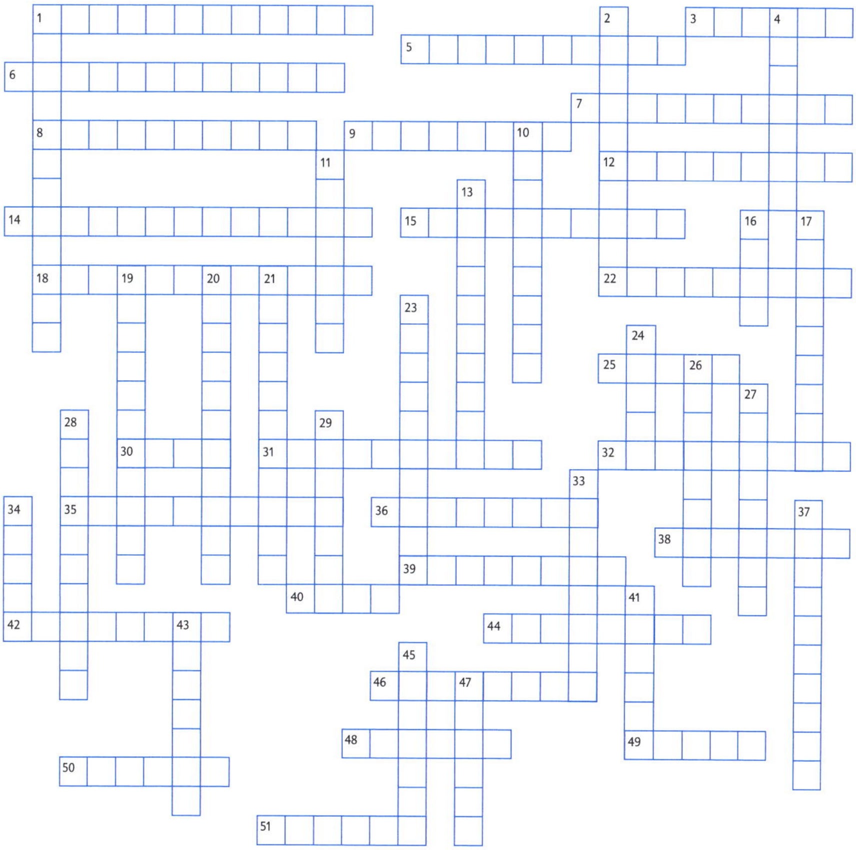

Across

1. Zeitgenosse; zeitgenössisch
3. Laufbahn
5. Siedlung
6. begeistert
7. ausreichend
8. erschöpfend
9. schließen, schlussfolgern
12. Vorfahren, Ahnen
14. Bleivergiftung
15. Vorsichtsmaßnahme
18. Unruhestifter, Störenfried
22. Seefahrer
25. verzögern, verspäten
30. Knochen
31. offensichtlich
32. Behandlung
35. Ausrottung
36. überzeugen
38. Überbleibsel
39. Skelett
40. drängen
42. Vorschlag
44. Meuterer

46. Wrackteile (eines Schiffes); Trümmer
48. Hunger, Hungersnot
49. treu, ergeben
50. im Stich lassen
51. streng, hart

Down

1. folglich
2. Vorschrift
4. Kaiser
10. anspruchsvoll, anstrengend
11. verurteilen, verdammen
13. Nachkomme
16. Blei
17. Proviant, Lebensmittel
19. unbewohnt
20. erfahren (adj.)
21. Bewerbung
23. einheimisch
24. sich beziehen auf
26. modern, fortschrittlich
27. sich beschweren, beklagen
28. ansteckend
29. Förderer; fördern
33. Völkermord
34. ausstatten
37. unbesiegbar
41. Schiff
43. erwerben
45. murren
47. Geleit, Geleitzug

Space

1 Text box

Flight into space

In the 20th century science had made enough progress to make space travel possible. Scientists had invented the techniques of how to propel, guide and control a rocket. The technical possibilities were there. What was needed was a push to set the US space programme in motion. That push came from the world of politics. In 1957 the Russians had put the first satellite Sputnik 1 into orbit. Two years later the spacecraft Lunik 3 circled the moon and sent back the first photos of the far side. The Americans were afraid of losing the "space race". In May 1961 President John F. Kennedy called for a space programme to land a man on the moon and return him safely to the earth "before the decade is out". The flight programme was named "Apollo".

The US space agency, NASA, started looking for astronauts. At first military test pilots were chosen to fly the spacecraft. They had to be less than 40 years old, in excellent physical condition, and no taller than 180 cm. Later NASA looked for a new type of astronaut, one who was not only physically and psychologically in top condition, but who also had a Ph. D. in medicine, engineering, or science. Six scientist-astronauts were selected in 1965, and in 1967 NASA selected eleven.

On July 16, 1969 the historic flight of Apollo 11 was launched from Complex 39 at the Kennedy Space Centre in Florida. In the spacecraft were Neil Armstrong, Edwin Aldrin and Michael Collins. When their spacecraft was in orbit around the moon, Armstrong and Aldrin climbed into the lunar module (LM), whereas Collins remained in orbit, piloting the command module. Then they separated the LM from the command capsule which took them down to the surface.

On July 20 the LM landed at the edge of Mare Tranquilitatis. "The Eagle has landed" was the message that was radioed around the world. A few hours later, Armstrong, wearing his space suit, climbed down the ladder and, at 10:56 p.m. stepped onto the surface of the moon. His first words were, "That's one small step for a man, but one giant leap for mankind." Soon after Aldrin joined him. The two astronauts spent more than two hours walking on the lunar surface.

Both astronauts found that walking and running was not too difficult for them, although the gravity on the moon is only one-sixth of the gravity on earth. They gathered 21 kg of soil samples. Heavy pieces of rocks had to be carried back to their LM. Armstrong and Aldrin took photographs and set up several experiments. They also erected an American flag and talked, by satellite communications, with US President Richard M. Nixon in the White House.

The flight of Apollo 11 attracted great interest around the world. Millions of people watched live television broadcasts from the moon. All three astronauts returned to the earth safely. On July 24 the vehicle splashed down in the Pacific Ocean near Hawaii.

Critics of the space flight programmes were afraid that astronauts who returned from the moon could carry with them living lunar organisms, unknown to us, and these might contaminate our planet. That's why the astronauts put on special "biological isolation garments" before they left the spacecraft. For security reasons Armstrong, Aldrin and Collins had to bear living in quarantine for three weeks. They remained in good health.

All in all, there were six manned landings on the moon: Apollo 11, 12, and 14–17. All lunar missions returned with samples of rock and soil to earth, weighing 384 kg in all. This mass of material was analysed by scientists in laboratories all over the world – not just in the United States. The more we learn about the moon, the more we will learn about the development of the solar system – and about our planet Earth.

641 words

Exercise 1 Understanding the text

Decide if these statements are true. Correct the false ones.

	true	false
a) In 1957 the Russian spacecraft Lunik 3 brought back the first pictures of the far side of the moon.	☐	☐
b) NASA wanted astronauts who were highly qualified pilots.	☐	☐
c) The American President wanted to win the space race against the Russians.	☐	☐
d) Scientists did not stand a chance to be accepted as astronauts by NASA.	☐	☐
e) Apollo 11 consisted of two parts: the lunar module and the command module.	☐	☐
f) On July 20, 1969 the three Apollo astronauts landed on the moon near the Mare Tranquilitatis.	☐	☐
g) Neil Armstrong was the first man on the moon.	☐	☐
h) This first landing on the moon was a big success for the Americans, but President Kennedy had wanted it to happen earlier.	☐	☐
i) After their return to earth the astronauts talked to President Nixon.	☐	☐
j) On the moon the astronauts carried out a lot of work.	☐	☐

k) Walking was not difficult, although on the moon people and things are heavier than on earth. ☐ ☐

____

l) On its return to earth Apollo 11 landed safely in the sea. ☐ ☐

____

m) Back at Kennedy Space Centre (Florida) the astronauts had to put on special isolation clothes. ☐ ☐

____

n) To make sure that the astronauts wouldn't bring back any illnesses they had to stay in isolation for three weeks. ☐ ☐

____

2 Word power

2.1 Some words to remember

aboard	an Bord
achievement	Leistung
adventure	Abenteuer
artificial	künstlich
assignment	Aufgabe, Kommando
audience	Publikum
booster rocket	Antriebsrakete
(to) broadcast	(TV, Radio) senden
commander	Befehlshaber
company	Firma; Begleitung
confrontation	Begegnung; Streit
contents	Inhalt
depth	Tiefe
(to) descend	herabsteigen
(to) develop	entwickeln
(to) discover	entdecken
engine	Motor, Maschine

exploration	Erforschung
(to) float	schweben
forecast	(Wetter-) Vorhersage
gravity	Schwerkraft
(to) guide	führen, leiten
imagination	Fantasie
(to) invent	erfinden
(to) launch	(eine Rakete usw.) starten; Start
lunar landing	Mondlandung
mankind	Menschheit
meeting	Treffen
message	Botschaft
mission	Auftrag
mutual	gegenseitig
orbit	Umlaufbahn, Kreisbahn
(to) pilot	steuern, (ein Flugzeug) führen
popular	beliebt
probe	Sonde (unbemannt)
progress	Fortschritt
(to) propel	antreiben
(to) prove	beweisen
re-usable	wieder verwendbar
sample	Probe (eines Minerals, von Blut usw.)
scientists	Wissenschaftler
(to) separate	trennen
solar panel	Sonnenkollektor
space shuttle	Raumfähre
spacecraft	Raumschiff
surface	Oberfläche
tolerance	Duldsamkeit
universe	Weltall
weightlessness	Schwerelosigkeit

2.2 Useful phrases

to set in motion	President Kennedy set the US space programme in motion.	in Bewegung setzen
to call for	Kennedy called for a space programme to land a man on the moon.	verlangen
to attract interest	The flight of Apollo 11 attracted great interest around the world.	Interesse wecken
to complete a mission	The Apollo 11 mission was successfully completed in 1969.	eine Mission (einen Auftrag) erfüllen
to take place	Joint American-Russian missions have taken place to mark the end of the race in space.	stattfinden

Exercise 2

Definitions: Space flight

What are these?

a) enormous balls of rock which orbit the sun ____________________

b) most of them are too far away for us; our sun is also one ____________________

c) an extremely strong engine used to launch a spaceship ____________________

d) a modern spacecraft that can be used more than once ____________________

e) name of the lunar landing module which Armstrong and Aldrin used ____________________

f) name of the US space programme whose aim was to land a man on the moon ____________________

g) unmanned spacecraft like Voyager 2 which was sent to Saturn ____________________

h) they supply a satellite with power by generating electricity from sunlight ____________________

Exercise 3

Cloze-Test: The making of the Star Trek series

Complete the text with words from this list.

adventure	broadcast	landed	successful
agreed	company	launch	surface
artificial	developed	orbit	universe
astronaut	dropped	race	
audiences	followers	set	

The story of the TV series Star Trek began in the early 1960s, a few years after the first ______________[1] satellite, the Russian Sputnik 1, was put into ______________[2] around the earth. This historic ______________[3] opened up an era called the "space ______________[4]" between the Soviet Union and the United States. Both nations developed intensive space programmes to explore the ______________[5] – and, of course, to prove to the rest of the world how much better either the Eastern Bloc or the Western Capitalist political system was.

Gene Roddenberry was an ex-police officer and he had written Westerns. In 1964 he ______________[6] the idea of a new space ______________[7] television series and presented it to the major US television companies. They were not too pleased with his idea and refused the script. But eventually, after many refusals and changes, the first episode of Star Trek was produced by a small ______________[8]. The film was sold to big NBC and ______________[9] on September 8, 1966. The episode was called "The Man Trap". In the beginning the series was not very ______________[10] in the eyes of the TV managers. The episodes did not attract large ______________[11]. As the ratings ______________[12], NBC announced that it wanted to stop the series after its second year.

But something extraordinary happened: thousands of loyal Star Trek fans wrote letters of protest to NBC, and, even more surprising, the TV company ______________[13] to produce episodes for a third year. That same year, 1969, Apollo 11 ______________[14] on the moon and ______________[15] Neil Armstrong became the first man to ______________[16] his foot on the moon's ______________[17]. This event added greatly to the popularity of the Star Trek series, which from then on kept winning more and more viewers and dedicated ______________[18].

Exercise 4 C-Test: Starship Enterprise (NCC 1701)

In the following text some words are incomplete. Only one or a couple of letters are given. Try to complete with words that fit the context.

He was bo__________[1] in Iowa. When he was thirteen he survived a mass killing on planet Tarsus IV in which he lost part of his family. He received his trai__________[2] at Starfleet Academy and after graduating was given his first assig__________[3] aboard the USS Farragut. Real fame came when at 31 he was made comm__________[4] of the Starship Enterprise which he led on its highly successful five-year mis__________[5] through space. His name: James T. Kirk.
He was a close friend of Captain Kirk. He was half human and half non-human. His mot__________[6] was a schoolteacher from Earth, his father a diplomat from the pla__________[7] Vulcan. He was the scie__________[8] officer aboard the Starship Enterprise. His name: Spock.
He served as chief medical officer abo__________[9] the Enterprise for some 27 years. His father had suffered from an illness that couldn't be cured; the only thing he could do for his father was to help him die. Shortly after that a cure for the illness was disco__________[10]. All through his life he carried the guilt for his father's death. His name: Dr. Leonard H. McCoy.
Millions of TV vie__________[11] from all over the world know these three and many more chara__________[12] from the TV series "Star Trek" – one of the most pop__________[13] TV shows ever made. Star Trek enjoyed such success that it created a large fan movement. At major mee__________[14] – or conventions – often more than 10,000 Star Trek fans – or "Trekkies" – turn up. Some of them even we__________[15] the costume of their favo__________[16] character from the TV series. They discuss the contents of individual episodes, the development of the characters, talk about details of the plot and the mes__________[17] of the Star Trek series: Peace, toler__________[18] and mutual underst__________[19]. The success of the TV programme inspired several other series, including the sequels "Star Trek: The Next Gene__________[20]", "Star Trek: Deep Space Nine" and full-length films made for the cin__________[21].

3 Language corner

3.1 Usage of words

tragen = *wear, carry, bear*

• *to wear* =	tragen (Kleidung, eine Brille etc.)	The astronauts had to wear spacesuits. *Die Astronauten mussten Raumanzüge tragen.*
• *to carry* =	tragen (mit den Händen)	The astronauts gathered soil samples which they had to carry back to their LM. *Die Astronauten sammelten Bodenproben, die sie zu ihrem Mondlandefahrzeug zurücktragen mussten.*
• *to bear* =	tragen (Verantwortung); ertragen	Flight controllers in Houston bore the main responsibility for the safety of the astronauts. *Die Flugkontrolleure in Houston trugen die Hauptverantwortung für die Sicherheit der Astronauten.* For security reasons Armstrong, Aldrin and Collins had to bear living in quarantine for three weeks. *Aus Sicherheitsgründen mussten Armstrong, Aldrin und Collins es ertragen, drei Wochen in Quarantäne zu verbringen.*

wählen = *choose, select, elect*

• *to choose* =	wählen (in ganz allgemeiner Bedeutung)	At first NASA chose military test pilots to fly the spacecraft. *Zuerst wählte die NASA (= sie entschied sich für) militärische Testpiloten, um die Raumschiffe zu fliegen.*
• *to select* =	sehr sorgfältig auswählen (z. B. durch Tests)	Six scientist-astronauts were selected in 1965. *1965 wurden sechs Astronauten, die auch Wissenschaftler waren, ausgewählt.*
• *to elect* =	durch Stimmabgabe wählen	John F. Kennedy was elected President of the USA in 1960. *John F. Kennedy wurde 1960 zum Präsidenten der USA gewählt.*

3.2 False friends

critic ≠ Kritik

• *critic* = der Kritiker	Critics of the space programmes were afraid that astronauts would bring back dangerous bacteria. *Kritiker des Raumfahrtprogramms befürchteten, die Astronauten würden gefährliche Bakterien ein-schleppen.*
• die Kritik = *criticism*	NASA had to face heavy criticism because of the high costs. *Die NASA musste sich wegen der hohen Kosten schwerer Kritik stellen.*

spend ≠ spenden

• *to spend* = verbringen	The two astronauts spent more than two hours on the moon. *Die zwei Astronauten verbrachten mehr als zwei Stunden auf dem Mond.*
• *to spend (money on/for)* = (Geld) ausgeben	The US government spent millions of dollars on the Apollo space programme. *Die US-Regierung gab Millionen Dollar für das Apollo-Raumfahrtprogramm aus.*
• spenden = *donate (money etc.), give (blood)*	The astronaut donated 10,000 dollars to Cancer Research. *Der Astronaut spendete der Krebsforschung 10 000 Dollar.*

4 Grammar spot: Conditional/if-clauses

In Konditionalsätzen drückt man eine Bedingung aus. Wir unterscheiden die beiden Satzteile **Bedingungssatz** (*if-clause*) und
Hauptsatz (*main clause*).

if-clause	**main clause**
If we learn more about the moon, Wenn wir mehr über den Mond lernen,	we'll know more about our earth. werden wir mehr über unsere Erde erfahren.

Probable condition (Typ 1: Erfüllbare Bedingung)

Im *if*-Satz steht eine Bedingung, die der Sprecher für erfüllbar hält . Wenn im ***if*-Satz** das **Präsens** verwendet wird, steht im **Hauptsatz** das **Futur I**.

if-clause	main clause
If you train hard, Wenn du fleißig trainierst,	you will become a good athlete. wirst du ein guter Sportler werden. (im Deutschen ist auch das Präsens möglich: ... wirst du ein guter Sportler.)

Improbable condition (Typ 2: Unwahrscheinliche Bedingung)

Im Gliedsatz steht eine Bedingung, deren Erfüllung der Sprecher für eher unwahrscheinlich hält. Wenn im ***if*-Satz** das **Präteritum** verwendet wird, steht im **Hauptsatz Konditional I**.

if-clause	main clause
If you got an invitation from NASA, Wenn du eine Einladung von der NASA bekamest (bekommen würdest),	would you like to fly into space? würdest du gern in den Weltraum fliegen?

Impossible condition (Typ 3: Irreale Bedingung)

Im Gliedsatz steht eine Bedingung, die nicht mehr erfüllt werden kann, da sich der Satz auf die Vergangenheit bezieht. Damit stellt diese Bedingung eine bloße Annahme dar. Wenn im ***if*-Satz** das **Plusquamperfekt** verwendet wird, steht im **Hauptsatz Konditional II**.

if-clause	main clause
If you had been the first man on the moon, Wenn du der erste Mensch auf dem Mond gewesen wärst,	what would you have said first? was hättest du zuerst gesagt?

Exercise 5 Practise your if-clauses

Supply the missing types.

Typ 1: If you are given the chance to fly into space, will you accept it?

a) Typ 2: ____________________

b) Typ 3: ____________________

c) Typ 1: ____________________

Typ 2: If you wanted to be an astronaut, you would have to pass lot of tests.

d) Typ 3: ______________________________

e) Typ 1: ______________________________

f) Typ 2: ______________________________

Typ 3: If the astronauts <u>had not brought back</u> rock samples from the moon, scientists <u>would have been</u> disappointed.

Exercise 6 Conditional: Mixed types

Supply the missing forms.

a) If there __________ (not, be) any gravity, things will float around in the air.

b) Things __________ (not, fall) to the ground if there weren't any gravity.

c) Astronauts __________ (not, can) survive in space if they didn't wear space suits.

d) Astronauts couldn't have walked on the moon if they ____________ (not, wear) space suits.

e) If we could travel at the speed of light, we __________ (can) visit other planets.

f) We could visit other planets if they __________ (not, be) so far away.

g) If the astronauts didn't do any exercise during their flights, their muscles __________ (get) weak because of weightlessness.

h) If satellites __________ (not, have) solar panels, they wouldn't have any energy for their instruments.

i) Weather forecasts _____________ (be) more precise years ago if meteorologists had had weather satellites earlier.

j) If there weren't any TV satellites in space, live broadcasts from other continents __________ (not, be) possible.

k) TV satellites wouldn't stay above the same place all the time if they __________ (not, move) in time with the Earth.

5 Writing desk

5.1 How to answer questions on the text

Was wird verlangt?

Questions on the text sind „textinterne" Fragen, d. h. die Antworten zu den gestellten Fragen sind im vorliegenden Text zu finden. Bei der Beantwortung dieser Fragen sollen Sie zeigen, dass Sie den Text insgesamt verstanden haben und in der Fremdsprache eine sinnvolle Antwort geben können. Sie stehen vor einer doppelten Aufgabe:

- Sie müssen im englischen Text die Stelle suchen, die eine Antwort auf die Frage gibt.
- Sie müssen die Frage auf Englisch möglichst mit eigenen Worten beantworten.

Wie gehen Sie vor?

Suchen Sie zuerst im Originaltext die Textstelle, die eine Antwort auf die Frage liefert. Markieren Sie die Stelle im Text. Doch das ist noch nicht Ihre Antwort! Versuchen Sie, die gefundene Information mit eigenen Worten wiederzugeben. In der Aufgabenstellung wird darauf oft ausdrücklich hingewiesen durch Anweisungen wie *„Answer these questions in your own words"* oder *„Do not copy from the text"*.

Im Original steht die sprachlich schwierigere Formulierung. Ihre Antwort soll die Textstelle in vereinfachter Form umschreiben oder erklären.

Beachten Sie besonders:

- Wie lang soll Ihre Antwort sein?

  Meist wird schon in der Aufgabenstellung darauf aufmerksam gemacht, wie umfangreich die Antwort ungefähr sein soll: *„Answer in 50–70 words"*. Wenn das nicht der Fall sein sollte, können Sie aus der Punktzahl, die für die Aufgabe angesetzt wird, ersehen, wie viel Sie schreiben sollen.

  Je mehr Punkte für die richtige Beantwortung angesetzt sind, desto ausführlicher muss Ihre Antwort sein, damit Sie die maximale Punktzahl erhalten.

  Für Kurzantworten („They liked it.") gibt es keine Punkte! Sie sollen ja nicht nur zeigen, dass Sie die richtige Antwort im Text aufspüren können, sondern auch, dass Sie über einen guten Wortschatz verfügen!

  Vermeiden Sie Wiederholungen ("and then …, and then …").
  Vermeiden Sie abgegriffene Verben ("be, have, get"). Verwenden Sie aussagekräftige Verben.
  Vermeiden Sie unklare Bezüge und allgemeine Formulierungen ("they, it, etc.").

Für weitere Tipps lesen Sie bitte Seite 114 „How to write a comment".

- Welche Zeitstufe sollen Sie in der Antwort gebrauchen?
  Orientieren Sie sich an der Zeit, die in der Frage verwendet wird. Wenn es dort heißt *„What do people in the United States think about …"*, dann ist das Präsens (Gegenwart) vorgegeben. Heißt es *„Why did so many people criticize the US space programme?,"* dann verwenden Sie am besten das Präteritum (Vergangenheit).

> Achten Sie darauf, dass Sie bei einer Zeitstufe bleiben und nicht zwischen verschiedenen Zeiten hin- und herwechseln. Man nennt einen solchen Wechsel „switching tenses" oder weniger freundlich „Zeitenmix".

5.2 Example: How to answer questions on the text

Unidentified flying objects

UFO is short for "Unidentified Flying Object", and means objects that cannot readily be identified by sight or radar. There have always been people who claimed that they had seen some strange apparition in the sky. One report of a UFO sighting, however, was different from the rest, because the eye-witness was quite reliable.

It happened on June 24, 1947. Kenneth Arnold, an American pilot, was alone in his small aeroplane high up in the skies over the state of Washington. Suddenly he saw nine circular objects crossing his flight path. The objects flew in formation at a speed of 1,900 kilometres per hour. When asked to describe their movement more clearly, Kenneth Arnold said they had looked like "saucers skipping over the water". This comparison was taken up by all media – and the new name "flying saucers" was coined.

Following the extensive news coverage, reports of UFO sightings received more and more publicity. They became a favourite topic of discussion and were talked and speculated about world-wide. Some people dismissed these reports as fairy tales, lies or hallucinations, whereas others believed them to be true descriptions of extra-terrestrial spacecraft.

Answer these questions in your own words (40–60 words each). Do not copy from the text.

a) Why was the 1947 report of a UFO sighting different from the rest?
b) How did people react to reports of UFO sightings?

Key

Antworten im Originaltext:

a) "the eye-witness was quite reliable" (lines 4/5)

b) "Some people dismissed these reports as fairy tales, lies or hallucinations, whereas others believed them to be true descriptions of extra-terrestrial spacecraft." (lines 15–17)

Selbstständige Formulierung:

a) The man who said he had seen the strange objects was an American pilot. In general, people tend to trust an intelligent man who knows something about flying planes and technology. So it seemed more likely that Kenneth Arnold told the truth.

b) Critics of these reports said they were not true. The so-called 'eye-witnesses' of UFO sightings had invented their stories themselves or they were mistaken in what they had seen or had just imagined it. Perhaps they had taken a balloon for a spaceship. However, there were others who thought the reports were true and did indeed supply information about ships from outer space.

Exercise 7 Answering questions on the text "Flight into space"

Answer these questions in your own words in about 30–60 words each. Do not copy from the text.

a) Why wasn't space flight possible in the 19th century?

b) Why was President Kennedy important for the US space programme?

c) What qualifications did you need to become a NASA astronaut?

d) Describe how a landing on the moon took place.

e) Explain what astronaut Neil Armstrong wanted to say with his first sentence spoken on the moon.

f) Why did the astronauts have to spend three weeks in quarantine after the flight?

Exercise 8 Guided writing: Making friends with E.T.

It is the middle of the night. A ship from outer space lands in the clearing of a forest. Strange-looking alien creatures leave the ship to explore the surroundings. All of a sudden, torches and flashlights cut through the night: Humans have got wind of aliens arriving and are trying to hunt down the unknown invaders.

Now you go on and complete the summary of the film E.T. Use all the words in their correct forms. You may have to add articles, prepositions etc. Make sure to use the right tense, too. Sometimes a passive form may be necessary.

Example:

little creatures / outer space / run / for their lives / back to / safety of their ship / leave / hostile planet Earth / hurry	The little creatures from outer space run for their lives back to the safety of their ship, leaving the hostile planet Earth in a hurry.

a) They / not realize / not all members of the crew / make it / back to ship in time.

____

____

b) One of them / leave behind / darkness of the woods / chase / by humans and dogs.

c) abandoned creature / escapes / backyard of a suburban house / a 10-year-old boy named Elliott / live / with his mother, sister and brother.

d) parents / separate / and / boy / feel / rather lost.

e) Elliott / find / extra-terrestrial (E.T.) being / hide / him from his mum / but / share his big secret / the neighbourhood kids.

f) all make friends / Elliott's new companion.

g) eventually / E.T. / take / Elliott's house.

h) for E.T. / rooms of the house / be / worlds full of surprises and novelties / must / discover.

i) E.T. / not know / all these things / need for / and how / use / and / have / a number of extremely funny adventures and amusing experiences.

j) Although E.T. and Elliott / become / best friends / the extra-terrestrial / let the boy know / not want to stay down here on this earth for ever: / want / go home.

k) "E.T. phone home", / keep telling / Elliott.

l) To all the kids' horror / E.T. / catch / officials from the space agency / want carry out / experiments on him and kill him.

____

____

But Elliott and his friends save E.T.'s life by helping him escape to the woods where a reunion with his compatriots has been arranged. E.T. makes it back to the spaceship already waiting for him, takes off for his planet, leaving a very sad Elliott and millions of movie-goers behind with tears in their eyes.

6 Fun and games

Exercise 9 Crossword puzzle

Try to sove the crossword puzzle.

Across

1. Raumfähre
3. Abenteuer
7. Inhalt
9. Wissenschaftler
11. (TV, Radio) senden
14. Schwerelosigkeit
17. Sonnenkollektor
19. Tiefe
20. Fantasie
22. entdecken
27. Firma; Begleitung
29. wieder verwendbar
34. Menschheit
35. schweben
36. Weltall
38. Motor, Maschine
39. antreiben
42. herabsteigen
43. zustimmen, vereinbaren
44. beliebt
46. beweisen
47. erfinden
48. Mannschaft

Down

2. Begegnung; Streit
3. künstlich
4. Antriebsrakete
5. Aufgabe, Kommando
6. Leistung
8. Fortschritt
10. Raumschiff
12. Befehlshaber
13. Duldsamkeit
15. Erforschung
16. Schwerkraft
18. (Wetter-)Vorhersage
21. Publikum
23. Oberfläche
24. Treffen
25. trennen
26. führen, leiten
28. gegenseitig
30. steuern, (ein Flugzeug) führen
31. Probe (eines Minerals, von Blut usw.)
32. Auftrag
33. entwickeln
37. Botschaft
40. Sonde (unbemannt)
41. (eine Rakete usw.) starten; Start
43. an Bord
45. Umlaufbahn, Kreisbahn

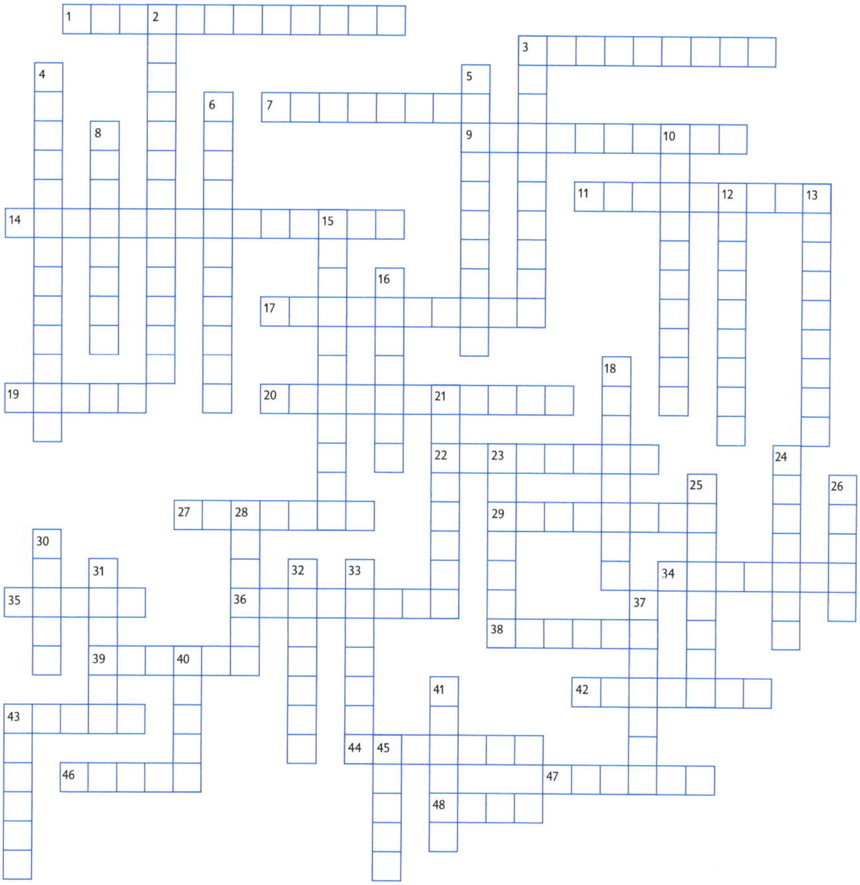

Exercise 10 Wordsearch: Space flight

Complete these words and try to find them in the word square.

AB__RD	C__W	GR___TY
AC_______NT	DE_TH	GU_DE
AD_____RE	DE___ND	IM_______ON
AR______AL	DE___OP	IN__NT
AS______NT	DI____ER	LA__CH
BO_ST	EN__NE	ME___NG
BR_____ST	EX_______ON	MI___ON
CO_____ER	FL_AT	MU__AL
CO____TS	FO____ST	OR_IT

PA_EL
PO___AR
PR_BE
PR____SS
PR__EL
RO__ET
SA__LE
SC______TS
SE____TE
SH___LE
SP______FT
SU___CE
UN____SE
WE__________ S

```
                        W
                      E E K
                    B T I X A
                  O A A G C P W
                R R Y P H S T L Q
              P A Y S I T L H S O N
            O P D R E S L O L U O R F
          P E R V V I T E K B I T O A R
        U S S W E T Q E S R T B R T B T F
      L T N E M N G I S S A G E A H L U I S
    A M A R E E T D D G N G C O D E V E L O P
  R J R C N I A U O D I E A L D R R P U M Z N D
T L P Y T C R R R Z G E S F X T A P L E P O R P G
  M I S S I O N E A X T S C E N O O E F H A A T
    U B B R F N M D D P M C O E R T R G O N I
      G R A V I T Y N E S R E V I N U B E B
        T F A R C E C A P S A N E I A L R
          L E N G I N E M T G I D R A O
            A L T R A T M M H E Q U C
              U P P B L S T O B N K
                T M S U R F A C E
                  U A M H Y H T
                    M S H W H
                      P L I
                        P
```

Mysteries

1 Text box

The Loch Ness monster

Every year during what journalists call "the silly season" – i. e. the summer months with little political news because all the world is on holiday – the legendary beast appears in the news again. Everyone then talks and speculates about the Loch Ness monster. Loch Ness is a lake in northern Scotland, about 39 km long, 2 km wide and about 230 m deep.

Why should Loch Ness be the home of the legendary animal? Why not some other lake in Scotland? The belief that a mysterious creature lives in the lake goes back to the Middle Ages. In AD 565 St. Columba, a missionary in Scotland, wrote in his diary that he attended the burial of a man who had been bitten to death by a water beast while swimming. For centuries people in the area have told each other the legend of the water horse, which pulled travellers under water until they drowned.

The legend really started in 1933 when the first motor road was built alongside the loch. Mr and Mrs John MacKay were driving along the new road when they saw something strange appearing from under the water surface: "an enormous animal which rolled and plunged until it disappeared with a huge splash." This is what they told reporters. The account of the MacKays was published in papers all over the world, causing a sensation and fascinating all readers. Was the beast a left-over dinosaur or just the result of a lively imagination – or too much whisky?

In 1934 Colonel Robert Wilson took a picture which was to become world-famous: it showed the "monster" with its head and neck very clearly visible on the water surface. More than 60 years later, in 1994, Christopher Spurling declared that the photo was a fake. He himself had made the model!

Over the past 60 years more than 3 000 people have claimed to have seen a "monster" of about 12–15 m length and no year comes to an end without a dramatic account of a new sighting. In 1972 an American scientific team found that "there seem to be more teapots in Loch Ness than anything else". Other investigators were convinced that Loch Ness's dark depths concealed not just one monster but a whole family of them. Environmentalists even demanded that the monster "Nessie" should be made a protected beast in order to prevent people from trying to catch or kill it.

A group of American university scientists caused great excitement when they announced they had succeeded in taking underwater photographs which proved the monster's existence without doubt. But when the photographs were shown to the world press everyone was rather disappointed. One reporter said that the photograph which was described as the best proof of Nessie's existence looked like "a set of bagpipes in a snowstorm". A British expedition even used sonar equipment, but failed to detect any beast. Most scientists remain sceptical of the existence of the "monster".

However, if it is ever established beyond doubt that Nessie does not exist, then the world will be a poorer place! And so too the area of Inverness where Loch Ness is located. Every year Nessie – or rather the vague promise of Nessie – attracts more and more tourists; and naturally a whole industry has sprung up on its shores, selling everything from souvenirs to snacks such as "monster hot dogs". The manager of the Official Loch Ness Monster Exhibition in Scotland says, "Tourists are more interested in Nessie than ever before." 583 words

Exercise 1 Understanding the text

Answer the following question in your own words. Do not copy from the text.

a) Why do we read in the summer months more about the Loch Ness monster than during the rest of the year?

b) How did the legend of the Loch Ness monster begin?

c) Why was 1933 a special year for the development of the legend?

d) What was found out about the "sensational" picture that Colonel Wilson had taken in 1934?

e) Have scientific teams succeeded in proving the monster's existence?

f) What did the world's press think about the photos presented by American university scientists?

2 Word power: Some words to remember

account	Bericht
A.D.	Anno Domini (n. Chr.)
(to) attend	besuchen, beiwohnen
(to) call for	auffordern
(to) claim	behaupten
(to) conceal	verbergen, verstecken
(to) convince	überzeugen
diameter	Durchmesser
disturbance	Störung
environmentalist	Umweltschützer
excitement	Aufregung
fake	Fälschung, Schwindel

hoax	Streich, Scherz
imagination	Fantasie
lake	See
mysterious	geheimnisvoll
phenomenon	Erscheinung
physicist	Physiker
plank	Planke, Bohle
(to) plunge	springen, tauchen
research	Forschung
retired	pensioniert
scale drawing	maßstabsgetreue Zeichnung
sheer	völlig, total
shore	Ufer
silly season	„Saure-Gurken-Zeit“
snack	Imbiss, Kleinigkeit zu essen
(to) splash	platschen, spritzen
wheat	Weizen

Exercise 2

Definitions: Mystery

Match the definitions with the corresponding words. Please note that there are more words than definitions.

beast	crop	footprint	motorway
burial	detect	investigator	pattern
circle	environmentalist	legend	scientific

a) a drawing or design ____________

b) a lower animal as distinguished from a human being ____________

c) a person concerned about the quality of life ____________

d) a story coming down from the past ____________

e) an impression of the foot on a surface ____________

f) ring, halo; a closed plane curve ____________

g) road with several lanes designed for high-speed traffic ____________

h) yield of a field; a plant that can be grown and harvested ____________

Exercise 3 Vocabulary grid: Secrets

Fill the squares with words from the list "Some words to remember". The word down in the bold squares is a synonym for turbulence.

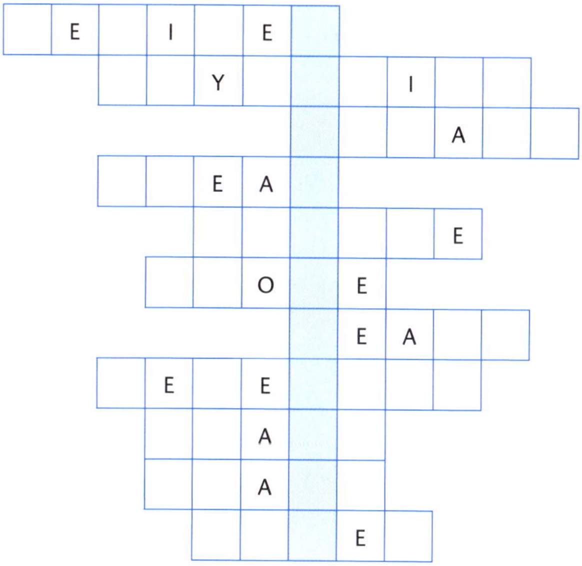

Exercise 4 Cloze-Test: Mysterious circles in wheat fields

Complete the text with words from this list.

arrived	explain	local
diameter	fields	neatly
discovery	huge	noticed

It was a bright and sunny morning in 1981 when farmer Timothy Jameson ____________[1] at one of his wheat ____________[2] at Headbourne Worthy in Hampshire and ____________[3] something he had never seen before. A very odd and ____________[4] circle had appeared in his field. The corn had been ____________[5] flattened into a large circular pattern of about 30 metres in ____________[6]. Farmer Jameson did not see any footprints, so he couldn't ____________[7] how the circle had got there. He told the reporter of his ____________[8] paper about his ____________[9] – and it was soon reported nation-wide.

Some words are scrambled. Try to restore the original word. To help you the first letter is given.

When in the following year more and more circles were (s-eihgdt) __________[10] in Hampshire, southern England, (r-hreesac) __________[11] into the mystery began. Thousands of experts (s-edtdiu) __________[12] the beautiful geometric formations. (B-soko) __________[13] on the subject were published. All authors were (c-noevdcin) __________[14] that the circles were not made by (m-na) __________[15]. "They are much too (p-icsree) __________[16] to be man-made hoaxes", one of the physicists (s-dai) __________[17].

Many (o-bervrses) __________[18] linked the circles to UFOs, claiming that they were (f-omder) __________[19] by a landing spaceship. They said that it was no coincidence that the (c-eicslr) __________[20] had appeared in southern England, (b-aesecu) __________[21] that area is also home to the (a-nnietc) __________[22] stone formations at Stonehenge.

From now on some words are incomplete. Only one or a couple of letters are given. Try to complete with words that fit the context.

Others dismi__________[23] this explanation as sheer non__________[24] and said, "Whatever causes these circles is as mys__________[25] better than science-fiction." Physicists spec__________[26] that an up to now unknown form of atmo__________[27] disturbance or some magnetic force had cre__________[28] the rings. The search for answers went on. For many years du__________[29] summer the papers were full of reports of new sightings and expla__________[30] of the supernatural phenomenon. To put an end to speculations two M.P.s called for the gov__________[31] to finance a serious scientific inve__________[32] of the rings in the wheat fields.

Translate the underlined words into German.

In July 1992 reporter Graham Brough phoned Pat Delgado to inform him of a newly discovered (__________)[33] spectacular ring in a wheat field near Sevenoaks, Kent. Delgado was a retired engineer (__________)[34] and had become a well-known specialist in the investigation of the mysterious crop circles. He was the author of a successful book about the rings called Circular Evidence (__________)[35]. It had sold more than 50,000 copies. In the book Delgado suggested that the patterns (__________)[36] were created by a "superior intelligence" – most likely extraterrestrial. When he saw the new circle, Delgado exclaimed, "This is the most wonderful moment of my research (__________)[37]. No human could have done this."

At that moment the reporter introduced Mr Delgado to two elderly men whom the journalist had brought along. "I'm sorry, Mr Delgado", one of them said, "but we have been fooling you. We made this circle last night!" The men were <u>landscape</u> (________________)[38] painters David Chorley, 62, and Douglas Bower, 67. To prove that they were telling the truth they had allowed the reporter to watch them and take photographs. Moreover, the two men admitted that for the past 13 years they had created as many as 25 to 30 new circles each growing season around southern England. Delgado was shocked, "We have all been tricked. If everything you say is true, people will think I'm an idiot!"

Exercise 5

Text reconstruction: The masters of the rings

Re-arrange these sentences. The text will tell you how the two men made the circles.

a) That was all they needed.

b) Then, at night, they drove around the countryside to a wheatfield which seemed suitable.

c) Their simple equipment which they used consisted only of a 4-ft.-long wooden plank and a ball of string.

d) The landscape painters explained how they made the circles.

e) First they prepared a scale drawing of the intended pattern.

1	2	3	4	5

Exercise 6

Translation: Wheat circles

Translate the words in brackets into English.

In 1978 Chorley and Bower were sitting in a pub wondering what they could do for a practical ______________[1] (Witz). As they had just read reports of flying-saucer sightings they decided to flatten some corn to make it appear as if a UFO had landed. To their ______________[2], (Enttäuschung) nobody took any notice of their first circles. In 1981 the sighting by farmer Jameson was reported in the press and all journalists wrote the circle was the work of ______________[3] (Außerirdischen). "We laughed a lot when we read the explanation in the paper," recalls Chorley. When they learned, however, that the government had been asked to put up money for an investigation they felt it was time to ______________[4] (zugeben) the hoax.

Pat Delgado and other circle specialists are recovering from their first shock. They say now, "Not all circles were made by humans. We will carry on ______________[5] (Forschung)." Millions of fascinated readers and, above all, UFOlogist like to ______________[6] (glauben) that there is a mystery behind the rings. If you ask them why, they will tell you, "Mysteries are fun!"

3 Language corner: Usage of words

Phrases with "to have"

to have lunch	zu Mittag essen
to have a drink	etwas trinken
to have a cold	erkältet sein
to have a game	spielen
to have a pleasant evening	einen netten Abend verbringen
to have sth. in mind	an etwas denken, etwas vorhaben
to have sth. done	etwas machen lassen
to have one's hair cut	sich die Haare schneiden lassen
to have a swim	schwimmen
to have a rest	sich ausruhen
to have a ride	fahren
to have a talk	sich unterhalten
to have a good time	sich amüsieren
to have a holiday	Urlaub machen, Ferien verleben

Exercise 7 Synonymous expressions

Match the phrases with the corresponding synonymous expressions.

phrase		**synonymous expression**	
1	to have in mind	a)	to eat a midday meal
2	to have lunch	b)	to enjoy oneself
3	to have a game	c)	to go to the hairdresser's
4	to have a rest	d)	to plan, to intend
5	to have a good time	e)	to play (football, cards)
6	to have one's hair cut	f)	to sit back, to put one's feet up

1	2	3	4	5	6

Exercise 8

Cloze-Test: Phrases with "have"

Use a phrase with "have" in these sentences.

a) I'm terribly thirsty; I must ____________ right away!

b) Dad isn't pleased with your coming home so late every night. He wants to ____________ with you.

c) Shirley, you have worked very hard these last few hours; ____________!

d) We don't have to do all this work ourselves, boss. I'll ____________ for us.

e) My nose keeps running; I think I ____________.

f) Anne and Robert have been married for eight years and they have never gone abroad in the summer. But this year they'll ____________ in France.

g) You went to the disco with Eric last night, didn't you? Did you _________?

4 Grammar spot

4.1 Tenses: Survey

Tenses	Active Voice	Passive Voice
Present	I see	I am seen
Future I	I'll see	I'll be seen
Future II	I'll have seen	I'll have been seen
Past	I saw	I was seen
Present Perfect	I have seen	I have been seen
Past Perfect	I had seen	I had been seen
Conditional I	I would see	I would be seen
Conditional II	I would have seen	I would have been seen

4.2 Tenses: Simple past – Present perfect

Eine besondere Lernschwierigkeit stellt die richtige Verwendung des *present perfect* (vollendete Gegenwart) dar, weil wir im Deutschen dazu keine Entsprechung haben. Bei uns ist es relativ gleichgültig, ob jemand sagt:

Beispiel
Gestern las ich ein interessantes Buch. → (= Präteritum/Imperfekt)
oder:
Gestern habe ich ein interessantes Buch gelesen. → (= Perfekt)

Uns ist klar, dass beide Vorgänge vergangen sind. Im Englischen können Handlungen, die in der Vergangenheit begonnen haben und in der Vergangenheit beendet wurden, nur im *simple past* wiedergegeben werden. Die Verwendung des *present perfect* ist eng an eine bestimmte Aussageabsicht des Sprechers/Schreibers geknüpft.

Simple past

Im *simple past* werden Handlungen wiedergegeben, die in der **Vergangenheit begannen und in der Vergangenheit abgeschlossen** wurden.
Das *simple past* ist die **typische Zeitform** für **Erzählungen** und **Berichte**.
Signalwörter: *ago, in 1934, in AD 565, last week/month/year, yesterday* etc.

In 1934 Colonel Robert Wilson took a picture of the Loch Ness monster.
1934 fotografierte Robert Wilson das Monster von Loch Ness.

Present perfect

Das *present perfect* wird benutzt, um auszudrücken, dass eine **Handlung in der Vergangenheit begonnen hat** und einen **Bezug zur Gegenwart** besitzt.
Signalwörter: *all year long, ever, for, since*

Since 1933 more than 3,000 people have claimed to have seen the "monster".
Seit 1933 haben über 3 000 Menschen behauptet, das "Monster" gesehen zu haben.

Exercise 9 Simple past – Present perfect

Put the verbs in brackets into the correct tense.

a) Hey, Jeff ____________ (ever/be) to Scotland?

b) Yes, I ____________ (go) there last year with my parents.

c) When you _________ (drive/progressive form!) along the lake, _________ (observe) anything mysterious?

d) No, I ____________ (not, see) the monster then if that's what you mean. But when we ____________ (go) into the museum I ____________ (look at) a giant-size model of Nessie.

e) For more than sixty years people __________ (claim) that they __________ (see) "Nessie". In 1934 one even __________ (say) he had taken a picture! But now, it __________ (prove/just/passive!) that the photo was faked.

f) I ____________ (never/believe) in that legend anyway!

5 Writing desk

5.1 How to write a comment

Was wird verlangt?
„Choose one of the following topics and write a text of 150 to 250 words …“ – so oder so ähnlich werden Sie zu einem Comment aufgefordert. Sie sollen sich in einem etwas längeren zusammenhängenden Text zu einer Frage äußern. Es geht weniger darum, dass Sie alle Gesichtspunkte darlegen bzw. ein Problem abschließend klären – das wäre angesichts der Kürze der Bearbeitungszeit zu viel verlangt. Vielmehr sollen Sie zeigen, dass Sie in der Fremdsprache argumentieren und einen Sachverhalt sprachlich angemessen darstellen können. Das ist eine sehr anspruchsvolle Aufgabe, die Sie aber mit vernünftiger Überlegung und Planung sicher beherrschen werden.

In der Themenstellung wird deutlich, welche Art von Comment Sie schreiben sollen.

- *Most people today know that Nessie does not really exist. Why do so many tourists travel to Loch Ness anyway?*
  Hier geht es um die Darstellung von Gründen, warum Touristen sich gegen besseres Wissen auf „Monstersuche“ machen. Mögliche Gründe wären: Neugierde, Spaß an Verrücktheiten, einige glauben doch daran.

  > Denken Sie hier bitte daran, dass Sie die Argumente nicht nur aufzählen, sondern einige Ihnen wichtig erscheinende herausgreifen und mithilfe von Belegen und Beispielen ausführlicher darstellen. Sie stellen die Argumente in der Reihenfolge „vom weniger Wichtigen zum Wichtigsten“ dar.

- *„Modern tourism brings more disadvantages than advantages!“ Discuss.*
  In der Aufgabenstellung werden Sie mit einer Aussage (siehe Anführungszeichen) konfrontiert. Meist wird eine etwas zugespitzte Behauptung zur Diskussion gestellt, die zu einer Stellungnahme geradezu herausfordert. Von Ihnen wird nun verlangt, Argumente für und gegen die Richtigkeit der These anzuführen *(Discuss.)* und dann Stellung zu nehmen. Auch hier sollten Sie keine Vollständigkeit anstreben, sondern sich – je nach Länge der erwarteten Antwort – auf einige wichtige Argumente pro Seite beschränken.

  > Achten Sie darauf, Argumente für **beide** Seiten – in unserem Beispiel die Vor- und Nachteile des Massentourismus – darzulegen, dann erst eine Abwägung vorzunehmen und eine persönliche Wertung abzugeben. Je stärker Sie die vorgelegte These anspricht bzw. reizt, desto größer ist die Gefahr der Einseitigkeit.

Bei einem Thema, das Ihnen auf den Nägeln brennt und zu dem Sie schon immer etwas sagen wollten (etwa im Bereich des Umweltschutzes oder der Friedenserhaltung), müssen Sie besonders vorsichtig zu Werke gehen. Schalten Sie also Ihren Verstand und Ihre Fähigkeit zur sachlichen Analyse voll ein! Lassen Sie sich nicht nur von Ihren Gefühlen leiten.

Wie gehen Sie vor?

1. Themenwahl und Argumentation
   a) Wählen Sie ein Thema aus, zu dem Sie etwas sagen können.
   b) Notieren Sie sich zunächst alle Punkte, die Ihnen zum Thema einfallen.
   c) Wählen Sie die Argumente aus, die Sie ausführen wollen – und können.
   d) Ordnen Sie Ihre Argumente nach der Wichtigkeit (vom weniger Wichtigen zum Wichtigsten).
2. Aufbau des Comment
   a) Einleitung (introduction)
   b) Hauptteil (arguments)
   c) Schluss (conclusion)
3. Sprachliche Ausarbeitung
   a) Zeigen Sie, dass Sie über einen guten Wortschatz verfügen!
   b) Erinnern Sie sich an Texte, die Sie zum Thema gelesen oder besprochen haben.
   c) Aktivieren Sie den Spezialwortschatz zu diesem Themenbereich.
   d) Vermeiden Sie farblose, abgegriffene Verben (have, get) und Adjektive (good, bad).
   e) Denken Sie daran, Ihre Sätze sinnvoll zu verbinden (siehe S. 77)
   f) Überprüfen Sie Ihren gesamten Text auf sprachliche Richtigkeit. Dabei kann Ihnen die folgende Checkliste helfen. Ergänzen Sie sie durch Ihre persönlichen „Lieblingsfehler“!

Checkliste zum Comment

Kein Zeitenmix:	eine Zeitstufe durchhalten (siehe Fragestellung, ob Präsens oder Präteritum)
3. Pers. Sg. -s:	*he knows*
Verneinung, Fragebildung:	mit *to do: Why do they come?*
if-Sätze:	Zeitenfolge beachten; kein *would/should* im *if*-Satz! *If I were you, I'd go with him.*
Wortstellung:	S P O = Subject – Predicate – Object mehrere Adjektive: Frequency – Manner – Place – Time
Indirekte Rede:	*He said he was interested.* („…, er sei interessiert.“)
kein Komma vor „that“:	*He said that he would be there.*

Kommas vor Relativsätzen:	*The tourists who knew the museum didn't go in again.* = nur die Touristen, die das Museum schon kannten (defining relative clause) – keine Kommas *The tourists, who knew the museum, didn't go in again.* = alle Touristen kannten das Museum schon (non-defining relative clause) – mit Kommas
much – many:	*much sugar* (nicht zählbar), *many friends* (zählbar)
this – these:	*this place – these places*
that – those:	that job – those jobs
since – for:	*since 1933, since Christmas* (Zeitpunkt) *for sixty years, for three weeks* (Zeitraum)

Beachten Sie besonders:

- Fallen Sie nicht mit der Tür ins Haus! Beginnen Sie Ihren Comment nicht mit „*Because* …" oder „*I think it is good that* …" – führen Sie durch eine Einleitung zum Thema hin. Stellen Sie sich vor, Sie schreiben für einen Leser – und nicht nur für den Lehrer, der Ihre Arbeit lesen muss!
- Denken Sie daran, dass es beim Comment im Wesentlichen darauf ankommt, dass Sie Ihre Fertigkeiten in der Fremdsprache nachweisen! Meistens gibt es für Inhalt und Sprache gleich viele Punkte. Sprachrichtigkeit ist also wichtig! Teilen Sie Ihre Bearbeitungszeit so ein, dass genügend Zeit zur sprachlichen Verbesserung bleibt.

5.2 Example: Comment writing

Themenstellung:
What problems can unemployment cause the individual concerned?

Vorüberlegungen:

arguments:
- jobless people get bored and depressed
- jobless people have less money

Lösung:

introduction: Every month new unemployment figures are published and they remind us that unemployment is one of the biggest problems the state is confronted with today. However, being out of work is very hard for the individual as well.

arguments: first argument:
It may be very nice for a person not to have to go to work for some time, but after a while he'll want to get back to work and do something useful. If you don't have a regular job you may get bored and you

have the feeling that you are not needed, that you are useless. This causes psychological problems.

second argument:
Unemployed people are entitled to draw unemployment benefit, which means the state pays them money, so that they are able to support their families. As this benefit from the state is only meant to help provide for the basic necessities, you'll soon find that you have less money than when you were working and perhaps earning extra money doing overtime. Now you find yourself with less money and you can't afford extra things, e.g. clothes, hobbies, holidays – all the things which make life so worthwhile.

conclusion: All in all, unemployment affects people's self-confidence and their emotional balance as well as their own financial situation and that of their families. Instead of paying huge sums in unemployment benefits the government should use the money to create jobs in the area of environment protection.

Exercise 10 Practice: Comment writing

Write a comment of 250 to 300 words on this topic.

The world would be a poorer place if somebody proved that Nessie does not exist.

King Arthur

1 Text box

The coming of King Arthur

When the Romans left the British Isles early in the 5th century a time of unrest and battles for power began. King Vortigern of Britain was an evil king who had killed all his rivals on his way to the throne. When the Picts and Scots attacked the Britons, Vortigern invited the Saxons from Germany and Denmark to fight his battles for him. In the end the Angles and Saxons fought against the Britons as well, killing them or driving them from their homes. The king himself fled into the mountainous regions of North Wales where he died.

Uther Pendragon defeated the Saxons and brought peace to the southern lands where he was king. On a stormy winter's night in the castle of Tintagel high above the Cornish sea a child was born to Uther and his wife Igrayne. Merlin, a wise man and wizard at the king's court, told the king about rumours of a plot to kill his son. To save the child's life Merlin left the castle at night on a secret path, hiding the baby prince under his cloak. No word was spoken of the boy's fate. A short time later King Uther was poisoned by the Saxons, and many of his followers were killed.

When the king was dead his knights fought amongst themselves for power. The years went by and there was no strong man to lead the Britons against the Saxon invaders. Then Merlin, the enchanter, who had heard of the constant battles, went to London to talk to the archbishop and they agreed on calling a meeting of knights for Christmas Day. During the church service a huge block of marble stone suddenly appeared in the churchyard. No one noticed how it had got there. A shining sword was stuck in it. Round the stone the archbishop, the lords and knights discovered these letters carved in gold: WHOEVER PULLS THIS SWORD OUT OF THIS STONE IS THE TRUE-BORN KING OF BRITAIN. Many knights jumped onto

the stone and tried to pull out the sword – but not one of them could move it even an inch. It was decided to send messengers round the country to call all knights to a tournament on New Year's Day. Perhaps the king could be found that way.

Among the knights who came to London were Sir Ector and his two sons, Kay and Arthur. Kay had just been made a knight, but Arthur was only sixteen and still too young. Kay realized that he had left his sword back at the inn where they had spent the night, so he asked Arthur to fetch it for him. Arthur rode back, but he found the inn closed and nobody answered his knocking. Wondering what to do now, he rode past the churchyard and saw the sword sticking in the stone. He jumped off his horse, ran to the stone, and without stopping to read he pulled the sword out and took it to his brother Kay, who recognised the sword at once, because he had tried to pull it from the stone the day before. Kay showed the sword to his father, shouting, "I have the sword from the stone, so I must be the King of Britain!" Sir Ector did not believe him, instead, he made Kay put the sword back into the stone, then he told him, "Pull it out!" Kay pulled and pulled but the sword wouldn't move. Then Arthur was told to have a go. He put his hand to the hilt and the steel slid easily out of the stone. Sir Ector and Kay knelt down at once. "Why are you kneeling? What is happening?" Arthur wondered. "You are the true-born King of Britain," said Sir Ector, "I am not your real father. Merlin brought you to me when you were a small child and asked me to bring you up as my own son."

They went to tell the archbishop and the knights, but no one believed them and the decision to choose a king was put off till Whitsun. Meeting in London again, they tried their luck at pulling the sword from the stone, but Arthur was the only one who could draw it out. So the crowd knelt down before him and all the knights and barons swore their loyalty to their new King Arthur.

With the help of the magic sword Arthur led his men to fight against the Saxons. After seven long years the invaders were finally driven back across the sea. Arthur set up his court at the ancient castle of Camelot and married Lady Guinevere.

770 words

Exercise 1 Questions on the text

Answer the following question in your own words. Do not copy from the text.

a) Why was it not a good idea of King Vortigern to ask the Saxons for help against the Picts and Scots?
b) Why did Merlin take the young baby away from the court of his father?
c) Why did Merlin go to London to see the archbishop?
d) Why did all the knights try to pull the sword from the stone?
e) Which fact shows that Kay was not an honest knight?
f) What did Arthur find out about his own past?
g) Why did the knights want to wait till Whitsun with their final decision?

Exercise 2 Synonymous expressions

Which word or phrases tell you that ...

a) the King of the Britons had asked the Saxons to battle in his place?
b) the native Britons had to leave their houses and farms?
c) no one talked about what happened to the baby boy anymore?
d) after Vortigern's death many of his followers wanted to be king?
e) that Kay knew the sword very well?
f) that Arthur drew out the sword without any difficulty?
g) that the knights did not choose Arthur as their King straight away?
h) that the knights assured Arthur that they would follow his orders?

2 Word power: Some words to remember

beneath	unter; unterhalb
churchyard	Kirchhof
cloak	Umhang, Mantel
(to) defeat	(jdn., eine Armee) besiegen, schlagen
(to) dress (a wound)	(eine Wunde) verbinden
(to) drive (from)	treiben, vertreiben
enchanter	Zauberer
evil	böse, übel
fairy	Fee

fate	Schicksal
(to) float	schwimmen, treiben
hermit	Einsiedler
hilt	Griff (eines Schwertes)
knight	Ritter
loyalty	Treue
magician	Zauberer
marble	Marmor
mist	Nebel
mortal	sterblich; tödlich
plain	Ebene
plot	Verschwörung; Handlung (eines Romans)
scabbard	Schwertscheide
shore	Ufer (eines Sees)
stroke	Schlag, Hieb
tournament	Turnier
unrest	Unruhe
wicked	böse, boshaft
wizard	Zauberer, Hexenmeister

Exercise 3 Words in a new context

Here are words from the Text Box "The coming of King Arthur". They are used in new and different contexts. Use the words in the right places. Please note there are more words listed than you actually need.

decision	hilt	luck	plot
discovery	kneel	magic	pull
evil	lead	move	recognize
finally	loyalty	notice	save

a) Has crime become a necessary __________ in our modern society?

b) After three hours walking through the woods, they __________ realised that they'd taken the wrong way.

c) Where does this motorway __________ to?

d) Many people believe that when they touch wood it will bring them __________.

e) Every Wednesday Muriel Scot would go to the cementry and __________ before her husband's grave.

f) He's always talking nonsense. Please, take no __________ of him.

g) That new medicine is very good for him, but he shouldn't expect __________.

h) A kidney donor could __________ the girl's life.

i) It is sometimes difficult to __________ voices on the telephone.

j) The elderly lady was shocked at the __________ that one of her sons was a member of a gang dealing with drugs.

Exercise 4 Vocabulary grid: Legends

Fill the squares with words from the list "Some words to remember".

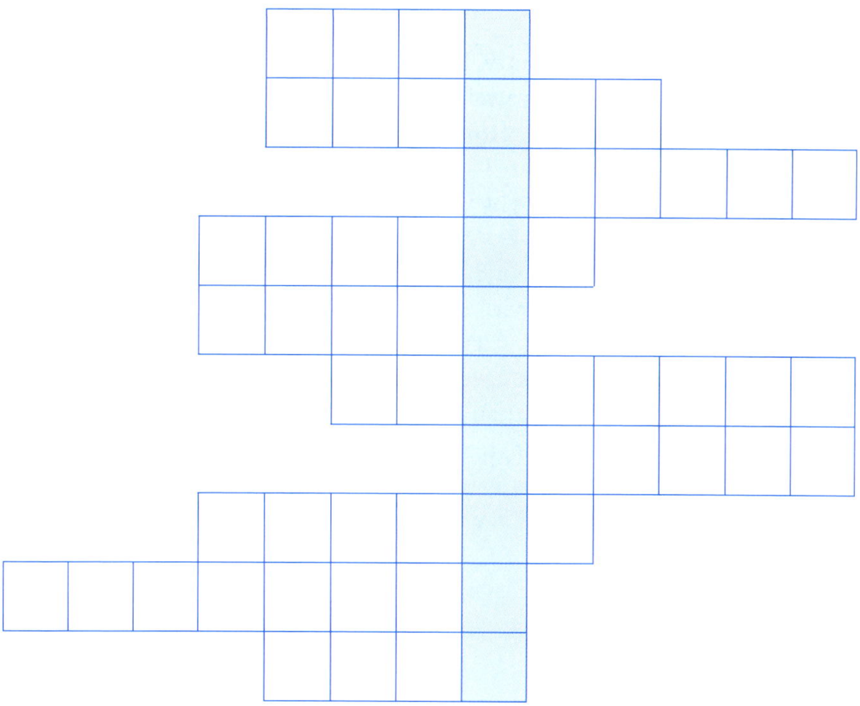

Across:
1. a secret plan against a person
2. a blow or hit
3. time of changes and fighting
4. man who does magic
5. treeless countryside
6. a case or covering for a sword
7. who will die; causing death
8. very bad
9. enchanter
10. cloud near the ground

Down:
a meeting of knights at which they fight and compete against each other to find out who is the best of them all; today you could say that players meet instead of knights.

Exercise 5 Cloze-Test: Tintagel today

Complete the text with words from this list.

board	enemies	path	view
born	fascinated	remains	waves
coast	location	situated	
connection	meetings	stone	

For centuries the impressive ______________ [1] of the castle has ______________ [2] visitors from all over the country. It is ______________ [3] high on a hill on the rough ______________ [4] of Cornwall near the little village of Tintagel: People call it "King Arthur's castle". However, when you have climbed the steep ______________ [5] to the top there is not much that you can see today: a number of low ______________ [6] walls which might be the ______________ [7] of a hall, of a well and perhaps a few graves. What is more breath-taking is the fantastic ______________ [8] of the rocks and the sea – and the thought of a legendary ______________ [9] of the castle with King Arthur. Could this be the place where Arthur was ______________ [10], where Merlin, the magician, hid the baby from his ______________ [11]? Merlin's Cave is the name of a rock formation down by the ______________ [12] that you can see from the top of the castle. Is this the place where King Arthur and his Knights of the Round Table held their ______________ [13]? At least this is what the villagers of Tintagel and the local tourist ______________ [14] want to make you believe.

Exercise 6 C-Test: How the legend began

Some words are incomplete. Only one or a couple of letters are given. Try to complete with words that fit the context.

It all be______[1] in the 12th century when Geoffrey of Monmouth reco______[2] the legend of King Arthur in his *History of the Kings of Britain*. He made Tintagel the scene where it all hap______[3]. Many writers fol______[4] who took up the story of Arthur and his great co______[5] at Camelot, among them was Alfred Lord Tennyson (1809–1892). Bet______[6] 1859 and 1888 he completed *Idylls of the King*, an Arthurian epic in 12 pa______[7]. In his *Memoirs*, Tennyson said of the *Idylls:* "It is not the history of one man or of one gene______[8], but a whole cycle of generations." All romantic writers of the nineteenth century kept ali______[9] the traditional conn______[10] with Tintagel Castle, not knowing what had rea______[11] happened at Tintagel in the past. There was no scien______[12] proof as archaeology was still its infa______[13]. The stories became extremely pop______[14], and the link between Arthur and Tintagel was stro______[15] than ever. But was Tintagel really Arthur's castle?

Exercise 7 C-Test: Searching for the truth behind the myth

Some words are scrambled. Try to restore the original word. To help you the first letter is given.

Archaeologists began (e-ianaxsovct) ____________[1] at Tintagel in 1933. They found out that the (r-nuis) ____________[2] we see today are remains of a Norman (c-taels) ____________[3] built in the 12 century. The (q-suinote) ____________[4], though, is: Why did Reginald, Earl of Cornwall, build a castle here at a (p-clea) __________[5] which is of little strategic (v-auel) __________[6]? Moreover, the castle could not have been an (i-nmotrpat) ____________[7] one, because it was only used for a relatively (s-rhto) ____________[8] time. People lived in it for only a (h-edudrn) ____________[9] years or so and by the fourteenth century it had (f-lanel) ____________[10] into disrepair. Later it was used as a (p-snroi) ____________[11]. So, that medieval castle could not have been Arthur's castle after all! If Arthur was not just a legendary (f-ugier) __________[12], if he did exist he lived in the sixth century, well before Tintagel was (b-ltui) ____________[13]. Consequently, the (l-kin) ____________[14] that Geoffrey had made was the result of (c-moeeplt) ____________[15] fantasy.

Exercise 8 Translation: The legend lives on!

Translate into English or German respectively.

Perhaps Geoffrey was ______________[1] (beeinflusst) by stories that Tintagel had been the place where the ancient (______________)[2] kings of Cornwall had built their fortress (______________)[3]. Some of the walls that we see today belonged to a chapel or a Celtic ______________[4] (Kloster) that was built 200 years before the castle. There are also finds which suggest (______________)[5] that the place was used even by the Romans. Maybe they had built an official station here on the road to the ______________[6] (Zinn) mines in Cornwall. So many traces (______________)[7] – but so many unsolved questions, too. Perhaps this is the ______________[8] (Grund) why such a large number of tourists still come to see the place, thinking that perhaps, after all, it really could have been the site (______________)[9] of King Arthur's castle!

3 Language corner: Usage of words

sea – lake

- *sea* = das Meer, die See
  sea wird verwendet zur Bezeichnung eines salzigen Gewässers, z. B. *the North Sea, the Dead Sea.* Nur ganz selten wird auch ein größerer Binnensee als *sea* bezeichnet: *the Sea of Galilee.*

After seven long years the invaders were finally driven back across the sea.
Nach sieben langen Jahren wurden die Eindringlinge schließlich über das Meer zurückgetrieben.

- *lake* = der See
  Der See, also das Gewässer, das von Land umgeben ist, wird als *lake* bezeichnet, z. B. *Lake Constance* (Bodensee), *Lake Geneva* (Genfer See), *the Great Lakes, the Lakes Superior, Huron, Michigan, Erie, and Ontario; Lake District (or the Lakes) in Cumbria.*

Arthur went down to the lake.
Artus stieg hinab zum See.

happy – lucky

• *happy* = glücklich *happy* wird verwendet zur Bezeichnung eines Gefühlszustands.	I was very happy when they told me that my brother was alive. *Ich war sehr glücklich (froh), als man mir sagte, mein Bruder sei am Leben.*
• *lucky* = glücklich *lucky* bedeutet „glücklich“ im Sinne von „Glück haben“, z. B. im Lotto, bei dem man selbst keinen Einfluss auf den Ausgang hat.	We were lucky to get home before the rain started. *Wir hatten Glück („Dusel“), dass wir nach Hause kamen, bevor der Regen anfing.*

hear – listen

• *hear* = hören *hear* bezeichnet die Fähigkeit des Hörens.	Can you hear me at the back? *Können Sie mich da hinten hören?*
• *listen* = zuhören *listen* bezeichnet das bewusste Zuhören, das Aufmerken, z. B. bei einem Vortrag.	Please listen to what I'm saying! *Hör mal bitte zu, was ich sage!*

Exercise 9 Practice: Test your language skills

Choose the right words to fill the gaps.

a) Thousands of poor Cuban migrants try to sail across the ____________ (lake/sea) to America.

b) "I enjoyed the book I've just read," says Emily. "After all, it had a ____________ (happy/lucky) ending – which is what I like."

c) The Everglades once covered the entire tip of Florida – about 4 million acres of wetland stretching from ____________ (Lake/Sea) Okeechobee in the north to the Gulf of Mexico in the south.

d) Lois cries, "Superman, if you can ____________ (hear/listen to) me, drop what you're doing and help me!"

e) British generals proposed a military land, ____________ (lake/sea) and air blockade against Serbia.

f) Our teacher has time to ____________ (hear/listen to) the worries and concerns of his students.

g) Scientists suspect that pesticides and other toxic chemicals are discharged into rivers and out to ______________ (lakes/sea), killing marine life.

h) Every day the immigrant told me he would be ______________ (happy/lucky) to work for money or food.

i) Billy Graham would practice sermons aloud in old sheds or in a canoe in the middle of a ______________ (lake/sea).

j) Nelson Mandela only used violence when the other side would not ______________ (hear/listen).

k) After the shooting, the criminal threw the gun in a ______________ (lake/sea).

l) At ______________ (Lake/Sea) World in Florida tourists can watch killer whales and dolphins.

m) Did you ______________ (hear/listen) about the tourist who got lost in the maze at Hampton Court?

4 Grammar spot: Modal auxiliaries

Die Verben werden im Englischen in drei Gruppen eingeteilt:

- Vollverben
- Hilfsverben *(to be, to do, to have)*
- modale Hilfsverben *(can, may, must, will, shall)*.

• Die **modalen Hilfsverben** haben für alle Personen nur eine Form (kein *-s* in der 3. Person Singular).	I must help my mother. She must help her mother. We must help our parents.
• Auf modale Hilfsverben folgt der Infinitiv ohne *to*.	You must work more.
• **Frage** und **Verneinung** werden ohne *do / does / did* gebildet.	Can I help you?
must not *(mustn't)* drückt ein Verbot aus.	You mustn't forget to do your homework for Monday! *Du darfst nicht vergessen …*
need not *(needn't)* drückt das Fehlen eines Zwangs oder einer Notwendigkeit aus.	You needn't do it right away. *Du brauchst sie nicht sofort zu machen.*

- Bestimmte Zeitformen (Futur, Perfekt, Plusquamperfekt) werden mithilfe eines **Ersatzverbs** (*substitute*) gebildet.

We will have to take a test soon.
Wir werden bald eine Prüfung machen müssen.

Survey: "can" in all tenses

Tenses	Positive forms	Negative forms
Present	I can work	I can't work I cannot work
Future	I'll be able to work	I won't be able to work
Past	I could work I was able to work	I couldn't work I wasn't able to work
Present Perfect	I have been able to work	I haven't been able to work
Past Perfect	I had been able to work	I hadn't been able to work
Conditional I	I could work I would be able to work	I couldn't work I wouldn't be able to work
Conditional II	I could have worked I would have been able to work	I couldn't have worked I wouldn't have been able to work

Survey: Substitutes

Modal	Substitute
can ("können")	to be able to
may ("dürfen")	to be allowed to
must ("müssen")	to have to
will ("wollen")	to want, to wish, to desire
shall ("sollen")	to be to

Exercise 10

Practice: Test your grammar – can

Form sentences and use the given time adverbials.

a) Fred can drive a lorry. When Fred was in the army he could drive a lorry.
After a few more driving lessons ____________________

b) Michelle can make her own dresses.
In a few years' time ____________________
Before she got married ____________________

c) James can play the guitar.
When his arm is better ______________________
A few years ago ______________________

d) John can go to the disco.
Tonight ______________________
Next Saturday ______________________

Exercise 11 Practice: Text your grammar – must

Put into simple past.

a) Jamie has to wash the dishes.

____

b) You mustn't see your present before your birthday.

____

c) You'll have to read that paragraph again.

____

d) My friend Bill has to go home early.

____

e) I must finish my essay.

____

f) Sandra mustn't go home alone.

____

g) You needn't pay for the meal yourself.

____

h) Jill won't have to take the test again.

____

Exercise 12 Practice: Text your grammar – negation

Put into the negative.

a) Zoe must be home before ten.

____

b) Miriam must wipe all the glasses.

____

c) We had to change our clothes.

____

d) He'll have to pay the workers in advance.

____

e) You must answer this letter at once.

____

f) I shall have to book my holiday tomorrow.

____

g) Omar had to fill in a landing card.

____

h) You must wait for me at the bus stop.

____

5 Writing desk

5.1 How to write a summary

Was wird verlangt?
Wenn Sie ein Summary zu schreiben haben, heißt das, dass Sie eine kurze Zusammenfassung eines vorliegenden Textes anfertigen sollen. Dabei muss das Original üblicherweise auf ein Drittel oder ein Viertel des ursprünglichen Umfangs reduziert werden. Also: Ein Originaltext von 600 Wörtern wird auf 150 bis 200 Wörter gekürzt. Das bedeutet, dass Sie zwei Drittel des Ausgangstextes über Bord werfen müssen. Welche Teile das sind, sollen Sie in dieser Übung lernen.
Die Aufgabe stellt zum einen hohe Anforderungen an Ihr Textverständnis und zum anderen an Ihre Fähigkeit, die wichtigste Aussage zu erkennen und knapp mit eigenen Worten wiederzugeben.

Wie gehen Sie vor?

- Gutes Textverständnis
  Stellen Sie zunächst sicher, dass Sie das Original gut verstanden haben. Dazu sollten Sie den Text mehrmals sehr sorgfältig lesen. Schlagen Sie die Ihnen unbekannten Wörter im Lexikon nach, denn nur so ist ein gutes Textverständnis gewährleistet.
  Lesen Sie „mit Bleistift und/oder Textmarker". Kennzeichnen Sie die Stellen, die Ihnen noch unklar oder schwer verständlich erscheinen. Vielleicht wird Ihnen die Bedeutung dieser besonderen Abschnitte bei einem dritten oder vierten Durchlesen klar.

- Unterscheidung zwischen wichtigen und „unwichtigen“ Passagen
  Was ist wichtig, was ist weniger wichtig? Eigentlich gibt es in einem Text keine „unwichtigen“ Passagen. Wenn der Verfasser selbst eine Aussage für wenig relevant gehalten hätte, hätte er diese nicht in seinen Text aufgenommen oder bei der Bearbeitung wieder gestrichen. Trotzdem können wir das Original kürzen.
  Jeder Autor möchte dem Leser klar und deutlich sagen, was er meint. Hier haben Sie soeben ein Beispiel dafür gelesen: *klar und deutlich*, das ist eigentlich dasselbe. Die Verdopplung dient *einzig und allein* (auch hier wieder) der Verdeutlichung. Um das Textverständnis zu sichern, bringt ein Verfasser mehrfach Beispiele und Belege für seine These. Oft wiederholt er zur Verdeutlichung einen bereits erwähnten Gesichtspunkt oder er vertieft ihn. Diese „nur“ der Klarheit dienenden Wiederholungen können wir weglassen und damit den Ausgangstext kürzen.
  Beim Summary eines erzählenden Textes müssen wir die ausschmückenden Passagen weglassen. Wichtig sind nur die Stellen, in denen die Handlung vorangetrieben wird.
  Wenn Sie „mit Bleistift und/oder Textmarker lesen“, kennzeichnen Sie die wichtigen Stellen, d.h. die Passagen, die wesentliche und neue Inhaltselemente enthalten. Unterscheiden Sie zwischen Hauptgedanken und Nebengedanken, zwischen neuen Gesichtspunkten und/oder weiteren Belegen und Beispielen für bereits Erwähntes.
- Textformulierung
  Schreiben Sie dann für jeden einzelnen Abschnitt des Originaltextes eine kurze Zusammenfassung. Achten Sie schon hier darauf, dass Sie einen im Ausgangstext kurzen Absatz auch entsprechend kurz zusammenfassen. Bei etwas längeren Textteilen darf auch Ihr Summary länger sein. Behalten Sie auf alle Fälle die insgesamt erlaubte Wortzahl im Auge!
  Denken Sie daran, eigene Formulierungen zu verwenden. Es genügt nicht, das Original zusammenzustreichen und ein paar verbindende Wörter hinzuzufügen. Sie sollen den Ausgangstext so weit wie möglich paraphrasieren. Hier wenden Sie an, was an anderer Stelle – im Vokabelteil einer erweiterten Textaufgabe – isoliert geübt wird: Sie ersetzen den ursprünglichen Text durch Synonyme (synonyms) oder Umschreibungen (paraphrases).

Checkliste zum Summary

- aus direkter Rede wird indirekte Rede
- Ich-Erzählungen werden in Erzählungen in der 3. Person (er, sie) umgeformt
- die Zeitstufe, die im Original verwendet wurde, wird beibehalten
- die Anordnung der Abschnitte wird beibehalten
- neue Gedanken, neue Beispiele zum Thema werden nicht eingeführt

5.2 Example: Summary writing

Write a summary of the following text of no more than 200 words.

King Arthur's magic sword: Excalibur

Arthur was crowned king and Merlin became his teacher. In a fight against Sir Pellinore Arthur was badly wounded and he also lost his sword. Merlin helped Arthur and took him to a hermit in the woods. The old man dressed Arthur's wounds and gave him medicine to drink. When Arthur told Merlin that he had lost his sword, the magician said, "The sword which you lost wasn't of any great value. But near here your own sword awaits you: it was made in Avalon by fairies, made for you alone. It is called Excalibur, and no one can stand against its stroke. It cuts through iron and steel and cannot break. With it you shall bring freedom and peace to your kingdom!"

After Arthur had recovered from his wounds, he and Merlin rode deeper and deeper into the forest, passed through a narrow valley until they arrived at a strange lake. All around it the hills rose darkly, but the water was of the clearest sunniest blue. The shore was covered thickly in fresh green grass and flowers. "This is the Lake of the Fairy Palace," said Merlin. "Beyond the lake lies the plain of Camlann where the last battle will be fought and where you will be killed by the Evil Knight. Beyond the plains lies Avalon, hidden in the mist and the mysterious waters. Now, go down and speak with the Lady of the Lake, while I wait here for you."

Arthur went down the steep path leading to the magic lake. He looked across the quiet blue water and there in the middle of the lake he saw an arm with a hand holding above the water a wonderful shining sword and a jewelled scabbard and belt. Then Arthur saw a beautiful woman walking across the water towards him. "I am the Lady of the Lake. I come to tell you that your sword Excalibur awaits you. It is very special. No other mortal hand can touch it; it was made for you alone. Now I must ask you for something in return."
"I swear to give you whatever gift you shall ask for," answered Arthur.

"You are still young and your reign has only just begun. Years of fame and glory lie ahead of you. But even the greatest king is mortal and one day you will die. When that day comes you must return this sword to the water, the element from which it came. Now, step into this boat," said the Lady of the Lake. Arthur saw a boat floating on the water before him and he got in. The Lady of the Lake stood on the shore, but the barge moved across the water as if unseen hands drew it. When Arthur came to the arm reaching out from under the water, he leaned out and took the sword. The arm and hand slid quietly beneath the water and was gone. The boat brought Arthur back to the shore where the Lady of the Lake had stood, but she had disappeared. Arthur climbed back to where Merlin was waiting for him and showed him the sword and scabbard. Merlin warned Arthur, "Look after that scabbard carefully, because as long as you wear that magic scabbard you shall lose but little blood, however badly you are wounded. After I am gone from you a wicked lady will try to steal the sword and the scabbard from you!" Then they rode on together and before long they reached the castle Camelot and all the knights welcomed their brave king. *595 words*

scabbard = Schwertscheide

Key

a) paragraph (originally 123 words)
After a defeat in a fight against Sir Pellinore the enchanter Merlin took the wounded King Arthur to a hermit for medical treatment. When Arthur worried about the loss of his sword, the wizard assured him that a much better one, Excalibur, was waiting especially for him. (47 words)

b) paragraph (originally 121 words)
After Arthur's recovery Merlin led him to the beautiful and magic Lake of the Fairy Palace, told him about Avalon and sent Arthur down to the water on his own to meet the Lady of the Lake. (37 words)

c) paragraph (originally 116 words)
Arriving at the blue lake Arthur saw a precious sword being held above the surface of the water. He met the beautiful Lady who made him familiar with the very special qualities of his new sword Excalibur. (37 words)

d) paragraph (originally 149 words)
She made Arthur promise to return Excalibur at his death and then sent him in a boat to the middle of the lake to collect his magic sword. Coming back to the shore Arthur realized the woman had gone. (39 words)

e) paragraph (originally 86 words)
When he had met up with Merlin again Arthur learned about the special protection which the scabbard offered. Merlin advised Arthur to look after sword and scabbard carefully and both rode back to Camelot. (34 words)

(altogether 195 words)

Exercise 13 Practice: Summary writing

Write a summary of a film you have seen recently or a book that you have read.

Child labour

1 Text box

Working youngsters

Do you earn some extra pocket money yourself? Do you work in a supermarket or fast food restaurant? Do you have a paper-round? How many hours do you do?

In the USA, 14- to 16-year-olds are allowed to work up to three hours on school days, but not after 7 p.m. and no more than 18 hours a week altogether. During a recent check investigators found that employers often disregarded these hour restrictions and that teenagers worked much longer. It was also discovered that many children were employed in jobs where they had to operate dangerous machinery, such as meat slicers. Most abuses of laws and regulations occurred in pizza parlours and supermarkets – all of them businesses which have always liked to hire teenagers to do the menial work there.

Child labour and the exploitation of minors are social evils of the 19th century. During the times of the Industrial Revolution children were employed in mines and factories where they worked long hours in dangerous and filthy conditions. In some cases children five and six years of age were forced to work from 13 to 16 hours a day. Before automatic machines were invented the

owners of mines and factories needed large numbers of cheap, unskilled labour. On the other hand, parents were so poor that they had to send their young children out to work, just to make ends meet. That left the children with no time to go to school, so they didn't learn how to read and write. Without any education later in life as grown-ups they had to be satisfied with employment in menial jobs.

Work for minors was full of risks. Numerous accidents happened to children. Because of their young age they often didn't obey the safety rules, of which there were few anyway. Children often played in dangerous places. More than one got caught with his clothes in a turning wheel and died before the engine could be stopped. The luckier ones escaped with bad injuries, but were crippled for the rest of their lives.

By the middle of the 19th century child labour had produced an enormous number of illiterate, diseased and crippled children. Poor families had not got out of poverty – on the contrary, they had become poorer still. The novelist Charles Dickens and the socialist Karl Marx brought the scandalous exploitation of children to the attention of a greater public. Due to their constant accusations and pressure on politicians the first significant British legislation against child labour was passed in 1878.

It became illegal to employ children under the age of 10. Children between the ages of 10 and 14 were only allowed to work every second day or half days. For all children Saturday became a half holiday.

In spite of all the regulation aimed at protecting the health of children and securing their education the laws were not always effectively enforced. Children still worked hard and long hours, not so much in mines and factories, but mostly in agriculture and in shops. There the laws could be broken quite easily because the children worked for their parents and nobody minded or complained.

In former times work for young people was hard – and pay was low. When boys left school at the age of 14 they almost always went to work in the same mine or factory as their father or older brothers. The boys were expected to make tea and look after tools. They were known as Kettle or Tool boys. The starting wage in the 1880s was about 6 pence a day, which was paid monthly. This was not the boys' own money to keep. They gave nearly all of it to their mother as their contribution to the upkeep of the family. *625 words*

Exercise 1 **Understanding the text**

Decide if these statements are true or false. Correct the false ones.

		true	false
a)	In the United States young people of 14- to 16-years of age may work up to three hours every day.	☐	☐
b)	Very often children work longer than they should, and in dangerous jobs, too.	☐	☐
c)	Before they had machines in the mines and factories children had less employment possibilities.	☐	☐
d)	Even very young children had to work to contribute to the income of the family.	☐	☐
e)	Apart from going to work children also had to attend school.	☐	☐
f)	In the 19th century many working children were unable to read or write.	☐	☐
g)	Charles Dickens and Karl Marx were two politicians who tried to improve the situation of working children.	☐	☐
h)	The new laws which limited the hours children were allowed to work were not respected by farmers and shop-owners.	☐	☐

2 Word power: Some words to remember

(to) abolish	abschaffen
abuse	Missbrauch
(to) affect	betreffen, beeinträchtigen
altogether	insgesamt
boredom	Langeweile

(to) borrow	sich (aus)leihen, borgen
(to) check	kontrollieren; Kontrolle
(to) disregard	nicht beachten
(to) doze	dösen, einnicken
exploitation	Ausbeutung
illiterate	des Lesens und Schreibens unkundig
investigator	Prüfer, Ermittlungsbeamter
(to) jeopardise	gefährden
labour	Arbeit, Arbeitskräfte
menial	niedrig, wenig angesehen
merchant	Kaufmann, Händler
merely	nur, bloß, lediglich
mill	Mühle; Fabrik (bes. Textilfabrik)
minor	Minderjährige(r)
(to) occur	geschehen, vorkommen, sich ereignen
orphan	Waise
restriction	Beschränkung
(to) secure	sichern, schützen, gewährleisten
significant	bedeutend, merklich
(to) slice	(ab)schneiden
unskilled	ungelernt

Exercise 2 Synonyms

Find synonyms in the main text for these words.

a) control ______________________

b) dirty ______________________

c) continuous ______________________

d) happen ______________________

e) adult ______________________

f) despite ______________________

g) guarantee ______________________

Exercise 3 Vocabulary grid: Labour

Fill the squares across with words to fit these synonyms and definitions.

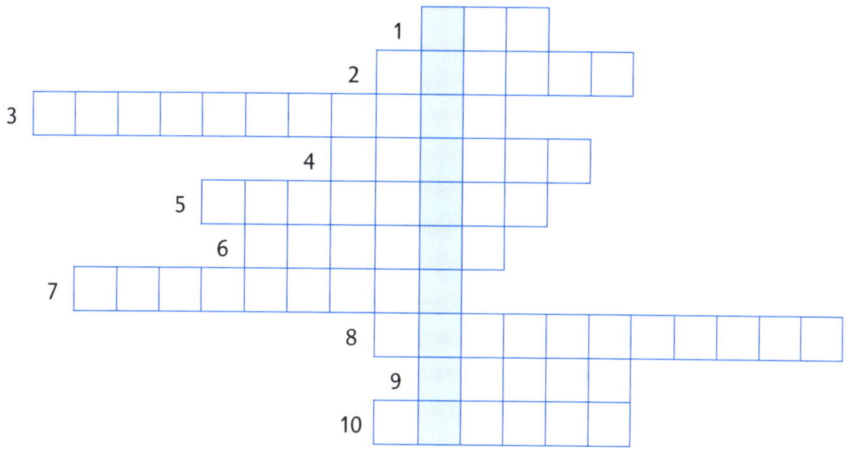

1. working place, profession
2. only
3. limitation
4. child with no parents
5. buys and sells goods
6. to guarantee
7. having no qualifications
8. important
9. cut
10. low-paid, less respected

The word in the darker squares down is a synonym for: endanger

Exercise 4 Cloze-Test: Child labour today

Complete the text with words from this list.

abolish	forced	outlawed	slaves
books	however	past	upkeep
century	mills	pay	
disappeared	orphans	services	

In the 18th ____________[1] in Great Britain, owners of cotton ____________[2] travelled around the country to collect ____________[3] and children of poor parents. The children were to work in the mills without any ____________[4]. The only return they received from their ____________[5] was their food. They worked like ____________[6] merely for the cost of their own ____________[7]. In some cases children who were five or six years old were ____________[8] to work up to 16 hours a day, but if you think that slavery was a scandal of the

__________[9] – you'll have to think again! The movement to __________[10] slavery began in the 18th century. Britain __________[11] (1807) the slave trade and abolished (1833) slavery in the British Empire. In the USA, slavery had also __________[12] in the North by the early 19th century. This is what the history __________[13] tell us – the reality, __________[14], is different.

Exercise 5 Prepositions: A sad report

Complete the following text with prepositions from this list.

of – from – of – in – of – in – off – of – in – in – of

________[1] spite ________[2] all social progress slavery still exists ________[3] our world today, and children are especially affected. The International Labour Organisation (ILO) reports that tens ________[4] millions ________[5] people around the globe, including children as young as six, are working ________[6] slavery.
The new centres ________[7] modern slavery are Third World countries and countries which suffer ________[8] the consequences ________[9] wars, rebellions and revolutions. ________[10] wars people are killed, houses are burnt down, farms are destroyed. People are driven ________[11] their land, and without their small fields parents are no longer able to feed their children.

Exercise 6 C-Test: Child labour in Third World countries

Some words are scrambled. Try to restore the original word. To help you the first letter is given.

The vast majority of working children live in developing countries. During the times of the (c-iilv) __________[1] war in Sudan (1992), small farmers were selling their young sons to travelling (m-tcaesrnh) __________[2] for as little as $70. Many parents saw no other (p-obtlsisiiy) __________[3] to keep their young ones (a-lvei) __________[4], which shows that until recently so-called "child catchers" were going (a-udrno) __________[5] countries and buying children from (h-epselsl) __________[6] parents. In Haiti more than 100,000 children were sold or (g-ievn) __________[7] away by poor families to do hard work as domestic (s-nveastr) __________[8] – not in the 19th century, but in the 1990s during a (p-dieor) __________[9] of social and political unrest after the first free presidential (e-lincoest) __________[10]. To make the children dependent on their (f-uuetr) __________[11] employers "child catchers" often give parents (m-oeny) ____________[12] to rebuild their homes for example. However, in their new jobs the children will never (e-nar) ____________[13] so much money to repay the (b-drowero) ____________[14] sums. So the families would (s-yat) ____________[15] in debt and dependence for ever.

Exercise 7 C-Test: Child labour in the USA

Some words are incomplete. Only one or a couple of letters are given. Try to complete with words that fit the context.

Child labour is still a problem in the USA today. To fight high labour co________[1] the garment industry in New York or fast-food restaurants in California emp________[2] more and more children using them as che________[3] workers. Ever younger children work ever lon________[4] hours at jobs no one else will take for the low pay. Children from imm________[5] families suffer most. They have no chance of compl________[6] to the authorities that they are being trea________[7] badly. Although laws and regulations do exist to sec________[8] their health and welfare, as workers without a per________[9] they are outlaws.

Translate into English or German respectively.

On the other hand, many ____________[10] (Arbeitgeber) argue that there is another side to the story. Teenagers who work after school learn discipline and ____________[11] (Verantwortung). If they were not working, many kids would be walking the streets doing nothing. Some might even turn to crime out of ____________[12] (Langeweile). Yet child-welfare advocates reply that they are not against teenagers working: they are against teenagers being ____________[13] (ausgebeutet). Teachers report that students who work late into the night often fall behind (____________)[14] in their homework, cannot concentrate and doze off (____________)[15] during class. Thousands of youngsters are jeopardising (____________)[16] their education, health and safety by working too many hours, too late at night, and in dangerous occupations (____________)[17]. So who pays the price in the end?

3 Grammar spot: Reported speech

In indirekter Rede werden Aussagen, Fragen oder Befehle wiedergegeben. Als Einleitungsverben der indirekten Rede (reporting verbs) stehen u. a. zur Verfügung: add, agree, answer, continue, emphasize, go on, know, mention, point out, remark, say, state, stress, tell, think, want to know.

So werden die **Pronomina**, die **Zeitstufe** und die **Adverbien** angepasst:

Pronouns

	Direct speech		Reported speech
Personalpronomen	I, you, we, you	→	he, she, they
Possessivpronomen	my, your our, your	→	his, her their
Demonstrativpronomen	this these	→	that those

Tenses

Keine Änderung der Zeitstufe

Steht das Einleitungsverb der Rede im **Präsens**, **Perfekt** oder **Futur**, wird die Zeitstufe der direkten Rede nicht geändert:

Tense	Direct speech		Reported speech	Tense
Present	John says / has said / will say, “I don’t like working in a factory.”	→	John says / has said /will say / (that) he doesn’t like working in a factory.	Present

Änderung der Zeitstufe

Steht das Einleitungsverb der Rede im **Präteritum**, wird die Zeit der direkten Rede um eine Zeitstufe zurückversetzt.

Tense	Direct speech		Reported speech	Tense
Present	Ian: “I work as a designer.”	→	Ian said (that) he worked as a designer. …, dass er als Grafiker arbeite.	Simple past
Simple past	Ian: “In 1995 I worked in an advertising agency in Wales.”	→	Ian said (that) in 1995 he had worked in an advertising agency in Wales.	Past perfect

Present perfect	Ian: "I haven't worked abroad."	→	Ian said (that) he hadn't worked abroad.	Past perfet
Future	Ian: "I'll visit Germany in the near future."	→	Ian said that he would visit Germany in the near future.	Conditional

Questions

	Direct speech		Reported speech
• Fragen werden eingeleitet durch *ask*, *want to know*, *wonder*.	Ian: "How much will I earn?"	→	Ian wanted to know how much he would earn.
• Steht in der direkten Rede kein Fragepronomen, wird *if* oder *whether* eingesetzt.	Ian asked his boss: "Can I work from home?"	→	Ian asked his boss if/ whether he could work from home.

Requests, advice and commands

Aufforderungen werden durch die Konstruktion **Verb + Objekt + *(not)* Infinitiv** wiedergegeben.
Durch die Wahl des Einleitungsverbs drückt man aus, ob es sich um eine höfliche Aufforderung *(to ask)*, einen Rat *(to advise)* oder einen strengeren Befehl *(to tell, to order, to command)* handelt.

	Direct speech		Reported speech
• **Polite request:** Eine höfliche Aufforderung wird durch ***to ask*** eingeleitet.	She said, "Please sign the application form."	→	She asked him to sign the application form.
• **Advice:** Ein Rat wird durch ***to advise*** eingeleitet.	The doctor said, "Don't work too much overtime."	→	The doctor advised him not to work too much overtime.
• **Command:** Ein Befehl wird durch ***to tell, to order, to command*** eingeleitet.	Foreman: "Hurry up, man!"	→	The foreman told him to hurry up.

Adverbials

Bei der Umwandlung von direkter Rede in indirekte Rede werden die Adverbiale wie folgt angepasst:

	Direct speech		Reported speech
Adverbial phrases of time	today	→	that day
	yesterday	→	the day before
	tomorrow	→	the following day
	next week/year	→	the following week/year
	now	→	then
Adverb of place	here	→	there

Exercise 8

Reported speech: Statements

To make people more aware of the problem of child labour today the International Labour Organisation invited journalists to a press conference in Geneva. David Graham attended the conference for the Manchester Herald. This is what the speaker of the ILO told the journalists:

"In spite of all social progress slavery still exists. Children are especially affected. The new centres of modern slavery are Third World countries. In wars people are killed, houses are burnt down, farms are destroyed. People are driven off their land, and without their small fields parents are no longer able to feed their children.
Child labour is still a problem in the USA. In New York and in California more and more children are employed as cheap workers. Young children work at jobs no one else will take because of the low pay. Children from immigrant families suffer most. They have no chance of complaining to the authorities that they are being treated badly. Although laws and regulations do exist to secure their health and welfare, as workers without a permit they are outlaws."

After the press conference journalist David Graham writes his article for tomorrow's paper.
Put the words of the speaker of the ILO into reported speech using as many reporting verbs as possible (point out / make it clear / emphasize / continue / go on / add etc.). Start like this:

At the press conference the speaker of the ILO said (that) in spite of all social progress slavery still existed.
He told the journalists …

Exercise 9 Reported speech: Questions

Mr Spencer, Timothy's teacher of English, noticed that Timothy's marks were getting worse and worse. So one day he asked Tim to come and see him after the lesson. These were the teacher's question.

a) Why are your marks getting worse?
b) Do you have any problems at home?
c) Do you have problems with your girlfriend?
d) Don't you want to go to school any more?
e) When do you go to bed at night?
f) What time do you do your homework?
g) Have you ever forgotten to do your homework?
h) Is your mother there when you come home from school?
i) Do you see your father every day?
j) Do you have any financial worries?

In the afternoon Timothy's friend James asks what Old Spencer had wanted to know. Give Tim's answer, starting "Old Spencer wanted to know / asked / inquired / wondered etc. ..."

Example:

Direct speech	**Reported speech**
What the teacher asked:	What Tim told his friend James:
How do you feel about school?	Old Spencer wanted to know how I felt about school.

Now you go on:

a) ______________________________
b) ______________________________
c) ______________________________
d) ______________________________
e) ______________________________
f) ______________________________
g) ______________________________
h) ______________________________
i) ______________________________
j) ______________________________

Exercise 10 Reported speech: Advice

Timothy told his teacher that he had taken a job in a supermarket to earn some extra pocket money. That's probably why he had not had enough time to do his school work properly. This is the advice Timothy received from his teacher:

a) Think about what's more important: pocket money or school.

b) Tell your parents about your job!

c) Don't work too many hours!

d) Don't do any hard manual work!

e) Avoid working before you have a test at school!

f) Work on Saturdays only!

g) Avoid working late at night!

h) Don' t do any shiftwork!

Timothy tells James what Old Spencer told him to do.
He told / advised me . . .

Example:

Direct speech	**Reported speech**
What Old Spencer advised him: Find an easier job!	What Timothy told James: He advised me to find an easier job.

Now you go on:

a) ______________________________

b) ______________________________

c) ______________________________

d) ______________________________

e) ______________________________

f) ______________________________

g) ______________________________

h) ______________________________

4 Writing desk: Letter writing

Was wird verlangt?
Sehr häufig werden Sie auf eine Aufgabenstellung stoßen, bei der Sie einen Kommentar zu einer Frage in Form eines Briefes abgeben sollen. Der Brief soll dann zumeist an einen (Brief-)Freund oder an eine Zeitung gerichtet sein.

Beispiel "*Write a letter to your English penfriend in which you tell him/her about …*"
oder "*Write a letter to the editor expressing your view on …*"

Wie gehen Sie vor?
Was den Inhalt Ihres Briefes betrifft, so gehen Sie im Großen und Ganzen wie beim Comment (siehe S. 114) vor. Schreiben Sie auch hier nicht ungeordnet drauflos, sondern bemühen Sie sich um eine übersichtliche Gliederung und sinnvolle Ausarbeitung Ihrer Argumente. In einem Leserbrief kommt es natürlich besonders darauf an, dass Sie andere Leser von Ihrer Meinung überzeugen. Hinzu kommt nun, dass Sie die äußere Form eines Briefes beachten müssen. Das ist ganz einfach, wenn Sie sich das allgemein gültige **Layout** und einige **Floskeln** einmal klar gemacht haben.

Example: Layout of a Letter

Letterhead:	your name and address
Inside Address:	The Guardian Weekly P.O. Box 19 Cheadle Cheshire SK81DD England
Date:	October 15, 20 ..
Salutation:	Dear Sirs,
BODY OF THE LETTER: reference (if any)	I read your article "Dealers on the move" of October 15, 20 .. with great interest and I would like to point out that … *or:* After reading your article …
Closing formula:	Yours faithfully,
Signature:	Full name/Christian name only

Phrases

	Anrede	Schlussfloskel
1. Personal Letter		
• an einen Freund/eine Freundin oder gute(n) Bekannte(n)	Dear Jim, Dear Jenny,	Yours, Love With love,
• an eine weniger gut bekannte Person	Dear Mr Palmer,	Best whishes, With best regards,
2. Business Letter/Letter to the Editor		
• an eine namentlich bekannte Person	Dear Mr Sunberry, Dear Miss Paull,	Yours sincerely,
• an eine nicht namentlich bekannte Person	Dear Sir or Madam, Dear Sir, Dear Madam,	Yours faithfully,

Beachten Sie besonders:

- Nach der Anrede und der Schlussfloskel steht jeweils ein Komma; in den USA setzt man nach der Anrede einen Doppelpunkt.
- Versuchen Sie auch beim Geschäftsbrief klar und einfach zu schreiben; vermeiden Sie altmodische Phrasen.

Exercise 11 Practice: Letter writing

Mrs Paull likes chocolates, she is especially fond of “Terry’s Gold”. However, when she opened the box she had received as a gift she was very disappointed. The chocolates didn’t look fresh at all, they looked rather old and grey – and they didn’t taste good. So she wrote a letter of complaint to the chocolate factory.

Use all the information and write Mrs Paull’s original letter of complaint to Terry’s in York.

This is the letter which she received after a few days:

Joseph Terry & Sons Limited
The Chocolate Works
Bishopthorpe Road
YORK, YO1 1YE
ALL COMMUNICATIONS ADDRESSED TO THE COMPANY AT YORK AND NOT TO INDIVIDUALS.

LMC /GEC
30th July, 20..

Mrs Mary Paull
5 Filmer House
Filmer Road
Fulham,
London SW6 7JE

Dear Madam,

Thank you for your letter. We are sorry to learn that you have recently been disappointed by the condition in which you have found our confectionery.
We regret, however, that as you did not send in the product for examination we are unable to ascertain the cause of the fault. From your letter, however, we suspect that this confectionery has been affected by unsatisfactory handling or storage conditions, despite the care that we take with the manufacture of our products, and the design of our protective packaging.
We hope that you will accept and enjoy the fresh All Gold Assortment which we are sending to you, under separate cover, together with our apologies for the disappointment and inconvenience you have been caused.

Yours faithfully,

Chambers

L. M. CHAMBERS (Mrs)
Consumer Service Department

5 Fun and games

Exercise 12 Wordsearch

Try to find the hidden words.

N	L	R	A	A	M	W	O	R	R	O	B	H	R	M
O	U	K	E	L	A	B	O	U	R	D	O	Z	E	H
I	N	V	E	S	T	I	G	A	T	O	R	R	I	Z
T	S	C	C	M	T	O	T	F	A	Q	E	R	R	V
A	K	C	I	N	D	R	G	F	X	L	D	U	T	S
T	I	L	L	A	I	C	I	E	Y	R	O	N	I	M
I	L	V	S	H	S	W	M	C	T	G	M	G	E	M
O	L	U	W	P	R	X	Q	T	T	H	N	G	B	M
L	E	T	A	R	E	T	I	L	L	I	E	V	E	M
P	D	T	B	O	G	A	Y	O	F	K	O	R	E	B
X	J	E	O	P	A	R	D	I	S	E	C	N	F	R
E	T	L	L	E	R	U	C	E	S	H	I	E	L	U
C	C	H	I	O	D	A	P	U	A	A	J	E	H	C
E	E	V	S	E	N	T	B	N	L	V	S	X	Q	C
Z	B	Q	H	T	A	A	T	L	I	Z	J	R	S	O

Lost in the jungle

1 Text box

The man who opened up the African continent

He almost didn't make it! Scotland's most famous explorer David Livingstone was nearly killed by a lion before he could start on his explorations in Africa which were to make him world-famous. Livingstone was born on March 19, 1813, in Blantyre, eight miles south of Glasgow in Scotland. When he was ten, young David began to work in a cotton-textile factory: six days a week from six in the morning until eight at night with a half hour break for breakfast and an hour for lunch. But Livingstone did not want to stay in the cotton mill forever – he wanted to become a doctor. So in 1826 he entered a medical school in Glasgow and attended classes in theology at the same time. Life was hard then because Livingstone had little money.

In 1838 he offered his services to the London Missionary Society, passed the test examination and was trained as a missionary. By 1840 Livingstone was a fully qualified doctor and missionary. In London he met Dr. Robert Moffat, another Scotsman, who told him about missionary work in Africa. David's interest in Africa was awakened – and in December 1840 his dream became true. Livingstone was sent as a medical missionary to South Africa. After an eventful and dangerous sea voyage he reached Kuruman on July 31, 1841, a remote settlement in Bechuanaland (now called Botswana) which was to become Livingstone's starting point for his explorations into regions where no white man had ever been.

Livingstone began his work among the black Africans of Bechuanaland. In 1843 the London Missionary Society gave him permission to establish a mission north of Kuruman. One day natives asked Livingstone to shoot a lion which had killed some of their sheep. Livingstone fired twice, but he only wounded the lion and before he could reload his gun, the animal attacked him and wounded his upper left arm. Livingstone was lucky to escape alive: one of his helpers was quick enough to shoot the lion dead. For three months Livingstone was badly ill. In order to recover from the attack, he visited the Moffats, fell in love with Robert Moffat's daughter Mary, and married her in 1845.

In 1849 he left the mission to explore the interior of the Black Continent. Travelling on cattle he and his party crossed the Kalahari Desert, suffering from the extreme heat and drought – and, above all, from the attacks from millions of mosquitos. On his journeys Livingstone was often in danger from hostile natives and wild animals. More than once he narrowly escaped death. Due to the damp and hot climate his health suffered badly: he lost weight and appeared to many a "mere bag of bones" because of his many attacks of malaria. But Livingstone's energy and stamina drove him on to many discoveries, among them Lake Ngami and the Upper Zambezi River. On November 16, 1855 he discovered the spectacular falls of the Zambesi which he named "Victoria Falls" after Queen Victoria. The waterfall is 1,6 km wide, with a maximum drop of 128 m.

Livingstone was the first white man to gather information about the African Interior and because of his explorations all contemporary maps had to be re-drawn. When Livingstone returned to Great Britain in 1856 he was greeted as a national hero. He met Queen Victoria in Windsor Castle, spoke about his discoveries in front of professors and scientists at all British universities, informing them about the beauties of the African continent but also about the cruelties of the slave trade which was carried on by the Arabian and Portuguese traders. Livingstone published his famous book *Missionary Travels and Researches in South Africa* in 1857.

611 words

Exercise 1 Understanding the text

Answer the following questions in your own words. Do not copy from the text.

a) What made life so difficult for young David Livingstone in Blantyre?

b) Why did Livingstone join the London Missionary Society?

c) How did Livingstone meet his wife Mary?

d) What made the explorations in Africa so difficult?

e) Which fact shows you that Livingstone was not only interested in the country but also in the people of Africa?

2 Word power: Some words to remember

abolition	Abschaffung
(to) appoint	ernennen
bag	Beutel, Tasche
cattle	Vieh, Rinder
contemporary	zeitgenössisch
defender	Verteidiger
(to) discover	entdecken
drought	Dürre
embarrassed	verlegen
(to) embrace	umarmen
(to) establish	errichten, einrichten
eventful	ereignisreich
eventually	schließlich
exploitation	Ausbeutung
(to) explore	erforschen
gamekeeper	Wildhüter
(to) gather	sammeln
interior	inner(e, er, es)
jungle	Dschungel
(to) kneel	knien
missionary	Missionar
poacher	Wilddieb
poaching	Wilddieberei
population	Bevölkerung
(to) pray	beten
(to) presume	vermuten, annehmen
publisher	Verleger
(to) reload	nachladen, neu laden
remote	entfernt
request	Wunsch, Verlangen

(to) rescue	retten
skirmish	Scharmützel, Auseinandersetzung
source	Quelle, Ursprung
stamina	Ausdauer
treatment	Behandlung
watershed	Wasserscheide

Exercise 2 Anagrams: Exploration

The letters of these words have been jumbled. Write down the original words using the definitions as your help.

Anagram	Word	Definition
a) BUERHPSLI	____________	a person or a company that produces and distributes copies of a book, newspaper, etc. for sale; a newspaper proprietor
b) AHGETR	____________	to come together; to collect, to pick (flowers)
c) RUSOEC	____________	a spring or fountain-head from which a stream issues (the ... of the Nile)
d) ESWTERDAH	____________	elevation or divide separating one river system from another
e) GURTOHD	____________	a long time without any rain; dry weather
f) AEBCMRE	____________	hold (a person) closely in the arms, esp. as a sign of affection
g) MEUSEPR	____________	to suppose that something is true; to take for granted
h) MIAATSN	____________	physical or moral strength to resist or withstand illness, fatigue, or hardship; endurance.

Exercise 3 Vocabulary grid: Search

Fill the squares with words from the list "Some words to remember". The word down in the bold squares means living or occurring at the same time.

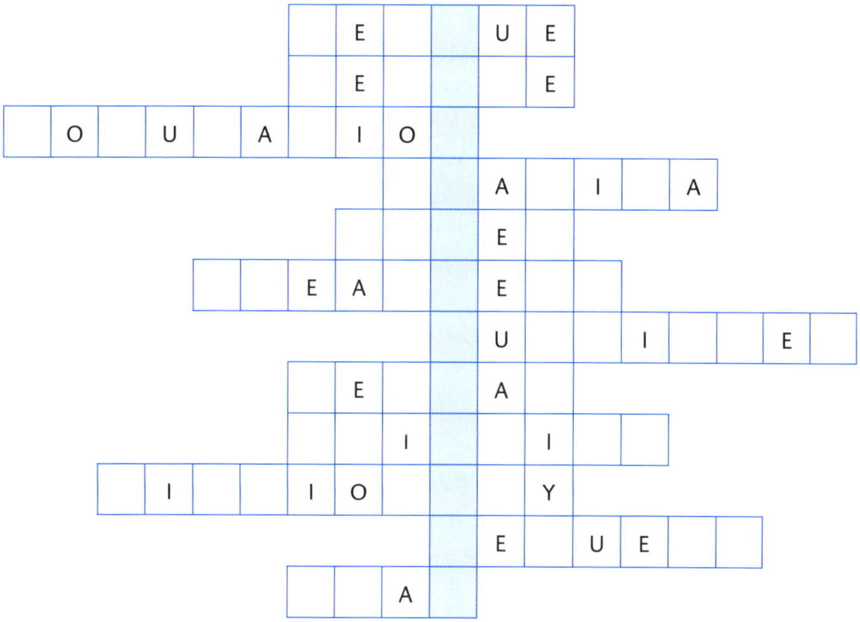

Exercise 4 C-Test: Exploring the black continent

Some words are scrambled. Try to restore the original word. To help you the first letter is given.

While he was back in England, Livingstone was appointed leader of a new "Zambesi Expedition" and returned to Africa in 1858. He discovered Lake Nyasa and (e-rxdloep) ____________[1] the country around the (l-kea) ________[2] to found a colony there. Steamboats were (s-ten) __________[3] on Livingstone's request to (e-bnale) __________[4] trade and a commercial exploitation of the area. April 27, 1862, (t-hhuog) __________[5], was one of the saddest days in David Livingstone's (l-fie) __________[6]: his wife Mary died and was (b-diuer) __________[7] at Shupanga under the shadow of a giant Baobab (t-ere) _________[8].
In order to (r-esai) _________[9] money for a new expedition into the (i-nerotir) __________[10] of Africa Livingstone (t-hhutog) __________[11] of

selling his (s-aatbteom) ___________[12] "Lady Nyasa", but he was afraid of the Portuguese buying it because he (f-dreae) ___________[13] they would use it in the slave trade. Livingstone had (b-eeomc) ___________[14] more and more worried about the (c-erlu) ___________[15] treatment of the (n-aeitv) ___________[16] population by Arab and Portuguese slave traders. In 1865, on a (v-iits) ___________[17] to England, Livingstone (c-mdoendne) ___________[18] the slave trade publicly, thus becoming one of the first (d-eernefsd) _______________[19] of the rights of the Africans. Friends and (a-edisrmr) ________________[20] put up money to finance Livingstone's next expedition to discover the (s-reoscu) ______________________[21] of the Nile and explore the (w-aseertdh) ___________[22] of central Africa. During these years the explorer suffered many illnesses for which there was no (m-iieecdn) ___________[23] available. A totally exhausted Livingstone discovered Lake Tanganyika – and for a long time the world did not hear of him and thought he had got lost and died.

Exercise 5 Cloze-Test: Dr Livingstone, I presume?

Complete the text with words from this list.

alive	day	just	side
beard	embrace	merchant	skirmishes
cabin	exhausting	newspaper	then
caravan	famous	probably	well
correspondent	fired	reached	workhouse

The man who rescued him was an adventurer, journalist and an explorer. His real name was John Rowlands, born on January 28, 1841 in Wales. As his family was extremely poor he grew up in a _____________[1]. When he was 16 he ran away to sea and sailed as a _____________[2] boy to New Orleans. He found work with an American cotton _____________[3] named Henry Morton Stanley. He liked the man and the name, so he changed his own and called himself Henry Morton Stanley from _____________[4] on. After fighting in the American Civil War in the Confederate army and later for the Union _____________[5], he became a special war _____________[6] for the New York Herald in 1867. Stanley reported on the battles and _____________[7] of the British army in Ethiopia.

The publisher of the Herald thought the readers of his _____________[8] would be more interested in about what had happened to the _____________[9] Scottish explorer David Livingstone, who was "lost" in East Africa, ______________[10] searching for the source of the Nile. So he told his reporter Stanley to try and find Livingstone instead of reporting on the war in Ethiopia. After an ______________[11] march of hundreds of miles through the jungle in the hot sun Stanley and his party ______________[12] the village of Ujiji in Tanzania. They ______________[13] their guns into the air to let the people know that a ______________[14] was coming. In front of a hut Stanley saw a white man with a grey ______________[15]. He looked very pale, tired and not ______________[16]. Stanley was so glad he had found the famous explorer ______________[17] and would have liked to run to him and ______________[18] him. But as there were so many natives around he felt embarrassed so he ______________[19] took off his hat and said, "Dr. Livingstone, I presume." The ______________[20] was November 10, 1871.

Exercise 6 C-Test: Lonely death

Some words are incomplete. Only one or a couple of letters are given. Try to complete with words that fit the context.

Stanley and Livingstone stayed tog__________[1] for a few months, became great friends and explored the north end of Lake Tanganyika. In March 1872 Livingstone car__________[2] on alone down the east side of the lake. He was very ill, and event__________[3] his servants built a hut for him to get some rest and reco__________[4]. But David Livingstone li__________[5] only for four days in the hut in Chitambo (today Zambia): On May 1, 1873 his servants found him knee__________[6] by his bed, his face resting on his han__________[7]. He had died while pra__________[8] to God – probably on April 30, 1873. In April 1874 the rema__________[9] of one of the greatest modern African explorers and one of the pion__________[10] in the abolition of the slave tra__________[11] were brought home to Great Britain and buried in Westminster Ab__________[12].

3 Language corner: Combinations and collocations

machen

Das deutsche Verb „machen“ wird im Englischen nicht immer mit *to make* übersetzt. Merken Sie sich die folgenden Wendungen.

to **make** a cake	einen Kuchen **machen**
to **make** a mistake	einen Fehler **machen**
to **make** progress	Fortschritte **machen**
to **take** an exam	eine Prüfung **machen**
to **take** a photo	ein Foto **machen**
to **take** a break	eine Pause **machen**
to **take** a holiday	Urlaub **machen**
to **do** one’s homework	Hausaufgaben **machen**
to **go** for a walk	einen Spaziergang **machen**
to **get** to the top (of one’s profession)	Karriere **machen**

Deutsche Wendungen mit „machen“ haben im Englischen diese Entsprechungen:

what is he doing?	was **macht** er?
what does he do (for a living)?	was **macht** er beruflich?
it gives me pleasure	das **macht** mir Freude
it gives me a lot of work	das **macht** mir viel Arbeit
that’s fun	das **macht** Spaß
don’t worry	**mach** dir keine Sorgen
that doesn't …worry me; I don’t care	das **macht** mir nichts
to **do** one’s homework	Hausaufgaben **machen**
to **go** for a walk	einen Spaziergang **machen**

Von den englischen Zusammensetzungen mit *to make* sollten Sie sich diese einprägen:

to **make** sure	sicherstellen, gewährleisten
to **make** a fuss	Aufhebens machen
to **make** ends meet	hinkommen, auskommen mit
to **make** the most of it	das Beste daraus machen
to **make** a point of	Wert legen auf etwas
to **make** fun of	verspotten

Exercise 7 German 'machen'

Which verbs are used with which nouns? Write the nouns in the proper places.

a photo(graph) / an exam / a mistake / a course / an offer / a film / a break / one's best / a holiday / one's (home)work / a noise / an effort / one's hair / notes / the best of something

make	do	take

Exercise 8 Usage: Survival in the South American jungle

Translate the words in brackets into English. Use the proper combinations with "to do, to make, to take" and show that you have understood the different usage of "to carry" and "to bear" (see p. 91). Mind the tenses!

James and Harry decided to book a survival training course in a camp in the jungle near Iquitos, Peru. After they had arrived at the lodge "Jungle Amazon Inn" their guide Jorge, of half Spanish, half Indio descent, ________[1] (machte einen Spaziergang) with them through the beautiful tropical gardens and told them a little of what they could expect. Next morning the three men left the lodge; they ________[2] (trugen) Wellington boots and ________[3] (trugen) machetes. In order to protect themselves against mosquitoes they were advised to ________[4] (tragen) long-sleeved shirts. Because of the humidity and the heat, James and Harry found it exhausting to ________[5] (tragen) their rucksacks. Now and again they ________[6] (verspotteten) of each other when they stumbled through the thick jungle and fell over. "Are you alright, Harry?" "Yeah, ________[7] (mach dir keine Sorgen)!"
"What are you ________[8] (machst du) with that camera, James?" "I'm just trying to ________[9] (zu machen) a photo of you!" he replied.
After a lengthy walk of more than four hours Jorge showed them what wood to collect for a fire and how to filter water from the Amazon River to make mate de coca, a special tea of the Indios. When they ________[10] (ihre

Arbeit gemacht hatten), they were glad to _______________[11] (eine Pause zu machen).
The two men and the guide stayed in the jungle for six days and five nights; they learned the basic rules of survival – e. g. as there are no roads always use a stream or river for orientation – in an unfriendly environment and learned how to _______________[12] (das Beste machen) of their situation. After returning safely to the lodge James and Harry agreed that _______________[13] (es Spaß gemacht hatte) to spend nearly a week in the wilderness.

4 Grammar spot: The participle

Wir unterscheiden folgende Formen:
- **Partizip Präsens** (= Infinitiv + *ing*, z. B. *driving, offering, singing)*
- **Partizip Perfekt** (= Infinitiv + *-ed, -d* bzw. bei unregelmäßigen Verben 3. Form der Stammformen, z. B. *driven, offered, sung)*

Syntactic compression

Die Partizipien werden häufig benutzt, um Relativsätze und Adverbialsätze zu verkürzen. Man nennt das in der Grammatik „syntactic compression" (Satzverkürzung).

Relativsätze

Aktivsätze werden mit dem **Partizip Präsens** verkürzt.

long version	shortened version
David Livingstone was the man who opened up the African Continent. David Livingstone war der Mann, der den afrikanischen Kontinent erschloss.	David Livingstone was the man opening up the African Continent.

Passivsätze werden mit dem **Partizip Perfekt** verkürzt.

long version	shortened version
Livingstone criticized the slave trade which was carried on by some traders. L. kritisierte den Sklavenhandel, der von einigen Händlern weiterhin betrieben wurde.	Livingstone criticized the slave trade carried on by some traders.

Adverbialsätze

Adverbiale Nebensätze können mit einer **Partizipialkonstruktion** verkürzt werden.

Adverbialsatz der Zeit

long version

When Livingstone saw the Victoria Falls for the first time, he could hardly believe his eyes.

Als Livingstone die Victoriafälle zum ersten Mal sah, traute er kaum seinen Augen.

shortened version

Seeing the Victoria Falls for the first time, Livingstone could hardly believe his eyes.

Adverbialsatz des Grundes

long version

As he felt exhausted, he told his servants to build a hut.

Da er sich erschöpft fühlte, wies er seine Diener an, eine Hütte zu bauen.

shortened version

Feeling exhausted, he told his servants to build a hut.

Time relation

Wenn man einen temporalen Adverbialsatz verkürzt, muss man besonders auf das Zeitverhältnis achten, in dem die Handlung des Gliedsatzes zur Handlung des Hauptsatzes steht.

Um auszudrücken, dass zwei Handlungen **gleichzeitig** verlaufen, wird das **Partizip Präsens** verwendet.

long version

As the explorers shared their last water supplies, they made plans about how to cross the desert more quickly.

Als die Forscher ihre letzten Wasservorräte teilten, machten sie Pläne, wie sie die Wüste schneller durchqueren könnten.

shortened version

Sharing their last water supplies, the explorers made plans about how to cross the desert more quickly.

oder (Konjunktion + Partizip):

When sharing their last water supplies, the explorers made plans about how to cross the desert more quickly.

Um auszudrücken, dass eine Handlung **zeitlich vor** einer zweiten liegt (d. h. dass sie bereits abgeschlossen war, als die andere begann), wird ***having* + Partizip Perfekt** verwendet.

long version	shortened version
After the explorers had used up their water supplies, they wondered how they could cross the desert more quickly. Nachdem die Forscher ihre Wasservorräte aufgebraucht hatten, fragten sie sich, wie sie die Wüste schneller durchqueren könnten.	Having used up their water supplies, the explorers wondered how they could cross the desert more quickly. oder (Konjunktion + Partizip): After using up their water supplies, the explorers wondered how they could cross the desert more quickly.

Beachte: In der deutschen Übersetzung steht im Gliedsatz das Substantiv, im Hauptsatz das Pronomen.

Having used up all their water supplies, the explorers wanted to get to the missionary station as quickly as possible.
Da die Forscher ihre gesamten Wasservorräte aufgebraucht hatten, wollten sie so schnell wie möglich die Missionsstation erreichen.

Exercise 9 Shortening sentences: Preserving wildlife in Africa

Shorten these sentences. Replace the relative and adverbial clauses by a different construction.

Example:

Tourists **who travel** to Africa want to watch wild animals in their natural surroundings.	Tourists **travelling** to Africa want to watch wild animals in their natural surroundings.

a) An international convention which was held (________________) in 1989 banned the sale of ivory.

b) Tourists who are interested (________________) in watching herds of elephants were pleased about the news.

c) As many African countries depend on (________________) tourism, they profited from the ban.

d) International organisations like Greenpeace which supported (__________) the move also pointed out a problem which arose (________________) from the ban.

e) As the countries increased (________________) the protected regions, they attracted more tourists.

f) The arrival of larger numbers of tourists spoiled parts of the areas that were meant (________________) to be protected.

Exercise 10

Replacing participle constructions: The War against poachers

Replace the underlined participle constructions, using relative or adverbial clauses.

Example:

The war against poaching begun by US naturalists many years ago has not been won in all states.	The war against poaching **which was begun** by US naturalists many years ago has not been won in all states.

a) The campaign for the protection of apes and rhinos started (________________) by US and Japanese scientists attracted the interest of the world public.

b) Cameramen made TV films showing (________________) the cruelties of poachers in the national parks.

c) TV viewers all over the world shocked (________________) by the pictures wrote letters of protest.

d) The civil war taking place (________________) in Rwanda almost destroyed one of the last homes of African mountain gorillas.

e) Several hundred farmers not having (________________) enough land to grow food invaded Rwanda's Volcanoes National Park.

f) The rebels seizing (________________) control of the park were Tutsis, an ethnic group trying (______________) to get back land lost (______________) more than three decades ago.

g) They destroyed a research centre run (________________) for nearly two decades by the American naturalist Dian Fossey, whose pioneering work with the great apes was made famous in the film "Gorillas in the Mist".

5 Writing desk: Translation

Die „goldene Regel" für gutes Übersetzen von der Fremdsprache in die Muttersprache lautet immer noch: „So wörtlich wie möglich und so frei wie nötig!" Damit meint man, dass Sie bei der Übersetzung eines Satzes die entsprechenden deutschen Einheiten nicht Wort für Wort aneinander reihen, sondern für den Sinn der englischen Originalversion eine möglichst getreue deutsche Wendung finden sollen. Das ist nicht immer leicht: Bei Witzen und Wortspielen scheint es überhaupt nicht zu klappen! Insbesondere dichterische Texte lassen sich kaum wortwörtlich in eine andere Sprache übertragen. Deshalb spricht man in diesem Bereich auch von eigenständigen kreativen Leistungen der Übersetzer – die aber nicht richtig gewürdigt werden, wenn man ihre Namen nur im Kleindruck an unauffälliger Stelle vermerkt.
Bei Klassenarbeiten und Prüfungen werden Sie es im Allgemeinen nicht mit dichterischen, sondern mit pragmatischen, nicht fiktionalen Texten zu tun haben. Wer sich in seiner Muttersprache gut auskennt und ein sicheres Stilgefühl entwickelt hat, wird mit der Herübersetzung wenig Kummer haben. Wer in Deutsch etwas schwächer ist, wird wohl zuweilen klagen: „Bei der Übersetzung bekommt man ja noch eine verkappte Deutschnote!" Nicht immer ist eine Wort-für-Wort-Übersetzung im Deutschen verständlich oder akzeptabel! „How do you do?" heißt nicht „Wie tust du tun?" – das würde kein Deutscher verstehen.
Wenn Sie gut vorbereitet sind, wird die Übersetzung viel von ihrem Schrecken verlieren. Die folgende Liste, die aus der Praxis heraus entstanden ist, soll Ihnen dabei helfen. Sie finden hier die grammatischen Bereiche zusammengestellt, in denen besonders häufig Fehler gemacht werden. Die Beispiele verdeutlichen, worauf Sie achten sollten und wie Sie eine Schwierigkeit meistern.

Häufige Fehlerquellen:

Schwerpunkt	Beachten Sie	Beispiel	Deutsche Übersetzung
Present Perfect	Dem entspricht im Deutschen oft das Präsens.	I have gone to this school for three years now.	Ich gehe schon seit drei Jahren in diese Schule.
***if*-clauses**	Die 2. Bedingung steht im Konjunktiv und nicht im Präteritum!	If I wrote to him, he would reply soon.	Wenn ich ihm schreiben würde, würde er bald antworten.
AcI-Konstruktion	Im Deutschen durch „dass" übersetzen.	We wanted them to come to our party.	Wir wollten, dass sie zu unserer Party kommen.
have* + obj + participle** ***had … cut	Im Deutschen mit „lassen" übersetzen.	Jim had his hair cut.	Jim ließ sich die Haare schneiden.
article	Im Deutschen öfter mit Artikel.	Man is about to destroy his own environment.	Der Mensch ist dabei, seine eigene Umwelt zu zerstören.
reported speech	Im Deutschen Konjunktiv Präsens.	Freddy said he was ill.	Freddy sagte, er sei krank.
there is, there are	Darf nicht mit „da ist", „da sind" übersetzt werden.	There are less unemployed people in Britain today than a few years ago.	Es gibt heute in Großbritannien weniger Arbeitslose als vor ein paar Jahren.
besonderer Plural: ***their lives***	Wird im Deutschen oft durch Singular wiedergegeben.	Four motorists lost their lives in an accident.	Vier Autofahrer kamen bei einem Unfall ums Leben.
may	Heißt nicht nur „dürfen".	Our friend Oliver may be ill.	Unser Freund Oliver ist vielleicht krank.
it/they/their	Auf das Bezugswort achten: Es muss dann im Deutschen „es, sie etc." heißen.	That was his first trip to England, and he enjoyed it.	Das war seine erste Reise nach England, und sie hat ihm Spaß gemacht.
Idiomatische Wendungen	Können nicht wörtlich übersetzt werden.	„How do you do?"	„Hallo." oder „Guten Tag!"

Exercise 11 Practice: Translation

Translate these sentences into German.

a) In the desert, there is water under the ground even though it hardly ever rains.

b) If there were/was more water, the farmers could grow more corn and maize.

c) If the water under ground reached the surface, it would make an oasis.

d) If a camel hasn't had anything to drink for a couple of days, it may drink as much as 20 buckets of water at a time.

e) For thousands of years the Bedouin people have been herding camels and sheep in the Arabian desert.

f) For generations, people in hot, dry countries have been using mud for building houses.

g) Most Arab women wear long black robes and face masks.

h) Many tribal peoples believe their dead ancestors to bring bad luck if they aren't looked after properly.

i) In Europe, horseshoes are believed to bring good luck.

j) Masai women, who live in East Africa, have their heads shaved to look more beautiful.

k) For special ceremonies tribal dancers often wear masks. Sometimes these are to hide them from evil spirits.

l) The guide explained that mud huts were often round, because walls with corners would crack more easily.

6 Fun and games

Exercise 12 Crossword puzzle

Try to solve the crossword puzzle.

Across
2. beten
4. Wildhüter
8. Behandlung
10. entfernt
11. Abschaffung
12. Quelle, Ursprung
13. verlegen (adj.)
15. Verleger
16. Scharmützel, Auseinandersetzung
18. Missionar
19. ereignisreich
20. Wilddieberei
21. Verteidiger
23. Dürre
26. ernennen
27. zeitgenössisch
28. Vieh, Rinder
29. Wasserscheide
32. erforschen
33. Wilddieb
34. Dschungel

Down
1. Beutel, Tasche
3. retten
5. schließlich
6. knien
7. Ausdauer
9. vermuten, annehmen
10. Wunsch, Verlangen
13. Ausbeutung
14. entdecken
17. inner(e, er, es)
22. errichten, einrichten
24. sammeln
25. Bevölkerung
30. umarmen
31. nachladen, neu laden

Exercise 13 Wordsearch

Try to find the hidden words.

```
            G K N H R C D
          T G M O L O E E X
        H N I K I N S V D G Y
      A N I M A T S E W O N A R
    S Y N O E E A N S R O M E T R
  E O P J P M R T K E I T L C F H Z
T U G U R P R U I V T M O U V U E E P
H C Z A O A A R O A A A T N M O T D R
N S Y R B L M C L B D T Z A A S E D E
E E A M L I S U P O D O S R E R D S S
E R E Y S I P K X L E K E U O R Y E U
Y V I H D O N B E I H H Q L O Q T K M
I L E X P E U P N T S E P U U O F N E
  O E N E U V B B I R X G N M Q Y M
    E L T T A C L O E H X E U X B
      L G F I B I N T E R I O R
        L N U M K K A P P A A
          P U L Q G W H B C
            G J X G V T E
```

Fame

1 Text box

The darker side of fame

When children are asked "What would you like to be when you grow up?" they often answer, "A famous football player, a pop star, a film star!" But have they ever thought that there is a darker side to fame and fortune?

He was 27. With his band Nirvana he had sold millions of CDs and had become one of the most successful rock heroes to millions. In April 1994 Kurt Cobain took a shotgun and killed himself. On receiving the news of her son's suicide Cobain's mother said, "Now he's gone and joined that stupid club. I told him not to join that stupid club." What she meant was that "stupid club" of young rock stars whose lives had ended before they had reached the age of 30. Rock legends like Jimi Hendrix, Janis Joplin, Jim Morrison and Sid Vicious had destroyed themselves with drug and alcohol abuse. Cobain, too, was a heroin user. Kurt had a very unhappy childhood. The divorce of his parents when he was eight hurt him deeply. His mother's new marriage did not turn out to be happy. The couple constantly argued and even threatened to kill each other. Kurt wanted to escape from this unpleasant world of the grown-ups and started taking drugs. The music of the punk groups also expressed his contempt of adult society. So after trying his luck at several jobs he formed a band of his own with two friends. They called the group Nirvana and produced their first album, called *Bleach*, in 1988.

Their second album *Nevermind* (1991) reached the top of the charts in no time, selling more than 10 million copies. Touring the USA and Europe brought money, fame – and also stress and more drug-taking. Cobain and his band became rich by telling the world how much they hated the establishment. They had started out as rebels against society, but the ironic and tragic thing happened: the outsiders, the outlaws became wealthy and famous. What followed was an identity crisis: "Teenage angst has paid off well/Now I'm bored and old," as Kurt Cobain sang in *Serve the Servants*. Another rock musician described his inner conflict caused by his transformation from outsider to idol like this: "Quick success brings a lot of difficulties. I'm being honest when I say that sometimes when I see a picture of the band or a picture of my face taking up a whole page of a magazine, I hate that guy." This, too, might have been the feeling that Kurt Cobain was no longer able to put up with and which led him to self-destruction.

The singer, dancer and songwriter Michael Jackson was the darling of the mass media but became the target of world-wide criticism, scorn and indignation when a young boy of 13 accused him of sexual abuse. Born on August 29, 1958, in Gary, Indiana, young Michael made his show debut at the age of five as the youngest member of his brothers' pop group the Jackson Five. Michael, a very talented dancer and singer, soon became the favourite with the audience. However, behind the scene things were different. The young boy suffered under his tyrannical father, who frequently told him off and beat him. In the end, Michael paid for his success as a performer and international show-business star with the loss of his childhood.

He left the family group and started a solo career. His albums *Thriller* (1982), *Bad* (1987), *Dangerous* (1992) and the videos of his songs belong to the most successful recordings ever made. Michael Jackson's dancing style, his very special way of dressing and his physical appearance made him a spectacular event on the stage. Because of his eccentric lifestyle, he became a frequent subject of the gossip columns in the trashy weeklies. His skin became whiter and whiter and there were rumours that plastic surgery had not only changed his face but also his character and personality.

Michael Jackson sought peace on his ranch "Neverland". This is the name of the fantasy land in a well-loved children's book. *Peter Pan* is a story about a boy who would not grow up written by the British novelist and dramatist Sir James Matthew Barrie in 1904. On his ranch Jackson surrounded himself with young boys. He said he loved children because he himself had been deprived of a normal childhood and wanted to create a paradise on earth for as many children as possible. The stress of being a superstar took its toll. Jackson admitted that he had become addicted to, for example, tranquillisers.

He turned to two women for help: film star Elizabeth Taylor and Lisa-Marie Presley, whom Michael later married. Lisa-Marie is the daughter of the "King" of rock and roll, Elvis Presley, who himself died on August 16, 1977, in Memphis, Tennessee, probably of drug and alcohol abuse – he yet another victim of tyrannical managers, demanding audiences, unscrupulous businessmen. All of these expect the superstar to continue playing a role and living up to the image that they have given him. What they do not consider are the feelings of the ordinary human being behind the glittering façade of show business. *860 words*

Exercise 1 Understanding the text

Answer these questions.

a) Why do people usually not think about the "darker side to fame and fortune"?

____

b) What did Kurt Cobain's mother mean when she told her son "not to join that stupid club"?

____

c) What was Cobain's childhood like?

____

d) Why did Cobain like punk music so much?

____

e) Why did success bring about an identity crisis?

____

f) Where are parallels in the lives of Kurt Cobain and Michael Jackson?

____

g) Take the example of Peter Pan. Why should somebody not want to grow up?

____

2 Word power

2.1 Some words to remember

abuse	Missbrauch
addicted	süchtig
adult	Erwachsen(er)
anthem	Hymne
appearance	Erscheinung, Aussehen
(to) argue	streiten
audience	Publikum
(to) christen	taufen
column	Spalte
contempt	Verachtung
cunning	listig, schlau, gerissen
(to) deprive	berauben
(to) destroy	zerstören
divorce	Scheidung
emergence	Aufkommen, Entstehen
envy	Neid
fame	Ruhm
fortune	Glück, Schicksal, Vermögen
gossip	Klatsch
indignation	Empörung
(to) mourn	trauern, betrauern
novelist	Romanautor
offensive	anstößig, beleidigend
outlaw	Geächtete(r)
performer	Darsteller, Bühnenstar
plastic surgery	Schönheitsoperation
promotion	Werbung
(to) release (an album)	(eine Platte) veröffentlichen
rivalry	Rivalität

rumour	Gerücht
scorn	Verachtung, Hohn
shotgun	Jagdgewehr, Schrotflinte
stupid	dumm
suicide	Selbstmord
(to) threaten	drohen
trashy weeklies	Regenbogenpresse
unscrupulous	skrupellos, rücksichtslos

2.2 Useful phrases

to pay off well	"Teenage angst has paid off well /Now I'm bored and old," Kurt Cobain sang in "Serve the Servants".	sich bezahlt machen, sich lohnen
to put up with sth.	Kurt Cobain was no longer able to put up with the stress.	etwas ertragen
to tell s.o. off	The young boy suffered under his tyrannical father, who frequently told him off and beat him.	mit jdm. schimpfen, jdn. ausschimpfen
to take its toll	The stress of being a superstar took its toll.	seinen Tribut fordern
to deprive s.o. of sth.	He had been deprived of a normal childhood.	jdn. einer Sache berauben
to live up to	Managers and fans expect the superstar to live up to the image that they have given him.	(den Anforderungen/ Erwartungen) entsprechen

Exercise 2 Anagram: Popularity

The letters of these words have been jumbled. Write down the original words using the definitions as your help.

Anagram	Word	Definition
a) TOPTENMC	__________	a feeling that a person is wholly bad and worthless
b) ATRNTEHE	__________	to say that one will do harm if a person does not do what is desired

c) TDISUP ____________ opposite of intelligent, clever

d) OENUTFR ____________ the good and evil that happens to people; great wealth

e) DRVOEIC ____________ legal separation of husband and wife by court of law

f) IGOSPS ____________ useless talk usually about other people and their mistakes

g) NEVOIFFSE ____________ causing anger; insulting and disgusting

h) RDEIEVP ____________ to take away from someone

Exercise 3 **Vocabulary grid: Public heroes**

Fill the squares with words from the list "Some words to remember". The word down in the bold squares decribes what a person looks like from the outside.

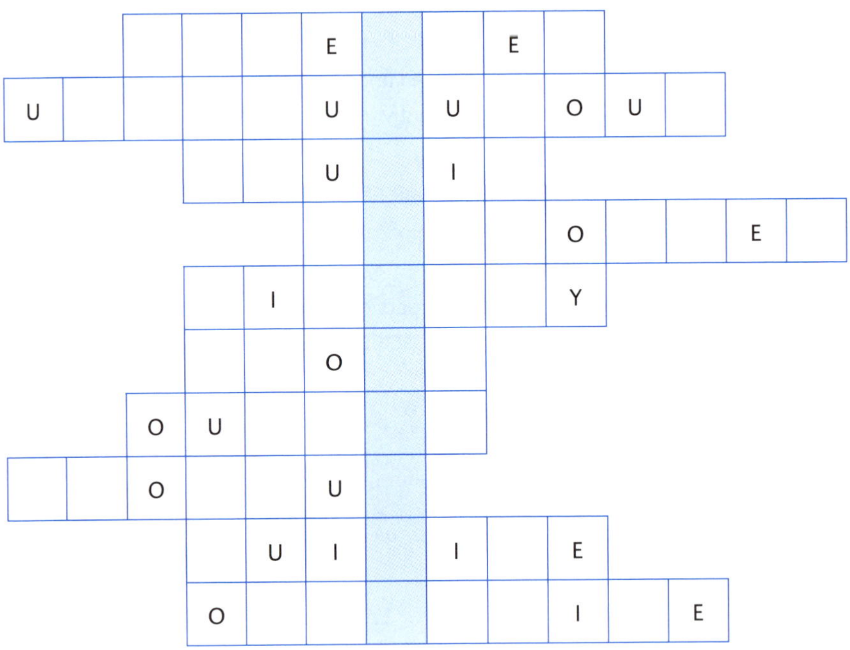

Exercise 4 C-Test: Tina Turner

Try to restore the original word. To help you the first letter is given.

Rhythm and (b-lesu) ______[1] singer Tina Turner was (c-ndihtrees) ______[2] Anna Mae Bullock in Nutbush, Tennessee, in 1939. She was (d-rvcisoede) ______[3] at the age of 17 by Ike Turner, a St. Louis band (l-redae) ______[4]. Ike changed her name to Tina, (m-redrai) ______[5] her and made her front singer of the Ike and Tina Turner (R-wieve) ______[6]. During most of her early years Tina was (e-iexldpot) ______[7] and treated badly by her (h-bunsda) ______[8]. When she finally walked out on him and the group (d-iugnr) ______[9] a tour, her career almost came to an (a-rbutp) ______[10] end. Concert promoters were so (f-iuusro) ______[11] that they would not book her for several years (a-dfwersart) ______[12]. Being half a million dollars in (d-tbe) ______[13], Tina Turner toured the cheap cabaret clubs to (s-rupopt) ______[14] her four children. In the early 80s she was rediscovered and made a (c-aokecmb) ______[15] with the album *Private Dancer*. She had an American (n-bruem) ______[16] one with "What's Love got To Do With It?" in 1984.

Exercise 5 Cloze-Test: Bob Dylan

Complete the text with words from this list.

anthems	following	live	recognized
appealed	hometown	met	records
before	inspired	movement	romance
career	late	name	signed
finished	led	reached	suffered

Bob Dylan, whose real ______[1] is Robert Allen Zimmerman, left his ______[2] in Minnesota in 1960 when he was 19. He had ______[3] a highschool rock-and-roll band, but the blues and country ______[4] that he heard on the radio ______[5] to him even more. He was particularly ______[6] by the works of Woodie Guthrie. His ______[7] began in New York City's folk clubs where he ______[8] people of the peace and civil rights ______[9] who liked his songs. Managers of the CBS record company quickly ______[10] the talent of the folk singer and ______[11] him up. The quality of his songwriting and his ______[12] performances rapidly won him an international ______________[13]. Dylan's songs "Blowin' in the Wind" and "The Times They Are A-Changin'" became ______________[14] of the peace movement of the ______________[15] 1960s and early 70s. A ______________[16] with the singer Joan Baez made them the king and queen of protest. When he ______________[17] a bad motorbike accident, it was feared that his career was ______________[18]. However, in 1975 he returned to show business but never again ______________[19] the unique position that he had enjoyed ______________[20].

Exercise 6 Text Reconstruction: John Lennon

Re-arrange the order of these sentences to form an article on the Life of John Lennon.

a) In 1965, the Beatles went to Buckingham Palace and were awarded the M.B.E. (Member of the British Empire).

b) He divorced his first wife Cynthia and married Yoko in 1969.

c) In 1980 he started work on a new album *Double Fantasy*.

d) John's first group was called "The Quarrymen", later they changed their name to "The Beatles".

e) The Beatles first played at the Cavern Club in Liverpool.

f) In 1966, John met a Japanese artist called Yoko Ono.

g) The American authorities tried to deport John, but in 1975 he won his battle against deportation.

h) In the Hilton Hotel in Amsterdam they spent several days in bed giving interviews about world peace: "Make love and not war!"

i) His aunt Mimi looked after him after his parents' divorce.

j) At school, John was bright, but lazy and failed all his exams.

k) They took part in demonstrations against the American bombing of Vietnam.

l) The group released their first single "Love Me Do" in 1962 when John got married.

m) After the release of the album *Imagine* (1971) John and Yoko left Britain to live in the United States.

n) John Winston Lennon was born in Liverpool on October 9, 1940.

o) On December 9, 1980 as John arrived home from a recording session, he was shot by an assassin outside his apartment in New York.

p) The following year John sent his M.B.E. back to Buckingham Palace, in protest against British involvement in Northern Ireland.

1	2	3	4	5	6	7	8	9	10	11	12	13	14	15	16

Exercise 7

C-Test: Bruce Springsteen

Some words are incomplete. Only one or a couple of letters are given. Try to complete with words that fit the context.

Bruce Springsteen was born in 1949 in Freehold, New Jersey, into a wor_____[1] class family. His mother was Italian and his father a hard-working Irish pri_______[2] guard and, later, a bus driver. Bruce was not a good pu_______[3] and often got into tro_____[4] with his teachers. At 13, he bou_____[5] a second-hand guitar and also tau_____[6] himself to play piano and harm_____[7]. He started his career as a musician by appe_____[8] in local bars and clubs. His songs were about desp_____[9] teenagers and their dreams of esc_____[10] and the hard times of fac_____[11] workers. His first album *Greetings from Asbury Park* (1973) was a com_____[12] flop, but in 1975 Born to Run estab_____[13] him as a successful performer. Springsteen's album *Born in the USA*, rele_____[14] in 1984, sold more than 13 million copies, thus becoming one of the best-sel_____[15] records of all time.

On sta_____[16] Springsteen wore the same clo_____[17] his father had gone to work in and became the singer of the blue-co_____[18] workers. With his songs about the yo_______[19] American working class Bruce Springsteen could aff_____[20] a comfortable life in a beau_____[21] villa in Beverly Hills, the ar_____[22] where the rich live. In 1994 he won an Oscar for *Streets of Philadelphia,* a song about AIDS vic_____[23] written for the film *Philadelphia* star_____[24] Tom Hanks.

Exercise 8 Translation: Public heroes

Translate into English or German respectively.

“That’s what show business is – sincere insincerity.”
Benny Hill (1925–92), British comedian

Rock’n’Roll music started in the 1950s with Chuck Berry, Bill Haley, Elvis Presley and was in the 1960s continued (__________)[1] by groups like the Beatles and the Rolling Stones. Since its emergence (__________)[2] it has been the sound of adolescents rebelling against the world in general and the parent generation __________[3] (im Besonderen). The loud, aggressive and sometimes offensive (__________)[4] rock music style appeals to young people because adults – “anyone over 30” – __________[5] (betrachten) it “the end of culture and civilisation”. The rock star __________[6] (wird) the representative of a youth in revolt.
Teenagers __________[7] (identifizieren sich) with their rock hero, believing that the image of the superstar as it __________[8] (erscheint) in the media is for real. But this image is created by cunning (__________)[9] managers and clever media people to __________[10] (fördern) record and video sales of a star or a group.
When Kurt Cobain died he __________[11] (war geworden) an idol for millions of youngsters who mourned (__________)[12] his death, lying on their beds listening to his music and not understanding why he had left and hurt them so much.
On the __________[13] (Veröffentlichung) of the Take That album *Nobody Else*, the papers ran promotion (__________)[14] articles telling their readers about how much the __________[15] (Mitglieder) of the group enjoyed (__________)[16] working with each other and that they were the best of friends: “The five teenage idols may be getting older but there are no __________[17] (Anzeichen) that they are becoming tired (__________)[18] of each other.” The reality was quite different: there was __________[19] (Rivalität) and envy among the musicians. When singer Robbie Williams eventually (__________)[20] left Take That, millions of young fans were shocked because they had always believed in what the media had told them about their idols.

3 Language corner

3.1 Combinations and collocations

Phrases with "to do"

to do a room	ein Zimmer sauber machen
to do German	Deutsch lernen
to do good	Gutes tun
to do one's hair	sich frisieren
to do one's homework	seine Hausaufgaben machen
to do the shopping	einkaufen
to do the supper	das Abendessen kochen
to do the washing	Wäsche waschen
to do the washing-up	(Geschirr) abwaschen
to do well in an exam	bei einer Prüfung gut abschneiden
what do you do (for a living)?	was machen Sie (beruflich)?
the car only does sixty	das Auto schafft nur sechzig

3.2 False friends

become ≠ bekommen

- *to become* = werden

Marilyn Monroe became one of the biggest stars of the American cinema.
Marilyn Monroe wurde einer der größten Stars des amerikanischen Kinos.

- bekommen = *to get, to receive*

Marilyn Monroe never received an Oscar.
Marilyn Monroe bekam nie einen Oscar.

famous ≠ famos

- *famous* = berühmt

Marilyn was famous because of her pinup photos.
Marilyn war berühmt für ihre Pin-up-Fotos.

- famos = *excellent*

Marilyn Monroe gave an excellent performance in "Some like it hot".
Marilyn Monroe lieferte eine famose Leistung ab/ spielte famos in „Manche mögen's heiß".

English word	Correct german	German word	Correct english
become	werden	bekommen	get, receive
famous	berühmt	famos	excellent
human	menschlich	human	humane
card	(Post-)Karte	Karte	ticket
concurrence	Gleichzeitigkeit	Konkurrenz	competition
meaning	Bedeutung	Meinung	opinion
self-consciousness	Befangenheit	Selbstbewusstsein	self-confidence
sensible	vernünftig	sensibel	sensitive
scrupulous	gewissenhaft	skrupellos	unscrupulous

Exercise 9 Usage: Phrases with "to do"

Use phrases with "to do" in these sentences.

a) Angie works as a chambermaid in the "The Haven" hotel. After the guests have had their breakfast she starts __________ all __________ in the house.

b) My English penfriend writes almost perfect German. He __________ for four years now.

c) Before mum starts the dinner, she __________ all __________ in the big supermarket.

d) My big sister goes to the disco every Friday night; before she leaves she spends three hours in front of the mirror to __________.

e) That was a tasty meal, Jim. But now I feel really tired. Could you help me __________, please.

f) You've worked more than enough, Charlotte. I hope you are __________ in your exam.

g) The Taylors seem to have loads of money. Do you happen to know what Mr. Taylor __________?

h) My old car drives me mad. It's a really slow coach: it only __________ 40 miles. I think I'll treat myself to a new one.

i) Now, Alfie, before you go out. Have you __________ for tomorrow?

Exercise 10

Usage: The tragedy of Marilyn Monroe

Use the right word in the empty spaces.

"My work is the only ground I've ever had to stand on."
Marilyn Monroe (1926–62)

Few people would say that Marilyn's acting was ______________[1] (famous/ excellent), but according to the ______________[2] (meaning/opinion) of actors who played in films alongside her she was a ______________[3] (sensible/ sensitive) creature. It is true, though, that MM was hard to work with.
Most of all, her extravagancies were due to the cruel treament she had received from ______________[4] (scrupulous/ unscrupulous) photographers and managers since she first started as a starlet and pin up girl.
She was born on June 1, 1926 as Norma Jean Baker, an illegitimate child who never knew her father. Growing up in poverty and misery didn't help her to develop any ______________[5] (self-confidence/self-consciousness).
A 21-year-old aircraft plant worker ______________[6] (became/got) her hero and rescued her from that dreadful background. Norma Jean married him when she was 16 and began working as a model for bathing costumes.
In order to ______________[7] (become/get) famous and earn more money she also started posing for pin-ups and glamour photos.
A Hollywood producer saw her photos, offered her a contract and renamed her Marilyn Monroe.
At first she was only given smaller roles because of the stiff ______________[8] (concurrence/competition) in the film industry, but eventually she played in major films, usually taking the role of the dumb blonde. Millions liked to see her that way and queued in front of the cinemas to buy ______________[9] (cards/tickets) for the latest MM film.
On August 5, 1962, she committed suicide by taking an overdose of sleeping pills, worried about getting old and losing her sex appeal.
She had always relied on other people's ______________[10] (meaning/opinion) too much. She had never found her own role in life, had always acted a part.
During her whole life she had been exploited by others and had never found the ______________[11] (human/humane) treatment she had been searching for since childhood.

4 Grammar spot: The gerund

Als Gerundium (*Gerund*) bezeichnet man ein substantiviertes Verb, d.h. ein Verb, das zum Substantiv gemacht wurde (durch Anhängen von *-ing: reading* = (das) Lesen).
Das Gerundium kann als Subjekt oder Objekt verwendet werden.

The gerund as subject

Das Gerundium kann Subjekt eines Satzes sein.	Listening to music is a favourite hobby of young people. *(Das) Musikhören ist ein beliebtes Hobby junger Menschen.*
Besonders häufig steht diese Fügung nach: • *there is no* = es lässt sich nicht	There is no denying that young people have more money today. *Es lässt sich nicht leugnen, dass Jugendliche heute mehr Geld haben.*
• *it's no use/no good* = es hat keinen Zweck	It's no use crying over spilt milk. *Es hat keinen Zweck, über verschüttete Milch zu weinen. (Sprichwort = Passiert ist passiert.)*

The gerund as object

Das Gerundium steht nach bestimmten Verben als Objekt.	Wendy enjoys going to the disco with Malcolm. *Wendy geht gern mit Malcolm in die Disco.*

The gerund after certain verbs

Es gibt eine Reihe von Verben, nach denen im Englischen das Gerundium stehen muss. Im Deutschen verwenden wir den Infinitiv. Prägen Sie sich diese Verben ein, nach denen die „*ing*-Form" (das Gerundium) steht!

admit	= zugeben	involve	= umfassen, mit sich bringen
anticipate	= vorwegnehmen, voraussehen	keep	= fortfahren, weitermachen
avoid	= vermeiden	mind	= etwas haben gegen
consider	= erwägen	miss	= vermissen
defer	= verschieben	pardon	= verzeihen
delay	= verschieben, verzögern	postpone	= verschieben

deny	= leugnen	prevent	= (ver)hindern
detest	= verabscheuen	recollect	= sich erinnern an
dread	= fürchten	resent	= übel nehmen
enjoy	= genießen	resist	= widerstehen
excuse	= entschuldigen	risk	= wagen
fancy	= Gefallen finden an	save	= retten, bewahren
finish	= beenden	stop	= aufhören
forgive	= verzeihen	suggest	= vorschlagen
imagine	= sich vorstellen	understand	= verstehen

Gerund and infinitive with different meanings

Einige Verben ändern ihre Bedeutung, je nachdem, ob das Gerundium oder der Infinitiv folgt.

to forget

Gerund

I'll never forget seeing Britney Spears live on stage.

Ich werde nie vergessen, wie ich einmal … sah. (= bezieht sich auf die Vergangenheit)

Infinitive

I won't forget to buy the latest Britney Spears CD!

Ich werde nicht vergessen (= daran denken), … zu kaufen. (= bezieht sich auf die Zukunft)

to remember

Gerund

I remember seeing the film "Lord of the Rings" for the first time when I was 15.

Ich erinnere mich, wie ich … gesehen habe, …

Infinitive

I must remember to lend you the DVD "Lord of the Rings: The Return of the King".

Ich muss daran denken (= darf nicht vergessen), dir … zu leihen.

to regret

Gerund

I regret having missed the film on TV.

Es tut mir leid, dass ich … verpasst habe.

Infinitive

I regret to miss your party next Saturday, because I'll be on holiday in France.

Es tut mir Leid, dass ich … verpassen werde.

to stop

Gerund	Infinitive
I stopped listening to the news on the radio. Ich hörte auf, die Nachrichten … zu hören.	I stopped to listen to the news. Ich hörte (mit meiner Arbeit) auf, um die Nachrichten zu hören.

to try

Gerund	Infinitive
I won't try getting any tickets for the Eminem concert – they'll be sold out anyway. Ich werde gar nicht probieren, Karten zu bekommen. (= einen Versuch machen)	I've tried to get tickets for the Eminem concert – but in vain. Ich habe (ernsthaft) versucht (= mich angestrengt), Karten zu bekommen. (= eine Anstrengung unternehmen)

Exercise 11 Gerund or infinitive?: Going out for the evening

Put the verbs in brackets into the correct form (gerund or infinitive). Add an appropriate preposition if neccessary.

Example:

Richard suggested ________ (going/ to go) to the cinema to see "The Return of the King".	Richard suggested going to the cinema to see "The Return of the King".

a) Alwyn admitted ____________ (having seen / to have seen)[118] the film before so he didn't really feel like ____________ (watching/to watch) it again.

b) Richard, however, said: "I think that film is well worth ____________ (seeing/to see) a second time."

c) But Alwyn wasn't convinced: "Who would want ____________ (going/to go) and see a film for the second time!?"

d) Anne interrupted before Richard could answer: "And what about me? Has anybody asked me what I would like ____________ (doing/to do) tonight?"

e) Alwyn: "Well, what about you then!? Would you prefer ____________ (going/to go) to the cinema, to a disco or to a restaurant?"

f) Anne: "I don't fancy ____________ (sitting/to sit) in a dark cinema for three hours. And I can't imagine the two of you ____________ (dancing/to dance) with me in the "2010 Club"! So let's go to MacBeef's!"

g) Richard: "I detest ____________ (eating/to eat) fast food that tastes of nothing!"

h) Alwyn: "If you don't enjoy ____________ (eating/to eat) out, why don't stay at home!"

i) Finally Anne said: "O, stop ____________ (arguing/to argue) and let's go and see the film, have a snack and go to the disco afterwards."

Exercise 12 Gerund as part of the predicate: Forming a band

Rewrite these sentences replacing the underlined words by the expressions given in brackets. Supply the right preposition if necessary and use the gerund!

Example:

It's impossible to know in advance if a song will hit the charts. (There's no way)	There's no way of knowing in advance if a song will hit the charts.

a) I think, many young people would like to play in a pop group. (to enjoy)

____

b) One day my friends Jeff and Morris suggested forming a pop group because our hobby is to make music. (to be interested)

____

c) They thought that it would not be too difficult for us to play a couple of numbers together. (to have no difficulty)

____

d) However, it was a big problem for us to find a room where we could rehearse. (to have difficulty)

____

e) Jeff and I would have liked to cover the latest hitparade hits, but many songs were too difficult and we'd never be able to play them. (to dream)

____

f) We didn't really know what songs to choose, when one night Jeff suggested, "Couldn't we pick some golden oldies that everybody likes?" (How about)

___

g) So in the end, we managed to rehearse some old Chuck Berry and Rolling Stones numbers. (to succeed)

___

h) Morris, our drummer, didn't like it when we went through a number again and again! (to be tired)

___

i) Although, in the end, we played quite well, we were still worried about how the crowd would react when we appeared live on stage. (can't stop)

___

j) It's absolutely impossible to tell in advance whether you will succeed or flop. (There's no way)

___

k) We are excited that we'll play at our youth club next Friday. (to look forward)

___

l) There is even a chance that we'll record one of our own number written by Morris. (possibility)

___

5 Fun and games

Exercise 13 Crossword puzzle

Try to solve the crossword puzzle.

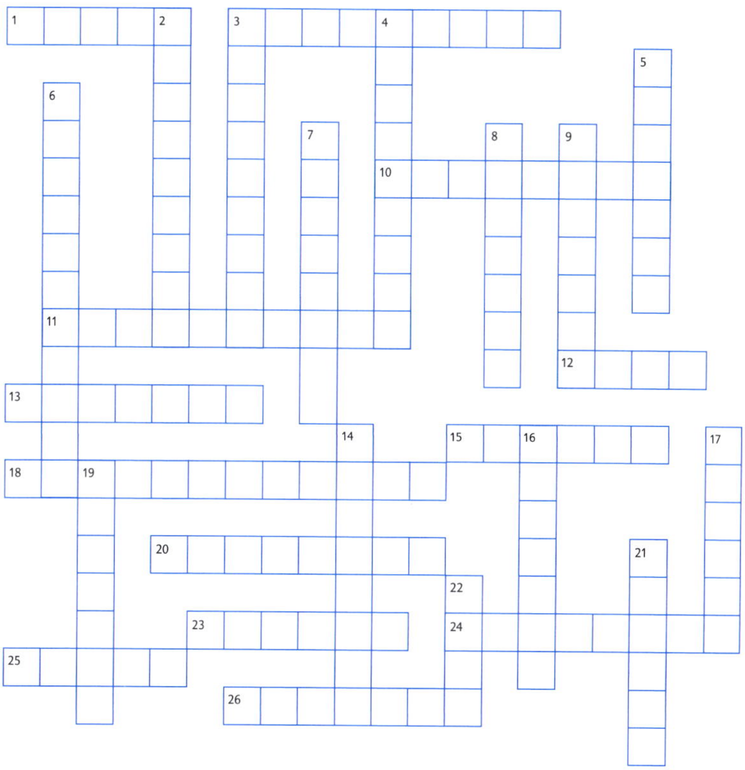

Across
1. Missbrauch
3. Werbung
10. Romanautor
11. Erscheinung, Aussehen
12. Neid
13. Rivalität
15. Klatsch
18. skrupellos, rücksichtslos
20. drohen
23. Spalte
24. süchtig
25. Erwachsen(er)
26. Glück, Schicksal, Vermögen

Down
2. Aufkommen, Entstehen
3. Darsteller, Bühnenstar
4. anstößig, beleidigend
5. zerstören
6. Empörung
7. Publikum
8. berauben
9. Scheidung
14. Verachtung
16. Selbstmord
17. dumm
19. Jagdgewehr
21. Geächtete(r)
22. Ruhm

Key

Born in the wrong age

Exercise 1 **Understanding the text**

A	B	C	D	E	F	G
2	6	4	5	7	1	3

Exercise 2 **Vocabulary grid: Law**

	A	C	C	U	S	A	T	I	O	N	
		P	U	N	I	S	H	M	E	N	T
	C	O	N	D	E	M	N				
	A	P	P	E	A	L					
			A	R	R	E	S	T			
		C	A	P	I	T	A	L			
	A	W	A	R	E						
A	B	O	L	I	S	H					
	C	O	N	V	I	C	T				
		B	A	I	L						
B	U	R	G	L	A	R	Y				
			B	E	T	R	A	Y			
C	H	A	R	G	E						
B	R	I	B	E	R	Y					
	C	R	E	D	I	B	I	L	I	T	Y

Exercise 3 **Cloze-Test: Working for social reforms**

1 century / 2 increased / 3 merchants / 4 misery / 5 search / 6 wages / 7 debts / 8 prison / 9 responsible / 10 injustices / 11 introduce / 12 dreadful / 13 aware / 14 underprivileged / 15 experienced

Exercise 4 Translation: Charles Dickens

1 clerk / 2 Schulden; verschuldete sich / 3 verhaftet / 4 seinen Lebensunterhalt verdienen / 5 warehouse / 6 prison / 7 Waise / 8 experience / 9 schlimmen / 10 Schließlich / 11 courts / 12 Romane / 13 cheap / 14 vertraut / 15 improvements

Exercise 5 C-Test: Oliver Twist – The boy from the workhouse

1 born / 2 orphan / 3 receive / 4 enough / 5 profit / 6 hungry / 7 cell / 8 eventually / 9 apprentice / 10 undertaker / 11 collect / 12 treated / 13 pickpockets / 14 care / 15 wallet / 16 jail / 17 completely / 18 criminal / 19 behaviour

Exercise 6 Asking questions

a) How old were Andrew Simms and Tom Roberts of Challacombe?
b) Who lost his farm more than three years ago?
c) What did Tom's father lose more than three years ago?
d) Why did he lose his farm?
e) Who(m) did the boys meet one day?
f) Who sentenced the boys to three months imprisonment for stealing?
g) When did crowds gather?
h) When was Bodmin prison built?
i) How many meals were the prisoners fed a day?
j) When did the children go back to their work?
k) When did Parliament pass the Youthful Offenders Act?

Exercise 7 Question tags

a) ... did you?
b) ...don't you?
c) ... did you?
d) ... couldn't you?
e) ... can you?
f) ... shouldn't you?
g) ... isn't it?
h) ... will you?

Exercise 8 Give synonyms and definitions: Child crime

a) youngsters = teenagers, young people
depressing = saddening, disturbing
delinquents = offenders
homes = families
entertaining = amusing, enjoyable, pleasant

b) criminologist = a person who studies crimes and criminals
to play truant = to stay away from school

Exercise 9 Guided writing: David Copperfield's childhood

a) When he comes back from Yarmouth David discovers that his mother has married Edward Murdstone.
b) Mr Murdstone brings his sister Jane to live with them.
c) Together the Murdstones make life for David and his mother unbearable.
d) David bites Mr Murdstone on the hand and is immediately sent to Salem House school.
e) He is put under the care of Mr Creakle, a sadistic headmaster.
f) David makes a few friends at the terrible school.
g) Suddenly his mother dies in childbirth.
h) Pegotty leaves to get married.
i) David is left alone, neglected by his stepfather.
j) When he is ten years old, David is sent to London to earn his living in the counting house of Murdstone and Grinby where he is almost starved to death.
k) His job is to wash and label wine bottles in a warehouse.
l) The warehouse is dirty, dark and full of rats.
m) David lodges with the optimistic Mr Micawber, who is always in great financial trouble.
n) When Mr Micawber is finally thrown into debtor's prison, David is again alone and without a home.
o) David leaves London for Dover where his great-aunt Betsey Trotwood lives.

Exercise 10 Wordsearch

U R I R Z H A
Y N S Y N O B C P
R N D P C N J R C R P
E H Y E E A O L U U T A E
S C L R R N R I U I S J J E A
I B U T A P A I S L R A T L E S L
M D R S N L R L P S D Q T B I O T T L
N O I T A G I T S E V N I O C C N R A
Y I B O D R V Y N F Q S O O I Y E I I
E A E D N U I P O N N R N V E R C A N
E W R Y E B L H C O M F N O E U O L E
B G Y T F J E O P C I O E D G J N C D
R I R W E O G S A S C T R H O R N F B
E A A D B E Q C G A U C F T E I F
Y R H R D A Z M M J F R T O G
W R C T T N N M E D N O C
A E V I D E N C E Z M
L S N Y C V S B C
X T E R X A T

Exercise 11 Crossword puzzle

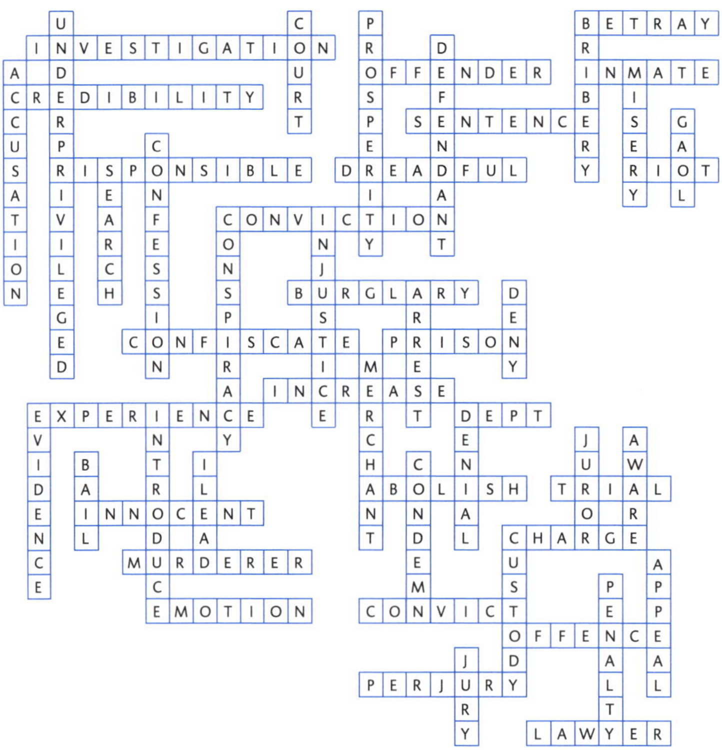

Detectives of the past

Exercise 1 Understanding the text

		true	false
a)	Schliemann had earned a fortune as a businessman.	✗	
b)	Schliemann wanted to try his luck searching for gold in Greece. *He wanted to prove that Homer was right.*		✗
c)	Schliemann thought that Homer's epic was the true historical report of a war between Greeks and Romans.	✗	
d)	Young Heinrich bought a book called *Illustrierte Weltgeschichte* for his father. *His father had bought it for him.*		✗
e)	Schliemann was certain that remains of the old Trojan city walls could still be found in the ground somewhere.	✗	
f)	Schliemann was very talented for learning foreign languages.	✗	
g)	In Greece Schliemann found remains of old walls which he thought had been part of Troy.	✗	
h)	Archaeologists later proved that the walls Schliemann had discovered were older still.	✗	
i)	Schliemann also excavated the gold coffin of King Agamemnon. *He found a gold mask which he thought was Agamemnon's.*		✗
j)	Although Schliemann did not use proper scientific methods he is important for the development of archaeology.	✗	

Exercise 2 Definitions: Archaeology

a) mummy
b) dig
c) pharaoh
d) battle
e) dictionary
f) method
g) dismiss
h) hill
i) treasure
j) excavate
k) civilisation
l) pave

Exercise 3 **Vocabulary grid: Archaeology**

	A	F	F	O	R	D								
			A	P	P	R	E	N	T	I	C	E		
						A	M	B	I	T	I	O	U	S
					B	U	R	I	A	L				
						G	R	A	V	E				
					C	H	A	M	B	E	R			
A	N	C	I	E	N	T								
			C	U	R	S	E							
D	E	P	A	R	T	M	E	N	T					
		C	O	N	T	A	I	N						
	C	O	F	F	I	N								

Exercise 4 **Cloze-Test: The tomb of Tutankhamen**

1 joined / 2 received / 3 assistant / 4 scientist / 5 Kings / 6 hand / 7 graves / 8 eventually / 9 desert / 10 give / 11 rewarded / 12 discoveries / 13 buried / 14 across / 15 beginning / 16 took / 17 destroy / 18 hole / 19 candle / 20 objects / 21 untouched / 22 pharaoh / 23 blood / 24 curse / 25 age / 26 ruled / 27 masterpiece / 28 display

Exercise 5 **C-Test: Mummies and tomb robbers**

1 spirit / 2 effort / 3 decay / 4 cruel / 5 corpse / 6 preserved / 7 drawn / 8 filled / 9 sweet / 10 Finally / 11 layers / 12 resins / 13 safe / 14 decorated / 15 valuable / 16 procession / 17 desert / 18 visited / 19 pyramids / 20 furniture / 21 extremely / 22 afford / 23 applied / 24 entrances / 25 chambers / 26 funeral / 27 archaeologist / 28 discovered

Exercise 6 **Usage: Early elephant hunters**

1 actually / 2 probably / 3 eventually / 4 became / 5 probably / 6 eventually / 7 probably / 8 perhaps

Exercise 7 Usage: The Curse of the dead pharaoh

1 became / 2 obtained / 3 current / 4 eventually; actually / 5 Eventually / 6 become / 7 became / 8 become / 9 eventually / 10 obtained / 11 become / 12 eventually / 13 become / 14 obtained / 15 actually; eventually

Exercise 8 Comparison of adjectives: The origins of man

1 most recent / 2 older / 3 oldest / 4 most detailed / 5 most fascinating / 6 most likely / 7 more likely / 8 most certainly

Exercise 9 Adjective or adverb?: Conserving the past

1 valuable / 2 good / 3 beautiful / 4 publicly / 5 extremely / 6 long / 7 exactly / 8 properly / 9 exceptionally / 10 difficult / 11 carefully / 12 numerous / 13 probably / 14 fairly / 15 worthless / 16 immediately / 17 real / 18 carefully / 19 just / 20 cautiously / 21 regularly / 22 finally / 23 hard / 24 correctly / 25 hardly / 26 clear / 27 recently

Exercise 10 Countries – Inhabitants – Languages

Country	Inhabitant	Language
Austria	Austrian	German
Belgium	Belgian	Flemish, French
Brazil	Brazilian	Portuguese
Britain	Briton	English
Canada	Canadian	English, French
Denmark	Dane	Danish
England	Englishman	English
Finland	Fin	Finnish
France	Frenchman	French
Germany	German	German
Greece	Greek	Greek
Holland/Netherlands	Dutchman	Dutch
Hungary	Hungarian	Hungarian
India	Indian	Hindi, English
Ireland	Irishman	English, Gaelic

Italy	Italian	Italian
Japan	Japanese	Japanese
Norway	Norwegian	Norwegian
Poland	Pole	Polish
Portugal	Portuguese	Portuguese
Russia	Russian	Russian
Scotland	Scotsman	English, Gaelic
Spain	Spaniard	Spanish
Sweden	Swede	Swedish
Switzerland	Swiss	German, French, Italian, Romansh (a Rhaeto-Roman dialect)
Turkey	Turk	Turkish
USA	American	English
Wales	Welshman	English, Celtic

Exercise 11 Give nouns

manage	management
certain	certainty
employ	employment
enter	entrance
foolish	foolishness
free	freedom
pay	payment
real	reality
sick	sickness
tender	tenderness

Exercise 12 Give adjectives

centre	central	read	readable
classic	classical	act	active
comfort	comfortable	agree	agreeable
comic	comical	eat	eatable
courage	courageous	forget	forgetful
duty	dutiful	harm	harmful

fashion	fashionable	pay	payable
mountain	mountainous	poison	poisonous
music	musical	think	thinkable
noise	noisy	use	useful

Exercise 13

Word families

noun (abstract)	**noun** (concrete)	**verb**	**adjective**
exploration	explorer	to explore	explorative
belief	believer	to believe	believable
collection	collector	to collect	collective
conviction	-----	to convince	convincing, convincible
destruction	destroyer	to destroy	destructive
discovery	discoverer	to discover	-----
entry, entrance	-----	to enter	-----
poverty	-----	-----	poor
preparation	preparer	to prepare	preparatory
remains, remainder	-----	to remain	-----
safety	-----	to save	safe
science	scientist	-----	scientific
supervision	supervisor	to supervise	-----
tale	teller	to tell	-----

Exercise 14

Wordsearch

```
D E T E R M I N A T I O N E V O L V E H
H Y X E I D E P A R T M E N T C F V Y P
P G S P Z C S M P M A S U O I T I B M A
T I B T L I I O P R S E F F Z D F D E T
N D I S C O V E R Y H T I E E Y L U R I
E R U S A E R T E G M T H N B U Y E C E
C Y E O H J E A N Q N L C G F R B F H N
S P M V B R P V T E Y E A D U M N M A C
E P O M R P U A I I R M A B A A R J N E
D V O T U E S C C P O E N H M C R J T K
O T K Y T M S X E T R N C G M E O D X C
Q T R E S E D E R D E T I O R S V W U X
C O F F I N R C R E E R E Q V A I W R W
J F F F D U O Y M P Y S N C F E V O R P
M K L O Y I F B D N I A T N O C R E E O
I B R R D R F U N E R A L R O E U Y U I
A T Y T Q I A R P W C M Y P O D S R D N
M H F F Y R U I R E M A I N S Y K C S Q
M H G Y E L L A V C O J Y K N I L R M E
U Q L N E M P L M F A X R P L P D G Y R
```

Exercise 15 Crossword puzzle

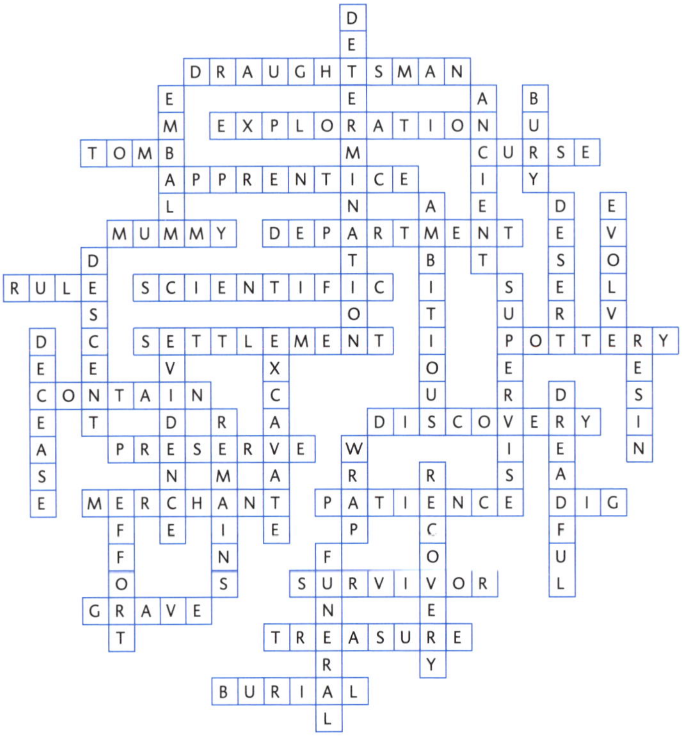

Adventures at sea

Exercise 1 Understanding text passages

a) Bligh and 18 men were put out in a small boat in the middle of the Pacific Ocean with few provisions. (l. 3/4)
b) Bligh very soon developed a love for the sea and the navy. (l. 12)
c) … he quickly made his way to the top. (l. 14)
d) Others turned out to be troublemakers. (l. 29)
e) With a crew of forty-six the ship was overcrowded. (l. 30)
f) Bligh's reactions were always insulting and aggressive. (l. 32/33)
g) … 18 crew members remained loyal to him … (l. 48/49)
h) The mutiny was completely unjustified. (l. 63)

Exercise 2 Questions on the text

a) Fletcher Christian and his supporters started the mutiny because they were no longer willing to put up with the strict treatment they had received from captain Bligh, who always demanded discipline and obedience.

b) In most novels and films William Bligh is usually presented as a captain who has no sympathy for his crew, who treats the sailors badly and does not know very much about seamanship.

c) Because of his exceptional qualifications Bligh quickly got ahead in the navy. The fact that the famous James Cook made Bligh an officer during the voyages to the Pacific also proves that young Bligh was a very good sailor and navigator.

d) The aim of Bligh's voyage to Tahiti was to supply the plantation owners of the British colonies in the West Indies with plants of the bread fruit tree, the fruit of which made up the staple diet for the slaves.

e) When they first met Fletcher Christian thought that William Bligh was a very competent captain from whom he would be able to learn a lot about navigation.

f) Friends of Bligh had asked him to include some of their acquaintances into his crew. As Bligh didn't want to offend anybody he finally ended up with more sailors than he really needed.

g) The good and easy life on Tahiti was a complete change for the sailors compared to the hard life on board during the voyage from England to the South Pacific. The crew could not collect the bread fruit plants immediately so they had plenty of time to be spoilt by the comforts of life on this island of paradise. In the end, they enjoyed living there so much that they were unwilling to accept orders from the officers. They would have preferred to leave the navy and stay on Tahiti for good.

h) The final ruling of the admirals and judges was that Christian and the mutineers had no right to rebel against their captain. William Bligh was cleared of any blame for the mutiny and carried on his career in the Royal Navy.

Exercise 3 Words in a new context

a) argument
b) appointment
c) accept
d) ask
e) arrived
f) demand

g) discipline
h) cruel
i) application
j) developed

Exercise 4 **Words with several meanings**

a) ask(ed)
b) collection(s)
c) condition(s)
d) consequence(s)

Exercise 5 **Vocabulary grid: Sea**

						A	D	V	A	N	C	E	D		
		A	P	P	A	R	E	N	T	L	Y				
				C	O	N	S	E	Q	U	E	N	T	L	Y
		A	P	P	L	I	C	A	T	I	O	N			
				A	T	T	E	M	P	T					
C	O	M	P	L	A	I	N								
	C	O	N	C	L	U	D	E							
						C	A	R	E	E	R				
					C	O	N	V	I	N	C	E			
			C	H	A	R	T								

Exercise 6 **Cloze-Test: The real Robinson Crusoe**

1 shoemaker / 2 control / 3 everyone / 4 quarrelling / 5 became / 6 vessels / 7 navigator / 8 discipline / 9 ashore / 10 own / 11 near / 12 uninhabited / 13 vegetation / 14 hunt / 15 enjoyed / 16 alone / 17 attract / 18 civilization / 19 lonely / 20 experience

Exercise 7 **C-Test: Francis Drake fighting the Spaniards**

1 sail / 2 voyage / 3 hero / 4 navigator / 5 ports / 6 convinced / 7 destroy / 8 mission / 9 fleet / 10 delayed / 11 conquer

Exercise 8 C-Test: The defeat of the Armada (1588)

1 served / 2 playing / 3 entered / 4 finish / 5 flagship / 6 attack / 7 defeated / 8 sank / 9 damaged / 10 wounded / 11 Spaniards / 12 power / 13 expedition / 14 failure / 15 contracted / 16 buried

Exercise 9 Usage: to take – to bring

a) brought
b) bring
c) take
d) take
e) bring, taken
f) take
g) bring
h) took
i) brought
j) take
k) taking

Exercise 10 Phrases with "to take"

A	B	C	D	E	F	G
5	1	7	2	3	4	6

Exercise 11 Some more phrases with "to take"

a) take place
b) take ... time
c) take ... time
d) take ... for granted
e) take into account
f) take advantage of
g) take care of
h) take for granted; take advantage of
i) took ... interest in

Exercise 12 Active and passive

a) The bread fruit trees are used as a cheap source of food by the plantations owners.
b) He will be asked to join by all his friends.
c) The older man was respected for his abilities as a seaman by Fletcher.
d) The son is being taught how to draw a chart by the old sailor.
e) Orders were not obeyed by the lazy sailors.

f) The ship had been burnt by the mutineers.
g) Bligh's voyage is regarded as a masterpiece in navigation (by us).
h) Seven of his 18 men were lost.
i) In 1817 he was buried in London.
j) The story has been used for a novel by two American writers.
k) A profit is still being made with the film on the mutiny by the MGM film company.

Exercise 13 Passive and active

a) The Egyptian embalmers took out all the organs and preserved them separately.
b) They only left the heart in place.
c) They drew the brain out of the head through the nose.
d) The Egyptian embalmers cleaned the body and filled it with spices and herbs.
e) They used bags of white powder, natron, to dry the body.
f) Finally they wrapped it in many layers of linen bandages.
g) The Egyptian embalmers put a mask over the face.
h) Then they put the body into a coffin.
i) The Egyptian embalmers used several coffins to protect the mummy.
j) They decorated the outer coffin finely.

Exercise 14 Give opposites: Nouns

a) advantage ≠ disadvantage
b) ability ≠ inability
c) appearance ≠ disappearance
d) armament ≠ disarmament
e) balance ≠ imbalance
f) decision ≠ indecision
g) honour ≠ dishonour
h) importance ≠ unimportance
i) literacy ≠ illiteracy
j) patience ≠ impatience

Exercise 15 Give opposites: Verbs

a) guide ≠ misguide
b) agree ≠ disagree
c) appear ≠ disappear
d) believe ≠ disbelieve
e) chain ≠ unchain
f) connect ≠ disconnect
g) do ≠ undo
h) fasten ≠ unfasten

i) like ≠ dislike
j) plug ≠ unplug
k) print ≠ misprint
l) understand ≠ misunderstand

Exercise 16 Give opposites: Adjectives

a) convenient ≠ inconvenient
b) able ≠ unable
c) agreeable ≠ disagreeable
d) breakable ≠ unbreakable
e) dependent ≠ independent
f) direct ≠ indirect
g) educated ≠ uneducated
h) effective ≠ ineffective
i) happy ≠ unhappy
j) kind ≠ unkind
k) legal ≠ illegal
l) lucky ≠ unlucky
m) pleasant ≠ unpleasant
n) safe ≠ unsafe

Exercise 17 Text production: Francis Drake, the pirate

1	2	3	4	5	6	7	8	9	10	11	12
c	i	l	a	e	k	d	h	f	j	g	b

Exercise 18 Wordsearch

Y	L	T	N	E	U	Q	E	S	N	O	C	D	J	E	D	J	I	T	S
L	E	R	B	N	O	I	T	U	A	C	E	R	P	A	L	O	Y	A	L
T	S	O	E	D	U	L	C	N	O	C	W	D	R	S	O	U	R	C	E
N	S	U	L	J	T	N	A	D	N	E	C	S	E	D	T	Q	F	S	D
E	E	B	K	G	C	W	R	E	C	K	A	G	E	L	B	M	U	R	G
R	V	L	M	C	G	N	I	T	S	U	A	H	X	E	A	F	O	Y	E
A	R	E	S	O	P	R	U	I	A	G	B	D	D	E	F	Y	E	D	E
P	M	M	Z	M	E	I	D	B	R	N	O	I	S	I	V	O	R	P	M
P	U	A	P	P	L	I	C	A	T	I	O	N	C	R	A	M	P	E	D
A	K	K	X	L	B	A	W	H	I	P	O	I	S	O	N	I	N	G	G
F	F	E	C	A	I	N	T	N	E	M	E	L	T	T	E	S	L	W	W
Q	E	R	C	I	C	N	K	I	G	N	I	D	N	A	M	E	D	T	B
Z	S	J	Y	N	N	S	S	N	T	D	A	O	E	G	L	A	F	R	J
Y	T	U	G	F	I	D	A	U	S	E	X	V	M	I	D	U	V	E	C
U	I	P	R	K	V	V	B	Y	L	O	I	T	T	V	W	G	G	S	H
R	Z	A	M	V	N	G	N	H	V	T	A	R	A	A	C	C	V	E	A
C	R	G	F	E	I	I	F	O	A	T	A	N	E	N	K	T	L	D	R
T	F	Y	M	G	T	V	C	N	C	C	C	A	R	E	E	R	G	C	T
L	F	P	J	U	Q	T	O	R	E	E	N	I	T	U	M	G	I	I	F
V	U	F	M	E	I	H	A	R	D	S	H	I	P	B	P	J	P	E	H

Exercise 19 **Crossword puzzle**

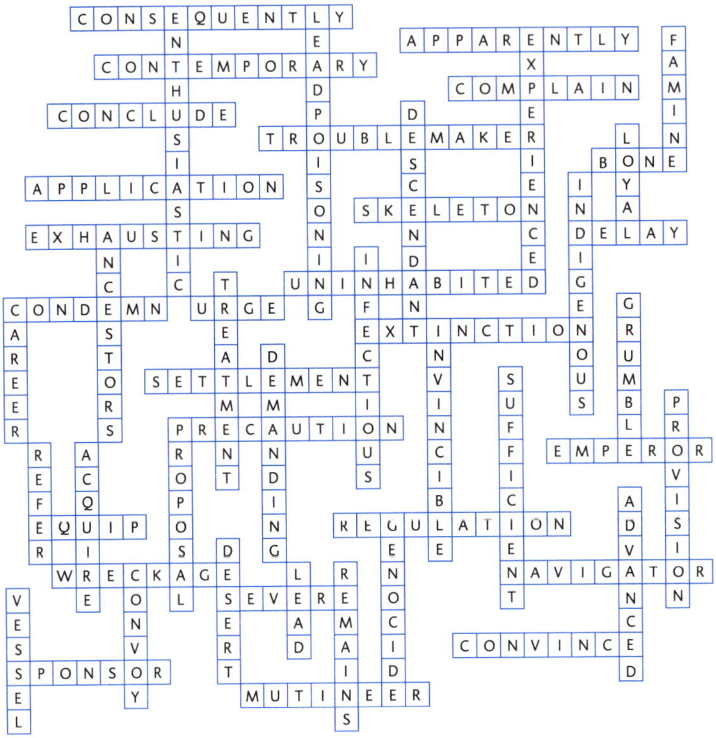

Discoveries

Exercise 1 **Understanding the text**

A	B	C	D	E	F	G
5	7	2	a	6	3	4

Exercise 2 **Cloze-Test: The search for the Northwest Passage**

1 convinced / 2 discover / 3 voyages / 4 route / 5 renewed / 6 traders / 7 urged / 8 decided / 9 experienced / 10 part / 11 led / 12 awarded / 13 appointed / 14 preparations / 15 supplies / 16 chosen / 17 unthinkable / 18 frozen / 19 survive / 20 trace

Exercise 3 C-Test: The tragic end of the Franklin expedition

1 everything / 2 missing / 3 equipment / 4 discovering / 5 received / 6 explorers / 7 stopped / 8 frozen / 9 surviving / 10 settlement / 11 deserted / 12 skeletons / 13 examined / 14 traces / 15 poisoning / 16 contained / 17 explains / 18 knowing / 19 found / 20 crew / 21 east / 22 sledge / 23 explorer / 24 transit / 25 tanker / 26 commercial / 27 useful

Exercise 4 Vocabulary grid: Explorers

					T	R	A	C	E				
						P	R	O	P	O	S	A	L
								N	A	T	I	V	E
			S	K	E	L	E	T	O	N			
							V	E	S	S	E	L	
						R	E	M	A	I	N	S	
							S	P	O	N	S	O	R
P	R	E	C	A	U	T	I	O	N				
							U	R	G	E			
			W	R	E	C	K	A	G	E			
				S	E	V	E	R	E				
			S	U	P	P	L	Y					

Exercise 5 Anagram: Discovery

a) search
b) navigator
c) convoy
d) refuge
e) famine
f) proposal
g) supply
h) trace

Exercise 6 Usage: economic – economical/historic – historical

a) economical
b) economic
c) economical
d) historical
e) historical
f) historical
g) economic
h) economic

i) economical
j) economic
k) economical

Exercise 7

Usage: a lot of/lots of/plenty of – much – many

1 much / 2 lots of / 3 A lot of / 4 much / 5 many / 6 much / 7 much / 8 many / 9 a lot of / 10 much / 11 many / 12 a lot of / 13 many

Exercise 8

Put into passive: Mixed tenses

a) The way to the "New World" was opened by Columbus.
b) The Indians were abused by the European invaders.
c) The destructive effects of colonisation are recognized by most U.S. citizens
d) A medal of honour will be received by an Indian civil rights activist.
e) More Indians are expected to vote in the next election by the Government.
f) A fund to help the indigenous peoples in America has been started by the United Nations.
g) The film "Dances With Wolves" was produced by Kevin Costner.
h) The Indians are portrayed as Noble Savages by (in) the film "Dances With Wolves".
i) Completely different languages are spoken by the Indian tribes.
j) A search for two old caravels of Columbus was started in 1930 by archaeologists.
k) The two ships of Columbus were discovered off the Jamaican coast in 1991 by deep-sea divers.
l) The importance of the discovery for the tourist industry is being stressed by the Jamaican government.

Exercise 9

Put into passive: Two objects

a) The European colonists were offered food by the natives.
b) The pioneers were shown the way through the desert by the friendly Indians.
c) The settlers were sent a warning by the Indian chief Red Cloud.
d) The Indian chief was handed a new rifle by the settlers.
e) Women were denied equal rights by some Indian tribes.
f) Wangari Maathai was awarded the Nobel Peace Prize by the Nobel Committee.

Exercise 10 Put into passive: Prepositional verbs

a) The creation of a development fund for Indians was agreed on by Latin American governments.
b) Newcomers to the reservation will be taken care of by the administration.
c) The young people in the Indian reservations must be looked after (by us).
d) All complaints will be dealt with as quickly as possible by the committee.

Exercise 11 Linking sentences: American Indians today

1 However / 2 because / 3 That means / 4 In the past / 5 But / 6 for / 7 but / 8 when / 9 As a result / 10 Unless

Exercise 12 Text reconstruction: Killing off the native population

1	2	3	4	5	6	7	8	9	10
j	g	i	c	h	e	a	d	f	b

Exercise 13 Extracting information from a text

1801 and 1805	Franklin takes part in the battles of Copenhagen and Trafalgar
1818	Franklin makes his first voyage to the Arctic
1819–1827	Franklin leads several expeditions to explore the northern coast of Canada and North America
1829	Franklin is knighted
1845	Franklin is appointed commander of an expedition to discover the Northwest Passage
July 26, 1845	expedition is last seen by a whaling vessel
1846	the two ships Erebus and Terror are stopped by ice
1847	Franklin dies
April 22, 1848	surviving men leave the ships and try to reach an Eskimo settlement on foot
1854	Robert McClure and his crew complete a passage from west to east
July 1857	ship Fox sails from England to search for the missing expedition

1880	US expedition discovers the wreckage of one of Franklin's ships
1903–1906	Norwegian explorer Roald Amundsen makes the first transit of the passage.
1969	US icebreaking oil tanker the Manhattan crosses the passage.
1980	Canadian anthropologist examines the bones of the crew.

Exercise 14 Crossword puzzle

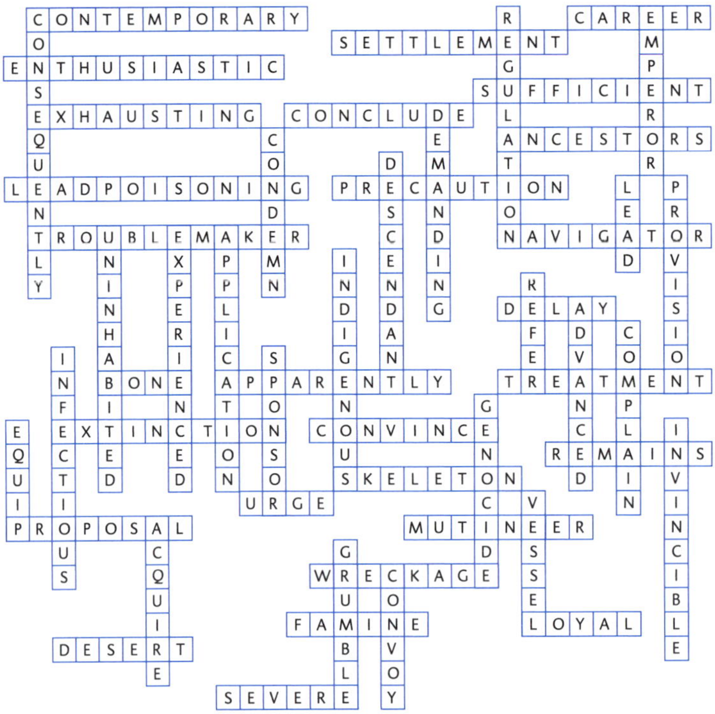

Space

Exercise 1

Understanding the text

		true	false
a)	In 1957 the Russian spacecraft Lunik 3 brought back the first pictures of the far side of the moon. *The Russian spacecraft Lunik 3 brought back the first pictures of the far side of the moon in 1959.*	☐	☒
b)	NASA wanted astronauts who were highly qualified pilots.	☒	☐
c)	The American President wanted to win the space race against the Russians.	☒	☐
d)	Scientists did not stand a chance to be accepted as astronauts by NASA. *NASA also looked for astronauts who were highly qualified scientists.*	☐	☒
e)	Apollo 11 consisted of two parts: the lunar module and the command module.	☒	☐
f)	On July 20, 1969 the three Apollo astronauts landed on the moon near the Mare Tranquilitatis. *Only two astronauts landed on the moon, the third one (Collins) remained in the command module circling the moon.*	☐	☒
g)	Neil Armstrong was the first man on the moon.	☒	☐
h)	This first landing on the moon was a big success for the Americans, but President Kennedy had wanted it to happen earlier. *Kennedy had demanded to land a man on the moon before 1970 ("before the decade is out"); so NASA was on time!*	☐	☒
i)	After their return to earth the astronauts talked to President Nixon. *The astronauts talked to the President from the moon.*	☐	☒
j)	On the moon the astronauts carried out a lot of work.	☒	☐
k)	Walking was not difficult, although on the moon people and things are heavier than on earth. *Walking was not difficult, because things are lighter on the moon.*	☐	☒
l)	On its return to earth Apollo 11 landed safely in the sea.	☒	☐

m) Back at Kennedy Space Centre (Florida) the astronauts had to put on special isolation clothes. ☐ ☒
The astronauts had to put on these special clothes before they left their capsule, i.e. when they were still floating in the sea.

n) To make sure that the astronauts wouldn't bring back any illnesses they had to stay in isolation for three weeks. ☒ ☐

Exercise 2 Definitions: Space flight

a) planet
b) star
c) rocket
d) shuttle
e) Eagle
f) Apollo
g) satellite, space probe
h) solar panels

Exercise 3 Cloze-Test: The making of the Star Trek series

1 artificial / 2 orbit / 3 launch / 4 race / 5 universe / 6 developed / 7 adventure / 8 company / 9 broadcast / 10 successful / 11 audiences / 12 dropped / 13 agreed / 14 landed / 15 astronaut / 16 set / 17 surface / 18 followers

Exercise 4 C-Test: Starship Enterprise (NCC 1701)

1 born / 2 training / 3 assignment / 4 commander / 5 mission / 6 mother / 7 planet / 8 science / 9 aboard / 10 discovered / 11 viewers / 12 characters / 13 popular / 14 meetings / 15 wear / 16 favourite / 17 message / 18 tolerance / 19 understanding / 20 Generation / 21 cinema

Exercise 5 Practise your if-clauses

a) If you were given the chance to fly into space, would you accept it?
b) If you had been given the chance to fly into space, would you have accepted it?
c) If you want to be an astronaut, you will have to pass a lot of tests.
d) If you had wanted to be an astronaut, you would have had to pass a lot of tests.

e) If the astronauts don't bring back rock samples from the moon, scientists will be disappointed.
f) If the astronauts didn't bring back rock samples from the moon, scientists would be disappointed.

Exercise 6

Conditional: Mixed types

a) weren't, wasn't
b) would not
c) couldn't
d) hadn't worn
e) could
f) weren't
g) would get
h) didn't have
i) would have been
j) wouldn't be
k) didn't move

Exercise 7

Answering questions on the text "Flight into space"

a) In the 19th century it was not yet possible to put a spacecraft into orbit. Scientists and engineers had not the know-how to construct a rocket which was powerful enough to carry a load and push it beyond the earth's field of gravity, nor had they the instruments to guide the spacecraft on its way through the universe.
b) President Kennedy was important because for rather political than scientific reasons he set the American space programme in motion. After the Russians had attracted the world's attention by launching the first satellite, Kennedy wanted to prove to the world that the technology of the capitalist Western society was not only equal but even superior to that of the Communist Soviet Union.
c) The first "generation" of astronauts the NASA was looking for consisted of mainly experienced pilots who knew everything about flying and were physically healthy and strong. In a later phase they also tried to find astronauts who had excellent qualifications as scientists.
d) After a journey of about three days an Apollo spacecraft reached an orbit around the moon. One astronaut stayed in the Command module, while two of his colleagues got into the small Lunar Module and landed on the moon's surface. After their explorations and activities they returned to the Command module which flew them home.
e) With his words, "That's one small step for a man, but one giant leap for mankind" Armstrong wanted to express that for him as the last link in a

chain of developments and invention it was only a small foot step onto the moon's surface, but for mankind the landing on the moon represented enormous progress. He had arrived at the final goal generations of scientists had worked for.

f) They had to spend three weeks in isolation because sceptics feared that the astronauts might have caught some unknown viruses or bacteria and brought them back to earth causing diseases for which there would be no medicine or antidote. So NASA thought it was better to put the astronauts into quarantine to make sure they were not incubating any illnesses and were in good health.

Exercise 8 Guided writing: Making friends with E.T.

a) They do not realize that not all members of the crew have made it back to ship in time.
b) One of them is left behind in the darkness of the woods, chased by humans and dogs.
c) The abandoned creature escapes to the backyard of a suburban house where a 10-year-old boy named Elliott lives with his mother, sister and brother.
d) His parents have separated and the boy feels rather lost.
e) Elliott finds the extra-terrestrial (E.T.) being and hides him from his mum, but shares his big secret with the neighbourhood kids.
f) They all make friends with Elliott's new companion.
g) Eventually E.T. is taken into Elliott's house.
h) For E.T. the rooms of the house are worlds full of surprises and novelties that must be discovered/he must discover.
i) E.T. does not know what all these things are needed for and how they are used and has a number of extremely funny adventures and amusing experiences.
j) Although E.T. and Elliott become best friends, the extra-terrestrial lets the boy know that he does not want to stay down here on this earth for ever: he wants to go home.
k) "E.T. phone home", he keeps telling Elliott.
l) To all the kids' horror E.T. is caught by the officials from the space agency who want carry out experiments on him and kill him.

Exercise 9 Crossword puzzle

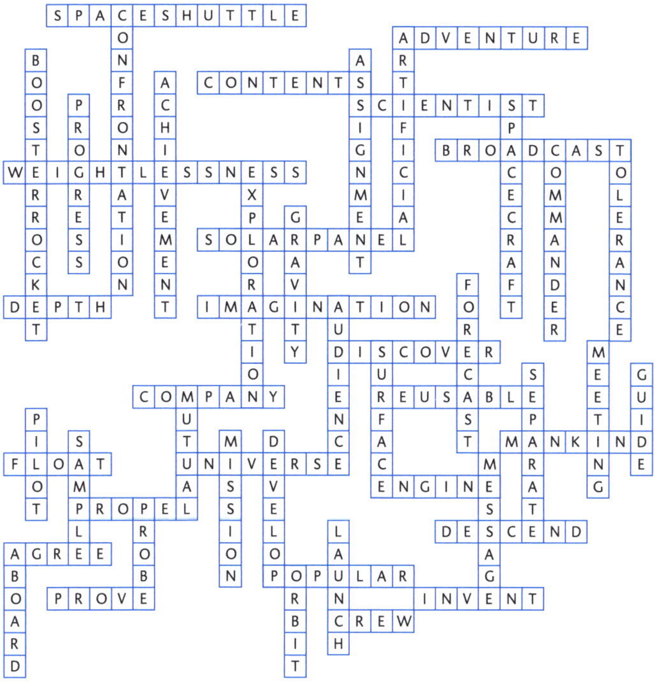

Exercise 10 Wordsearch

W
E E K
B T I X A
O A A G C P W
R R Y P H S T L Q
P A Y S I T L H S O N
O P D R E S L O L U O R F
P E R V V I T E K B I T O A R
U S S W E T Q E S R T B R T B T F
L T N E M N G I S S A G E A H L U I S
A M A R E E T D D G N G C O D E V E L O P
R J R C N I A U O D I E A L D R R P U M Z N D
T L P Y T C R R R Z G E S F X T A P L E P O R P G
M I S S I O N E A X T S C E N O O E F H A A T
U B B R F N M D D P M C O E R T R G O N I
G R A V I T Y N E S R E V I N U B E B
T F A R C E C A P S A N E I A L R
L E N G I N E M T G I D R A O
A L T R A T M M H E Q U C
U P P B L S T O B N K
T M S U R F A C E
U A M H Y H T
M S H W H
P L I
P

Mysteries

Exercise 1 Understanding the text

a) Journalists need something interesting and sensational to write about. When there is nothing much to report – as it happens every year during the summer months, because people are away on holiday – they sometimes invent stories or write again about some old-time favourites like the "monster" of Loch Ness to attract the readers' attention.

b) The legend dates back to the days of the Irish monk and missionary St. Columba, who lived in the 6th century. He mentioned the fact that he had been to the funeral of an unfortunate man, who had been killed by a water beast in Loch Ness. From then on people believed that there was a monster in the lake.

c) From 1933 on tourists could reach Loch Ness more easily because a motorway had been built around the lake. A couple travelling in the area claimed they had seen a monster in the lake. Their report was readily taken up by journalists who informed their readers about this "sensational sighting", thus giving the legend a new push.

d) The sensational picture which was often published and thought to be a proof of Nessie's existence did not really show the monster. It was the photograph of a "model monster" a couple of friends had made to fool the public.

e) Although some teams who investigated the lake thought they had found some evidence of the monster or even a whole family of them, most scientists had to admit that they could not find any real proof that Nessie existed.

f) The press people were rather thrilled when an American team affirmed they had managed to take pictures of the monster underwater. However, when the photos were presented to the press, the journalists were rather annoyed: the photos did not show anything, only stretches of murky water.

Exercise 2 Definitions: Mystery

a) pattern
b) beast
c) environmentalist
d) legend
e) footprint
f) circle
g) motorway
h) crop

Exercise 3 Vocabulary grid: Secrets

R	E	T	I	R	E	D					
		P	H	Y	S	I	C	I	S	T	
						S	P	L	A	S	H
		W	H	E	A	T					
				P	L	U	N	G	E		
			S	H	O	R	E				
						B	E	A	S	T	
		R	E	S	E	A	R	C	H		
			P	L	A	N	K				
			S	N	A	C	K				
				S	H	E	E	R			

Exercise 4 Cloze-Test: Mysterious circles in wheat fields

1 arrived / 2 fields / 3 noticed / 4 huge / 5 neatly / 6 diameter / 7 explain / 8 local / 9 discovery / 10 sighted / 11 research / 12 studied / 13 Books / 14 convinced / 15 man / 16 precise / 17 said / 18 observers / 19 formed / 20 circles / 21 because / 22 ancient / 23 dismissed / 24 nonsense / 25 mystery / 26 speculated / 27 atmospheric / 28 created / 29 during / 30 explanations / 31 government / 32 investigation / 33 entdeckten / 34 Ingenieur / 35 Beweis / 36 Muster / 37 Forschungsarbeit / 38 Landschaft

Exercise 5 Text reconstruction: The masters of the rings

1	2	3	4	5
d	e	c	a	b

Exercise 6 Translation: Wheat circles

1 joke / 2 disappointment / 3 extra-terrestrials / 4 admit / 5 research / 6 believe

Exercise 7 Synonymous expressions

1	2	3	4	5	6
d	a	e	f	b	c

Exercise 8 Cloze-Test: Phrases with "have"

a) have a drink
b) have a talk
c) have a rest
d) have it done
e) have a cold
f) have a holiday
g) have a good time

Exercise 9 Simple past – Present perfect

a) have you ever been
b) went
c) were driving / did you observe
d) didn't see / went / looked at
e) have claimed / have seen / said / has just been proved
f) have never believed

Exercise 10 Practice: Comment writing

"Nessie sighted again!" The sensational headline in the tabloid and the dark and unclear picture accompanying the article boosts sales tremendously. Readers want to know everything about the latest discoveries in Loch Ness – and are a little disappointed when after reading the article they come to the conclusion that there still is no definite proof of the monster's existence. However, at the same time most are somehow relieved that there is also no definite proof that Nessie does not exist!

We live in a world today where man seems to have everything under control. Modern technology and rational business techniques have done away with uncertainties. Statistics tell politicians and managers what people think, how they will vote, and if they will buy some new product. With his research man seems to be able to find out everything.

We use modern scientific equipment to reveal the secrets of nature. Satellites travel into the depths of space to distant worlds, electronic microscopes plunge

deep down into the microcosms to disclose unknown worlds. There seems no place left for amazement, surprise and wonder.
Progress in medicine has enabled people to live healthier and longer, the introduction of machines and computers into the work process has made work easier – we enjoy all these benefits of scientific advances and no one would like to turn back the clock to the 19th century.
But there are times when people look for an escape from rational reckoning and all the technical devices which seem to make our world more impersonal and colder. This desire explains the success of the Star Wars and Star Trek series, of films like Back to the Future and of books by Stephen King, all of which provide "food for our imagination" and which lead us into a world of fantasy.
The Loch Ness monster, too, is part of this beloved world. So let Nessie live, even though the beast might not exist – or the world will be a poorer, a colder place.

330 words

King Arthur

Exercise 1 Questions on the text

a) It is true, the Angles and Saxons helped Vortigern to stay in power, but in the end they saw an opportunity to take possession of Britain for themselves and consequently did not only fight against Vortigern's enemies and rivals but also turned on the native Britons.
b) The enchanter Merlin had heard that there were plans to kill the baby son of the king by ambitious knights who wanted Arthur out of the way in order to claim the throne for themselves.
c) After the death of King Uther a time of great unrest broke out: the knights could not decide who was to be their leader and quarrelled amongst each other. Merlin went to London to see the archbishop and talk about how they could put an end to the fighting and killing.
d) There was an inscription on the stone which said that the knight who could pull the sword from the stone was the real king of Britain.
e) Arthur, who did not realise how important the sword was, gave it to his brother Kay. Kay showed it to his father and wanted to make him believe that he himself, Kay, had pulled it from the stone.

f) Arthur learned that he was not Sir Ector's own son, but that in reality he was the son of King Uther and that the faithful Merlin had taken him to Sir Ector to be raised in safety.
g) The knights could not believe that young Arthur was to be their king, so they decided it would be better to wait for a few months before reaching the final decision.

Exercise 2 Synonymous expressions

a) Vortigern invited the Saxons from Germany and Denmark to fight his battles for him (l. 4)
b) driving them from their homes (l. 6)
c) No word was spoken of the boy's fate. (l. 14/15)
d) ... his knights fought amongst themselves for power. (l. 17)
e) ... he had tried to pull it from the stone the day before (l. 44/45)
f) ... the steel slid easily out of the stone (l. 49/50)
g) ... no one believed them and the decision to choose a king was put off till Whitsun. (l. 54/55)
h) the knights and barons swore their loyalty (l. 58)

Exercise 3 Words in a new context

a) evil
b) finally
c) lead
d) luck
e) kneel
f) notice
g) magic
h) save
i) recognize
j) discovery

Exercise 4 Vocabulary grid: Legends

				P	L	O	T					
				S	T	R	O	K	E			
							U	N	R	E	S	T
			W	I	Z	A	R	D				
			P	L	A	I	N					
					S	C	A	B	B	A	R	D
							M	O	R	T	A	L
			W	I	C	K	E	D				
M	A	G	I	C	I	A	N					
				M	I	S	T					

Exercise 5 Cloze-Test: Tintagel today

1 location / 2 fascinated / 3 situated / 4 coast / 5 path / 6 stone / 7 remains / 8 view / 9 connection / 10 born / 11 enemies / 12 waves / 13 meetings / 14 board

Exercise 6 C-Test: How the legend began

1 began / 2 recorded / 3 happened / 4 followed / 5 court / 6 Between / 7 parts / 8 generation / 9 alive / 10 connection / 11 really / 12 scientific / 13 infancy / 14 popular / 15 stronger

Exercise 7 C-Test: Searching for the truth behind the myth

1 excavations / 2 ruins / 3 castle / 4 question / 5 place / 6 value / 7 important / 8 short / 9 hundred / 10 fallen / 11 prison / 12 figure / 13 built / 14 link / 15 complete

Exercise 8 Translation: The legend lives on!

1 influenced / 2 alten / 3 Festung / 4 monastery / 5 vermuten lassen / 6 tin / 7 Spuren / 8 reason / 9 Ort

Exercise 9 Practice: Test your language skills

a) sea
b) happy
c) Lake
d) hear
e) sea
f) listen
g) sea
h) happy
i) lake
j) listen
k) lake
l) Sea
m) hear

Exercise 10 Practice: Test your grammar – can

a) After a few more driving lessons he will be able to drive a lorry.
b) In a few years' time she will be able to make her own dress.
Before she got married she could make her own dress.
c) When his arm is better James will be able to play the guitar.
A few years ago James could play the guitar.
d) Tonight John can go to the disco.
Next Saturday will be able to go the disco.

Exercise 11 Practice: Test your grammar – must

a) Jamie had to wash the dishes.
b) You weren't allowed to see your presents before your birthday.
c) You had to read that paragraph again.
d) My friend Bill had to go home early.
e) I had to finish my essay.
f) Sandra wasn't allowed to go alone.
g) You didn't have to pay for the meal yourself.
h) Jill didn't have to take the test again.

Exercise 12 Practice: Test your grammar – negation

a) Zoe doesn't have to/need not be home by ten.
b) Miriam doesn't have to/need not/needn't wipe all the glasses.
c) We didn't have to change our clothes.
d) He won't have to pay the workers in advance.
e) You don't have to/need not answer this letter at once.

f) I shan't have to book my holiday tomorrow.
g) Omar didn't have to fill in a landing card.
h) You don't have to/need not wait for me at the bus stop.

Exercise 13

Practice: Summary writing

Individuelle Lösung

Child labour

Exercise 1

Understanding the text

	true	false
a) In the United States young people of 14- to 16-years of age may work up to three hours every day. *Not every day, only on school days.*	☐	☒
b) Very often children work longer than they should, and in dangerous jobs, too.	☒	☐
c) Before they had machines in the mines and factories children had less employment possibilities. *More children were employed.*	☐	☒
d) Even very young children had to work to contribute to the income of the family.	☒	☐
e) Apart from going to work children also had to attend school. *Many of them had no time to go to school.*	☐	☒
f) In the 19th century many working children were unable to read or write.	☒	☐
g) Charles Dickens and Karl Marx were two politicians who tried to improve the situation of working children. *Darwin was a writer, Marx was a journalist.*	☐	☒
h) The new laws which limited the hours children were allowed to work were not respected by farmers and shop-owners.	☒	☐

Exercise 2

Synonyms

a) check (l. 6)
b) filthy (l. 14)
c) constant (l. 33)
d) occur (l. 10)

e) grown-up (l. 21)

f) in spite of (l. 39)

g) secure (l. 40)

Exercise 3 Vocabulary grid: Labour

									J	O	B							
								M	E	R	E	L	Y					
R	E	S	T	R	I	C	T	I	O	N								
							O	R	P	H	A	N						
				M	E	R	C	H	A	N	T							
					S	E	C	U	R	E								
	U	N	S	K	I	L	L	E	D									
								S	I	G	N	I	F	I	C	A	N	T
									S	L	I	C	E					
								M	E	N	I	A	L					

Exercise 4 Cloze-Test: Child labour today

1 century / 2 mills / 3 orphans / 4 pay / 5 services / 6 slaves / 7 upkeep / 8 forced / 9 past / 10 abolish / 11 outlawed / 12 disappeared / 13 books / 14 however

Exercise 5 Prepositions: A sad report

1 in / 2 of / 3 in / 4 of / 5 of / 6 in / 7 of / 8 from / 9 of / 10 in / 11 off

Exercise 6 C-Test: Child labour in Third World countries

1 civil / 2 merchants / 3 possibility / 4 alive / 5 around / 6 helpless / 7 given / 8 servants / 9 period / 10 elections / 11 future / 12 money / 13 earn / 14 borrowed / 15 stay

Exercise 7 C-Test: Child labour in the USA

1 costs / 2 employ / 3 cheap / 4 longer / 5 immigrant / 6 complaining / 7 treated / 8 secure / 9 permit / 10 employers / 11 responsibility / 12 boredom / 13 exploited / 14 vernachlässigen / 15 einnicken / 16 gefährden, aufs Spiel setzen / 17 Arbeiten

Exercise 8 Reported speech: Statements

At the press conference the speaker of the ILO said (that) in spite of all social progress slavery still existed. He told the journalists that children were especially affected. The new centres of modern slavery were Third World countries. He continued that in wars people were killed, houses were burnt down, farms were destroyed. People were driven off their land, and without their small fields parents were no longer able to feed their children.

He went on that child labour was still a problem in the USA. In New York and in California more and more children were employed as cheap workers. He added that young children worked at jobs no one else would take because of the low pay. Children from immigrant families suffered most. They had no chance of complaining to the authorities that they were being treated badly. He said that although laws and regulations did exist to secure their health and welfare, as workers without a permit they were outlaws.

Exercise 9 Reported speech: Questions

a) Old Spencer wanted to know why my marks were getting worse.
b) Old Spencer asked if I had any problems at home.
c) He inquired if I had problems with my girlfriend.
d) He wondered if I didn't want to go to school any more.
e) Old Spencer wanted to know when I went to bed at night.
f) Old Spencer asked what time I did my homework.
g) He inquired if I had ever forgotten to do my homework.
h) He wondered if my mother was there when I came home from school.
i) Old Spencer wanted to know if I saw my father every day.
j) He asked if I had any financial worries.

Exercise 10 Reported speech: Advice

a) He advised me to think about what was more important: pocket money or school.
b) He told me to tell my parents about my job.
c) He told me not to work too many hours.
d) He advised me not to do any hard manual work.
e) He told me to avoid working before I had a test at school.
f) He advised me to work on Saturdays only.
g) He told me to avoid working late at night.
h) He advised me not to do any shiftwork.

Exercise 11 Letter writing

Mary Paull
5 Filmer House
Filmer Road
Fulham
London SW6 7JE

24th July, 20..

Joseph Terry & Sons Limited
Bishopthorpe Road
YORK YO1 1YE

Your confectionery "Terry's Gold"

Dear Sir or Madam,

I am very fond of your chocolates "Terry's Gold". For years I have been a regular customer, and up to now I have never had any reason for complaint.
However, I must tell you that on opening the box I received today I was very disappointed. The chocolates didn't look at all fresh, in fact, they looked rather old and grey – which put me off from tasting them.

I have never come across a box of your chocolates in such poor condition before, so I felt I had to let you know as the quality of your confectionery is usually of a superior standard.

Yours faithfully,

Mary Paull

Mary Paull (Mrs)

Exercise 12 Wordsearch

N	L	R	A	A	M	W	O	R	R	O	B	H	R	M
O	U	K	E	L	A	B	O	U	R	D	O	Z	E	H
I	N	V	E	S	T	I	G	A	T	O	R	R	I	Z
T	S	C	C	M	T	O	T	F	A	Q	E	R	R	V
A	K	C	I	N	D	R	G	F	X	L	D	U	T	S
T	I	L	L	A	I	C	I	E	Y	R	O	N	I	M
I	L	V	S	H	S	W	M	C	T	G	M	G	F	M
O	L	U	W	P	R	X	Q	T	T	H	N	G	B	M
L	E	T	A	R	E	T	I	L	L	I	E	V	E	M
P	D	T	B	O	G	A	Y	O	F	K	O	R	E	B
X	J	E	O	P	A	R	D	I	S	E	C	N	F	R
E	T	L	L	E	R	U	C	E	S	H	I	E	L	U
C	C	H	I	O	D	A	P	U	A	A	J	E	H	C
E	E	V	S	E	N	T	B	N	L	V	S	X	Q	C
Z	B	Q	H	T	A	A	T	L	I	Z	J	R	S	O

Lost in the jungle

Exercise 1 Understanding the text

a) Young David had to work long hours in the cotton-textile factory. He worked for fourteen hours a day and had only two breaks of one and a half hours altogether. In addition, his family was very poor.

b) Livingstone joined the London Missionary Society because he had studied medicine and theology and he hoped the Society could train him as a missionary and offer him a suitable post.

c) Dr. Robert Moffat was a Scotsman who worked as a missionary in Africa in the immediate neighbourhood of Livingstone. After he had been attacked and wounded by a lion, David Livingstone was cared for by the Moffat family. There he met his future wife Mary, the daughter of Dr. Moffat.

d) The extremes of the climate in Africa made Livingstone's work very difficult: it was hot and damp. The distances which had to be covered were enormous, too.

e) Livingstone was not only interested in the continent Africa, but also in its people. He deeply condemned the slave trade and on his visits to Europe he exercised his influence to make Europeans aware of the unbearable situation of the Africans.

Exercise 2 Anagrams: Exploration

a) publisher
b) gather
c) source
d) watershed
e) drought
f) embrace
g) presume
h) 13 stamina

Exercise 3 Vocabulary grid: Search

						R	E	S	C	U	E						
						R	E	M	O	T	E						
P	O	P	U	L	A	T	I	O	N								
								S	T	A	M	I	N	A			
							K	N	E	E	L						
				T	R	E	A	T	M	E	N	T					
									P	U	B	L	I	S	H	E	R
						R	E	L	O	A	D						
						S	K	I	R	M	I	S	H				
		M	I	S	S	I	O	N	A	R	Y						
									R	E	Q	U	E	S	T		
						P	R	A	Y								

Exercise 4 C-Test: Exploring the black continent

1 explored / 2 lake / 3 sent / 4 enable / 5 though / 6 life / 7 buried / 8 tree / 9 raise / 10 interior / 11 thought / 12 steamboat / 13 feared / 14 become / 15 cruel / 16 native / 17 visit / 18 condemned / 19 defenders / 20 admirers / 21 sources / 22 watershed / 23 medicine

Exercise 5 Cloze-Test: Dr. Livingstone, I presume?

1 workhouse / 2 cabin / 3 merchant / 4 then / 5 side / 6 correspondent / 7 skirmishes / 8 newspaper / 9 famous / 10 probably / 11 exhausting / 12 reached / 13 fired / 14 caravan / 15 beard / 16 well / 17 alive / 18 embrace / 19 just / 20 day

Exercise 6 C-Test: Lonely death

1 together / 2 carried / 3 eventually / 4 recover / 5 lived / 6 kneeling / 7 hands / 8 praying / 9 remains / 10 pioneers / 11 trade / 12 Abbey

Exercise 7 German 'machen'

make	do	take
a mistake	one's best	a photo(graph)
an effort	one's (home)work	an exam
an offer	one's hair	a break
a film		a holiday
a noise		a course
the best of sth.		notes

Exercise 8 Usage: Survival in the South American jungle

1 went for a walk / 2 wore / 3 carried / 4 wear / 5 carry / 6 made fun / 7 don't worry / 8 doing / 9 take / 10 had done their work / 11 take, have a break / 12 make the best / 13 it had been fun

Exercise 9 Shortening sentences: Preserving wildlife in Africa

a) held
b) interested
c) Depending on tourism, many African countries …
d) supporting / arising
e) Increasing the protected regions, the countries attracted …
f) meant

Exercise 10 Replacing participle constructions: The war against poachers

a) which was started
b) which showed
c) who were shocked
d) which took place
e) who did not have
f) who seized / which tried / which they had lost
g) which was run; had been run

Exercise 11 Translation

a) gibt es
b) Wenn es mehr … gäbe
c) Wenn … erreichen würde
d) trinkt es vielleicht
e) halten die Beduinen
f) verwenden
g) Die meisten
h) glauben, dass ihre toten Vorfahren Unglück bringen
i) sollen Glück bringen
j) lassen ihre Köpfe rasieren
k) Diese sollen sie verstecken
l) rund seien … Risse bekämen

Exercise 12 Crossword puzzle

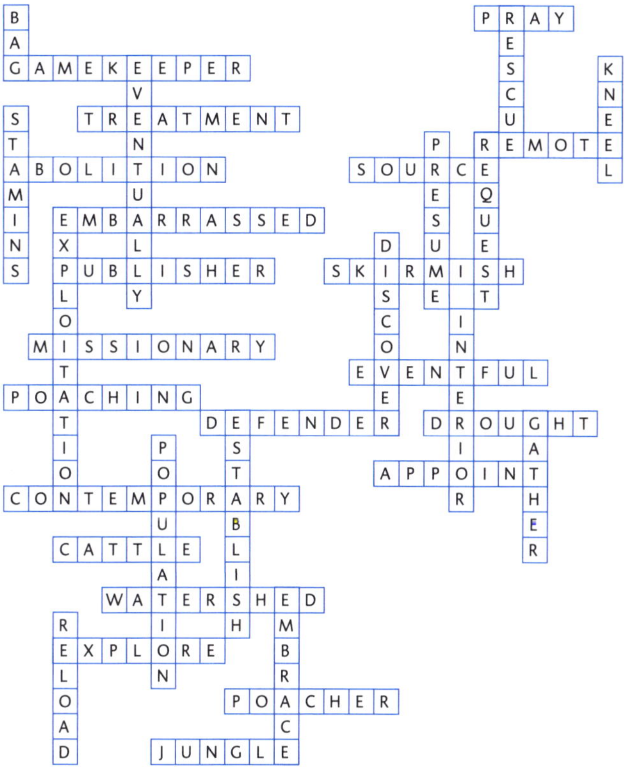

Exercise 13 Wordsearch

G K N H R C D
T G M O L O E E X
H N I K I N S V D G Y
A N I M A T S E W O N A R
S Y N O E E A N S R O M E T R
E O P J P M R T K E I T L C F H Z
T U G U R P R U I V T M O U V U E E P
H C Z A O A A R O A A A T N M O T D R
N S Y R B L M C L B D T Z A A S E D E
E E A M L I S U P O D O S R E R D S S
E R E Y S I P K X L E K E U O R Y E U
Y V I H D O N B E I H H Q L O Q T K M
I L E X P E U P N T S E P U U O F N E
O E N E U V B B I R X G N M Q Y M
E L T T A C L O E H X E U X B
L G F I B I N T E R I O R
L N U M K K A P P A A
P U L Q G W H B C
G J X G V T E

Fame

Exercise 1
Questions on the text

a) Where there is light, there is also darkness, but people only want to see the beautiful side. They know the stars and their lives from reports in the media. Magazines nearly always show the splendour and the wealth the stars enjoy. Readers only get to hear the fairy tale side of being famous, which is to be successful and glamorous.

b) She meant that her son should not follow the bad example of some young rock stars, e. g. Jim Morrison and others who had wasted their lives by taking drugs and when they had finally come to the end of the road they had killed themselves.

c) He was very unhappy as a child, especially after the separation and divorce of his parents. He stayed with his mother, who remarried, but her new marriage wasn't a happy one. The couple behaved very aggressively and Kurt didn't feel safe and secure in that atmosphere.

d) He liked that sort of music because the punk rockers rebelled against society and Kurt felt the same way: he was disgusted with the world of the adults and wanted to scream out his hatred at it.

e) The group started as outsiders who wanted to be different from society. But success turned them into (nearly) "everybody's darling". They were now liked by many, and had thus lost their original starting point as rebels. They had nothing left to say.

f) Both stars had an unhappy childhood. Kurt was very depressed and sad because the marriage of his parents ended in divorce and his mother could not find happiness in her new marriage. Michael's father never treated his son like a father should. He was not a person young Michael could have turned to. In their careers as stars both lived under extreme pressure and finally took tablets or drugs.

g) Normally, young people cannot wait to grow up; they want to be accepted as adults as soon as possible. Some start smoking just to show others that they aren't children any longer. Few, like Peter Pan or Michael Jackson, might wish to stay children for ever because they like the innocence and the naiveté that we associate with childhood. Perhaps they want to avoid or postpone the day when they have to become independent and accept responsibility for their own decisions.

Exercise 2 Anagram: Popularity

a) contempt
b) threaten
c) stupid
d) fortune
e) divorce
f) gossip
g) offensive
h) deprive

Exercise 3 Vocabulary grid: Public heroes

		T	H	R	E	A	T	E	N				
U	N	S	C	R	U	P	U	L	O	U	S		
			S	T	U	P	I	D					
					P	E	R	F	O	R	M	E	R
			R	I	V	A	L	R	Y				
			S	C	O	R	N						
		O	U	T	L	A	W						
S	H	O	T	G	U	N							
			S	U	I	C	I	D	E				
			O	F	F	E	N	S	I	V	E		

Exercise 4 C-Test: Tina Turner

1 blues / 2 christened / 3 discovered / 4 leader / 5 married / 6 Review / 7 exploited / 8 husband / 9 during / 10 abrupt / 11 furious / 12 afterwards / 13 debt / 14 support / 15 comeback / 16 number

Exercise 5 Cloze-Test: Bob Dylan

1 name / 2 hometown / 3 led / 4 records / 5 appealed / 6 inspired / 7 career / 8 met / 9 movement /10 recognized / 11 signed / 12 live / 13 following / 14 anthems / 15 late / 16 romance / 17 suffered / 18 finished / 19 reached / 20 before

Exercise 6 Text reconstruction: John Lennon

1	2	3	4	5	6	7	8	9	10	11	12	13	14	15	16
n	i	j	d	e	l	a	f	b	h	p	m	k	g	c	o

Exercise 7 C-Test: Bruce Springsteen

1 working / 2 prison / 3 pupil / 4 trouble / 5 bought / 6 taught / 7 harmonica / 8 appearing / 9 desperate / 10 escape / 11 factory / 12 commercial / 13 established / 14 released / 15 best-selling / 16 stage / 17 clothes / 18 blue-collar / 19 young / 20 afford / 21 beautiful / 22 area / 23 victims / 24 starring

Exercise 8 Translation: Public heroes

1 fortgeführt, fortgesetzt / 2 Aufkommen, Entstehen / 3 in particular / 4 anstoßig / 5 consider / 6 becomes / 7 identify / 8 appears / 9 gerissenen / 10 promote / 11 had become / 12 betrauerten / 13 release / 14 Werbe- / 15 members / 16 Spaß hatten, gern / 17 signs / 18 überdrüssig / 19 rivalry / 20 schließlich

Exercise 9 Usage: Phrases with "to do"

a) doing the rooms
b) has been doing German
c) does the shopping
d) do her hair
e) do the washing-up
f) doing well
h) does for a living
h) does
i) done your homework

Exercise 10 Usage: The Tragedy of Marilyn Monroe

1 excellent / 2 opinion / 3 sensitive / 4 unscrupulous / 5 self-confidence / 6 became / 7 become / 8 competition / 9 tickets / 10 opinion / 11 humane

Exercise 11 Gerund or infinitive?: Going out for the evening

a) having seen / watching
b) seeing
c) to go
d) to do
e) to go
f) sitting
g) dancing
h) eating
i) eating
j) arguing

Exercise 12 Gerund as part of the predicate: Forming a band

a) would enjoy playing
b) we are interested in making
c) we would have no difficulty in playing
d) we had difficulty in finding
e) we couldn't dream of playing
f) How about picking
g) we succeeded in rehearsing
h) was tired of going
i) we could not stop worrying
j) There's no way of telling, There is no telling
k) we look forward to playing
l) possibility of recording

Exercise 13 Crossword puzzle

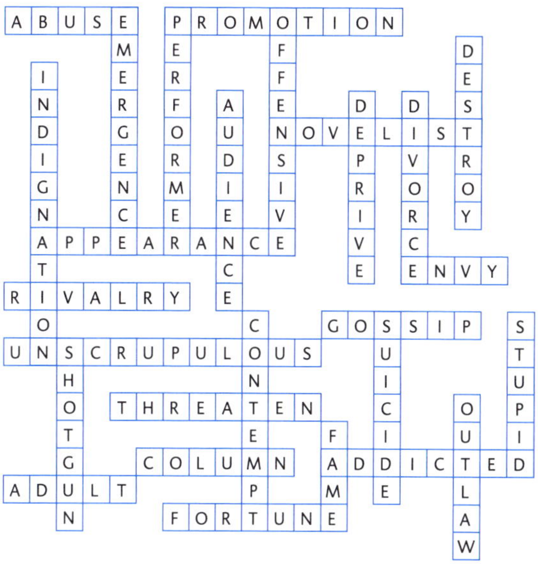

Ihre Meinung ist uns wichtig!

Ihre Anregungen sind uns immer willkommen. Bitte informieren Sie uns mit diesem Schein über Ihre Verbesserungsvorschläge!

Titel-Nr.	Seite	Vorschlag

Bitte hier abtrennen

Zutreffendes bitte ankreuzen!

Die Absenderin/der Absender ist:

- ☐ Lehrer/in in den Klassenstufen: ____
- ☐ Fachbetreuer/in
  Fächer: ____
- ☐ Seminarlehrer/in
  Fächer: ____
- ☐ Regierungsfachberater/in
  Fächer: ____
- ☐ Oberstufenbetreuer/in
- ☐ Schulleiter/in
- ☐ Referendar/in, Termin 2. Staatsexamen: ____
- ☐ Leiter/in Lehrerbibliothek
- ☐ Leiter/in Schülerbibliothek
- ☐ Sekretariat
- ☐ Eltern
- ☐ Schüler/in, Klasse: ____
- ☐ Sonstiges: ____

Unterrichtsfächer: (Bei Lehrkräften!)

____

STARK Verlag
Postfach 1852
85318 Freising

17-V1T

Bitte ausfüllen und im frankierten Umschlag
an uns einsenden. Für Fensterkuverts geeignet.

Kennen Sie Ihre Kundennummer?
Bitte hier eintragen.

Absender (Bitte in Druckbuchstaben!)

Name/Vorname

Straße/Nr.

PLZ/Ort

Telefon privat

Geburtsjahr

E-Mail-Adresse

Schule/Schulstempel (Bitte immer angeben!)

Bitte hier abtrennen

(Bitte blättern Sie um)

17-V1T